► **Coincidences** ▼

▶ **Coincidences** ▼
Chance or Fate?

KEN ANDERSON

BLANDFORD

A Blandford Book

First published in the UK 1995 by Blandford
A Cassell imprint
Cassell plc, Wellington House
125 Strand, London WC2R 0BB

Originally published as two volumes, *Coincidences* (1991) and *Extraordinary Coincidences*, by HarperCollins Publishers, Sydney, Australia. This abridged and combined edition is published by arrangement with the author, Ken Anderson, and HarperCollins Publishers, Australia.

Distributed in the United States by Sterling Publishing Co., Inc.
387 Park Avenue South, New York, NY 10016–8810

**A cataloguing-in-Publication Data entry for this title is available
from the British Library**

ISBN 0–7137–2523–0

Typeset by Keystroke, Jacaranda Lodge, Wolverhampton
Printed and bound in Great Britain by
Biddles Ltd, Guildford and King's Lynn

This one is for Lonesome Sam

▶ Contents ▼

► **Preface** ▼

The material presented here amounts to what is believed to be the largest collection of coincidences yet gathered in one book. It comes from a wide variety of sources: my own research over a number of years; readers of my previous books on the subject, my daily newspaper column and articles; radio and TV audiences who have phoned or written as result of my appearing on a show; and acquaintances, friends and colleagues. For the help of all these generous people I am most grateful.

However, the book is not merely a collection of fascinating anecdotes and the like. It attempts to look at the thorny question of the *meaning* – if any – of coincidences in, I hope, as objective a way as possible.

As the philosopher Arthur Schopenhauer wrote, the real significance of coincidences exists only in relation to the individual who experiences them; for other people, for whom they have no significance, these coincidences pass unnoticed into the background of everyday life. Like most unqualified assertions, though, this is not totally correct. As we shall see, there are many coincidences involving others that cannot but fail to impress the rest of us.

On this point, it is often argued that to dwell on 'trivial' coincidences when discussing the phenomenon is to belittle the possible importance of 'significant' coincidences. In this book there are what many people would consider a goodly number of 'trivial' coincidences rubbing shoulders with the significant events. Yet I do not consider it is intellectual laziness to leave them 'unsorted'. For one thing, as Schopenhauer is more or less saying, what may be considered trivial to one person is significant to another. For example, that a child was born at eight minutes past 8 p.m. on 8/8/88 draws from the sceptics a scornful, 'So what? With so many children born every minute, somebody had to be!' However, the child and the parents find it significant – and so might others: the baby was Princess Beatrice, the first child of the Duke and Duchess of York. How many princesses are born at such a moment in time? A second point to bear in mind is that coincidences are essentially random, non-repeatable events which do not 'sort' themselves; we have the big with the small, the major with the minor, and in some chapters I purposely present them in this manner to give a flavour of the way they occur.

Finally, I would like to say that while many coincidences provide an essentially wry, amusing look at life, they can also offer those of us who develop a heightened awareness of them insights and guidance. Developing such an awareness is not hard to do. I believe this book will help you in the pleasing task.

I am very grateful to all those who have given permission to use material, including those who have written to me with anecdotes and other information. Every effort has been made to contact holders of copyright material but in some cases the source has been untraceable.

I am also very grateful to the Blandford editors and staff for their highly professional editing, painstaking checking and attention to detail of this work. The reader has benefited from their unsung labours!

▶ Introduction ▼

Let us preview briefly the chapters in this book.

Chapter One An overview which includes definitions of coincidences and the various beliefs and arguments about what lies behind the phenomenon. Are they nothing more than statistical quirks, random anomalies in the greater scheme of things that can be largely explained by application of the theories of probability? Do they give us tantalizing glimpses of some as yet unknown principle of nature or psychic powers such as ESP? Are they evidence of a non-causal side of life that balances the causal?

Chapter Two Another aspect of coincidences is the Clustering Effect, as proposed by Austrian biologist Paul Kammerer. Events do occur in 'runs': accidents, mass shootings, etc. Research shows that people of certain professions and occupations 'cluster' under a particular star sign or signs, and the 'mystery of woman' creates birth clusters. What is the reason? Is such a seemingly illogical effect simply part of the hidden principle that many believe lies behind coincidences?

Chapter Three A fresh look at two of the best-known cases of significant coincidences in an examination of non-deliberate predictions: the fate of the *Titanic* and the disclosure of top-secret D-Day codewords in a crossword puzzle.

Chapter Four The mystery of numbers and coincidences is examined: how numbers influence us all, using as an example the manner in which that most mysterious of all numbers, 9, dogged Beatle John Lennon to his death. We also see coincidences in dates of crimes, disasters, political and other events.

Chapter Five A person loses a ring or some other small object only to have it turn up in the stomach of a fish – a prize coincidence tale whose origins are to be found in history. This chapter examines whether the Fish-stomach Effect is merely apocryphal or whether it is one of many stories that have their origins deep in our psyche? Is it genuine?

Chapter Six The search for coincidences in the literary world is one of the most active scenes and also, for obvious reason, one of the best recorded. This chapter shows too how easily and eerily art imitates life, including stories of authors whose plots become the subject of other writers' books and the way coincidence is used in plots – and how we have come to accept such contrivances. It also looks at coincidences and Nostradamus' predictions.

Chapters Seven to Ten These are filled with anecdotes randomly selected and generally unrelated. They can be used by those who prefer, or only have time, to dip into this book.

Chapter Eleven A curious phenomenon is examined here: people, both famous and poor, who are unrelated yet are born at the same time often look alike and go on to live similar lives, in some cases dying at the same time. They are Time Twins. The chapter has many cases of children, or their mothers, who in some mysterious manner appear to delay or hasten births so they will take place at the precise moment another baby is born.

Chapter Twelve The famous and infamous, and how coincidences have shaped their actions – for example, the similar moustaches worn by the world's greatest monster, Hitler, and the world's greatest comedian, Chaplin. What coincidences linked the two men?

Chapter Thirteen   Consists mainly of amazing anecdotes told by those who took part in conflicts in all parts of the world – for example, the coincidence that impelled Wing-Commander Basil Embry to make his legendary escape from the Germans in 1940.

Chapter Fourteen   Looks in detail at the interrelationship between premonitions and coincidences, concentrating on even more anecdotes. In what way do the two phenomena differ?

Chapter Fifteen   Should you keep a diary of coincidences? This chapter includes extracts from one kept by a woman and the contents certainly appear to suggest uncanny influences at work in her life. There are also extracts from my own co-incidence diary.

I will finish this introduction with an anecdote which is typical of many sent to me by people who find coincidences have meaning in their lives.

In his letter a man in his twenties related that he had taken an interest in psychology and borrowed from his local library *Jung and the Story of Our Time* by Laurens Van der Post. He was half-way through before he lost interest and returned the book. Two days later a friend of his sister was walking along a busy street in a city many miles from where he lived when she spotted on the pavement a copy of the same book. She picked it up. The friend mentioned her find when she next spoke to the man's sister, and the sister responded by saying he had begun studying psychology. As a result the friend sent him the book. 'It came back to me,' he wrote. 'I took it as a sign that I *had* to finish that book, which I did.'

I can only hope that readers of this book feel the same way, no matter how it came into their hands.

CHAPTER ONE

Overview, Definitions and Beliefs

Conversation between two students:

'How would you describe coincidences?'

'That's funny. I was just about to ask you the same question!'

It is this suggestion of extrasensory perception, or other unknown powers at work, that is so much a part of the allure of coincidences.

Let's look at some examples.

Inspirational case A nun of the Good Samaritan order who works at a St Vincent de Paul centre in Sydney found a man sleeping in the car park one evening. She brought some blankets and made him as comfortable as possible. Next morning when she checked on him, he was obviously ill. She opened her purse; it contained only a $A5 note and some small change. She called a cab and gave the driver the note to take the man to hospital. That afternoon as she was parking her car at the centre a starling began fluttering about over the bonnet. It had a piece of paper in its beak which it dropped near the car. The nun picked it up. The 'paper' was a $A5 note.

Useful case Kath McCauley, a radio producer, sent me a tape of a programme on coincidences, leaving me with a problem. As it was a reel-to-reel tape, I could not play it because, like most people these days, I have a cassette player.

I was left frustrated. I had been looking forward to hearing the tape, but instead I had to put it aside, wondering when I would ever get the chance to hear it.

That same afternoon, walking to the post office, I passed a woman who was weighed down by a heavy object she was carrying by a strap over her shoulder. It took me another ten or so steps before I registered what the object was – a reel-to-reel tape recorder.

When I retraced my steps and confronted her, she was initially, and understandably, cautious. Then recognition dawned. 'We're neighbours,' she said. Sure enough, she had recently moved into a house a few doors from mine. Further, she was also a journalist and had just started some part-time radio work, hence the professional reel-to-reel over her shoulder. She pointed out that she did not normally carry one; she was due to do an interview that night. 'I was going to catch a taxi home,' she mused, adjusting the bulky weight of the machine. 'I don't know what made me decide against it.'

By the end of the day I had used her machine to transcribe the programme. I did have a bit of difficulty explaining to my benefactor the part about the subject of the programme that was on the reel . . .

Uncanny case Narelle Dickerson attended a sales representatives' conference a few years ago at which she met a woman from another branch office in a town hundreds of miles away. They found themselves drawn to one another and soon struck up a conversation. Narelle found that, like her, the other woman was the mother of blonde-haired identical twin daughters. She was stunned when in further conversation she found they had been born within a few hours of one another. Her daughters had been named Kylie and Jodie, while the other woman had called hers Kylie and Jacqui. All had the same interests.

Coincidences are a universally accepted phenomenon. However, they do not excite controversy in the way other unproven phenomena – UFOs, dowsing, near-death experiences, for example – do. Until, like the student, we go in search of *meaning*.

Early in my research I approached academics, who told me the subject was not an acceptable field of study. I was surprised and argued that coincidences are common occurrences, yet no one can say definitively what they *mean*, or even if they have meaning. Surely this deficiency in our best-known phenomenon had inspired scientists to probe the realms of the possible and philosophers to muse? What about in literature? Where would plots in books and films be without them? Why, in short, are they not worth studying?

Dr Philip Kellman, a Fulbright psychology scholar, had a straightforward answer: 'Because it's very hard to get evidence. That is, it's hard to get the kind of evidence or statistics that are the basis of an acceptable study. For example, if a patient tells you he dreamed the prime minister had resigned and that day the PM does resign, it becomes an event and everybody talks about it. But how many people have dreams that don't come true and, statistically, what is the likelihood of dreaming this purely by chance? That's why it's so very hard to assess coincidences in most cases.'

As I have since discovered, Kellman was arguing about the most common of coincidental experiences, where you hear or run into someone you have just been thinking about, or, as in his argument, something happens to somebody you had a feeling about. More often than not, the argument goes, you don't run into a person you are thinking about, and the prime minister doesn't resign after your feeling that he will – a feeling which may, after all, be just wishful thinking. If I had known then what I now know, I would have asked, 'But how about when you run into somebody in circumstances that are coincidental that you have not been thinking about?' One case on my files concerns two men who live hundreds of miles apart: one day both went fishing from a jetty in a small village and, being the only two there, they got to talking; they discovered they were long-lost half-brothers! Many other coincidence encounters are so incredible they make the people-you-are-thinking-about-that-you don't-meet argument look feeble.

I did not pursue the matter and the doctor, in his conciliatory tone, continued: 'One thing to keep in mind is that scientific scepticism just asks the question, "How can we be sure?" A lot of scientists will say, "Chance, nothing like that ever happens," but it is just as dogmatic to be certain it doesn't happen as it is to be certain that it does.'

Kellman was sincere, and was being obliging in even agreeing to discuss the subject with me, considering, as he said, that he knew of no research on the subject. He went even further, obviously realizing by now that he was dealing with an innocent abroad (well, each to his own field of expertise!). He had not been much help, he said, so he would ask a colleague if he knew of any studies on the subject of 'synchronicity' (a term for coincidences coined by the pioneering psychiatrist Carl Jung, as we shall see).

Dr Chris Clark, the colleague, later told me how surprised he was by this request: 'Philip asked me if I knew of any studies being done into synchronicity and I suddenly realized it was the word I had been trying to think of for the past few days, following a chance conversation about Jung. It was an accidental conversation and I cannot remember when I had last had occasion to mention either Jung or synchronicity – they are not words used around here [the psychology department]. The chances of the conversation and the question coming shortly afterwards are extraordinary.'

In telling this story against himself, Chris agreed quite happily that he was adding to the store of anecdotal coincidence material from reliable persons.

While coincidences are frozen out of conventional research, there have been a number of international scientific conferences on the near-death-experiences (NDE) phenomenon, even though the number of NDE cases is minuscule compared with significant coincidences. At first glance this is puzzling, although Dr Kellman touched on the reason, which is that NDE stories are similar, therefore they are convenient for study because they provide *repeatable* data – a primary requirement for conventional scientists in search of new fields of glory. On the other hand, coincidence data are varied and more often than not individual cases are seemingly unrelated; the material is anecdotal. As for incidence, coincidence is as likely to happen today as in a thousand years from now and its improbability is no guarantee against its occurring. In fact, a view is growing – slowly – in research circles that anecdotal material of any nature, awkward as it is to classify, may be worth looking at.

Currently, in broad terms there are those who believe coincidences are nothing more than statistical quirks, random anomalies in the greater scheme of things that can be largely explained by the application of theories of probability. Then there are those who believe in other explanations: coincidences as a tantalizing glimpse of some as yet unknown principle of nature, coincidences as evidence of a non-causal side of life that balances the causal and coincidences as evidence of psychic powers.

Coincidence and chance

Before we discuss these various attitudes we should look at a definition of coincidence. Do we simply go along with those who are happy to call it 'something out of the ordinary', 'an unlikely event', 'luck', 'divine providence' or, most commonly, 'chance'?

Descriptions such as the above are obviously inadequate for our purpose. In fact, chance is the alternative word I have come across most often for coincidence. Are 'coincidence' and 'chance' interchangeable – that is, do they have the same meaning? Scientists, especially physicists, tend to use the word 'chance' vaguely, even ambiguously at times, or with different shades of meaning. Indeed 'chance' is used by most of us in this way in everyday life, often linked to form a phrase with 'blind', 'pure', 'sheer' or some other adjective. It is not surprising that such loose usage should extend into a subject in which so many terms are not specifically defined. Even in those areas where 'chance' is specifically used (science, philosophy, psychology and theology), it has different shades of meaning.

Does 'chance' have a specific purpose, a 'law' under which it operates? Emile Borel, in *Probabilities and life* (1962), gives this reply (he calls it an answer): 'It would seem [it] should be in the negative, since chance is in fact defined as the characteristic of the phenomena which follow no law, phenomena whose causes are too complex to permit prediction.'

Borel goes on to observe that, following the lead of Galileo, Pascal and many other eminent thinkers, mathematicians have built a science, the calculus of probabilities, upon the 'laws' of that utilitarian word.

Harry Edwards, a Sceptics organization official, says most people do not understand the laws of chance in relation to coincidence. If a coincidence is postulated with a 100,000 probability, many people will consider it a most unlikely event. That this is not so is evidenced by the number of lotteries drawn on most days of the week. Every winner is betting against odds of about 100,000 to one. So too with coincidences.

Edwards claims: 'If we consider the number of "events" that occur every second, then it would be a remarkable world indeed if every "event" was totally unique and there were no coincidences.'

On the basis of his argument, coincidences can be lightly dismissed as no more than an aberration, even the most amazing of them being probable on the basis of some supposed finite measure of the number of 'events' that happen in the world each day. It is the monkey-tapping-at-a-typewriter assertion: give the monkey long enough and it will come up with the works of Shakespeare. It shouldn't surprise anyone that not all agree with arguments of this sort.

In his book *On Time* (1982), Michael Shallis argues that chance implies that the unlikely is being compared with a model of supposedly random events. The danger in this supposition is that there may not be any such real thing as randomness, just as infinity is a purely abstract concept (p. 139).

Shallis adds that to dismiss coincidence as merely due to chance, or as 'one of those things', is to ignore the real problems of randomness, to appeal inappropriately to probability theory and to discount the idea of a purposeful universe (p. 139).

Chance is not to be separated from formal definitions of coincidence, judging by two dictionaries I checked at random: **Coincidence** a striking occurrence of two or more events at one time apparently by mere chance (*Macquarie*); the chance occurrence at the same time or place of two or more events that appear to be related or similar (*Penguin Reference*).

Some may say that it is a matter of semantics, but part of what I wanted to do in formulating a clear definition was to get away from the word 'chance'. It is too dismissive, it gets in the way of a clear understanding of coincidences, it stymies thought and it is somehow an inadequate description for many coincidences.

For example, on 1 April 1930, London evening newspapers reported that two men, each named Butler, both butchers by occupation, had been found shot (one in Nottinghamshire, one near London). One was named Frederick Henry Butler, the other David Henry Butler. They were not related and had not known one another. Both had shot themselves with pistols and both were found by the side of their cars.

Chance?

After tinkering for some time I came up with this definition: *Two or more seemingly unrelated incidents come together in time to create an event and that event is the coincidence.* No mention of chance. Note the time element. Originally, for the sake of simplification, I had assumed a relevant time period. Time is important because it is the only barrier to the impossible.

Coincidences and the theory of probabilities

Having made some attempt at a definition, we can now return to those arguments for and against the meaning of coincidences, starting with probability. No discussion of coincidence is possible without attempting to deal with the vexed question of its relationship to probability. Coincidences, with nowhere else to go, have been welded to the probability theory in much the same manner as the paradoxical theory itself has been wedded to mathematics to form a sort of *ménage à trois* in which the marriage itself works, although nobody understands why.

The first major treatise on probability dates back to the early 1700s, when Swiss mathematician Jacob Bernoulli described it as 'the art of conjecture'. Over the next century or so, it came to be seen as a guide for weighing up assumptions.

Today probability is part of the fabric of science, not to say everyday life. For example, the whole insurance and assurance industry is based on probability. We are subject to it daily. For example, when we want to cross a busy road we work out the probability of being able to do so and act when the probability of a safe crossing is high. (Of course, we should keep in mind that one study has shown more pedestrians have been hit when crossing an intersection with the lights than against them!) Another study by an American parapsychologist suggests some of us may use probability at a subconscious level. The parapsychologist spent several years collecting statistics with the aim of finding out whether people avoided trains that had been involved in an accident. He compared the total number travelling on the same scheduled train on the preceding seven, fourteen, twenty-one and twenty-eight days prior to the accident. His results showed that in all cases there were fewer people on board when the accident occurred than could have been expected based on the earlier figures.

There is no question that the law of probability functions, or of its efficacy within its limits. Arthur Koestler admits in *The Challenge of Chance* (1973), 'without it the edifice of modern science would collapse' (p. 210).

In his *A Philosophical Essay on Probabilities* (1812), the great astronomer P. S. Laplace, who viewed the theory of probabilities basically as common sense reduced to calculus, said it has made us appreciate with exactitude what exact minds feel by a sort of instinct, often without being able to give a reason for it.

Problems in this relationship come when we try to claim coincidences as non-causal events, ungoverned by the theories of probability. I ran into a perfect example a few years ago. Appearing on a TV show in front of a live studio audience, I asked the producers beforehand to help me carry out an experiment which would, I hoped, show coincidences surround us more than we realize.

I had not been on the show before and thought for some reason that the audience comprised about thirty people. It averages 150 (plus millions of viewers). On this particular day there were about 130 present. In any case, before the show started we organized the audience to provide the day and month of their births, but not the year. As a result, on air, we were able to point out that in this randomly selected group of people there were three pairs, each with matching birth dates. There were gasps of wonder as we announced the results and the cameras picked up the six dual birthday people. I sat back, pleased and somewhat relieved. I would have been quite content if only one matching birthday had been found in that audience. Instead we had three matches and one pair's birthday was Christmas Day.

So far as I was concerned, it had been a pleasing way of

illustrating before millions of viewers one aspect of coincidence, even though it could have fallen flat . . .

I had based the experiment on the famous birthday problem of the mathematician Warren Weaver. He has estimated the odds that at least two people will share the same birthday at better than 50/50 among a group of only twenty-three randomly chosen people. In his *Lady Luck and the Theory of Probability* (1963), Weaver says he mentioned these odds at a dinner meeting of high-ranking army officers. Many of them refused to believe it. Noticing there were twenty-two people at the table, one suggested they each in turn announce their birthdays. They worked around the table. Not one matched. Then the waitress spoke up. Apologizing for the interruption, she said, 'I'm the twenty-third person in the room and my birthday is 17 May, just like the general over there.'

Now, where I drew the wrath of the purists was in saying that the birthday matches had defied probability and relied on coincidence. A polite letter arrived from a chartered accountant who provided figures which showed that by the time fifty people have been gathered, the chances of a birthday match are 97 per cent. The chances are 100 per cent with seventy-three people, according to a computer printout he enclosed. 'You had a 97 per cent chance of finding three matching birthdays among 150 people and you did!' the accountant concluded.

Not being a mathematician, I felt somewhat chastened. I was being told it was nothing to get excited about. (He overlooked the point that there were less than this number present on this day.) But then I began to wonder, what if none of the less than 150 people present had had matching birthdays? Would mathematicians have been excited enough to write and tell me of this odds-defying event? What if by chance six people met and there was the same result, three matching birthdays? Say we had asked the audience if any had been born on the most significant birthday in the Christian calendar, Christmas Day, and two had stood up? Would we be dealing with probability, impossibility or coincidences in these scenarios?

As for containing our excitement when we come across something seemingly unusual, well, natural human reactions must be taken into account: feelings of surprise or bemusement, or that something odd is going on, are often scoffed at by the sceptics, alarmed that too much may be read into these events. However, such responses are natural and certainly not sinister, or necessarily a denial of the balance of probabilities or a body of learning such as mathematics. They are, however, reactions generally soon forgotten for the mundane matters of everyday life.

I subsequently came across an article by Professor John Allen Paulos in which he points out, in a discussion on the Weaver problem, that 'one must gather together 367 people (one more than the number of days in a leap year) in order to *ensure* that two of them share a birthday'. Although that is stating the obvious, it serves to show that the 100 per cent probability figure for seventy-three people is no more than that, a probability, not a certainty. Given that, the three matching birth dates in our impromptu survey must be considered as impressive as many in the studio (and presumably millions of viewers) felt them to be. Incidentally, Paulos, Professor of Mathematics at Temple University in the USA, in the Summer 1991 edition of *Skeptical, Inquirer*, goes on to say that 253 people are needed for a 50 per cent chance that one of them has a specific birth date – such as Christmas Day.

To his credit, Paulos is one of those scientists who does admit openly 'coincidences, after all, *are* sometimes quite significant' – a rare sentiment indeed for a person in his position.

> *'A reasonable probability is the only certainty'*
> – E. W. HOWE

Let us digress briefly to consider the relationship between certainty and coincidences.

Colin Wilson argues that the basic peculiarity of human nature is the need for uncertainty and crisis to keep us on our toes. 'One day it may be that we shall learn to keep the will alert as automatically as we now breathe, and if that happens, we shall be supermen living on a continual level of "peak experience",' he asserts, adding that until we do achieve 'this new degree of self-determination, life had better remain as bewildering and paradoxical as possible'.

Another proponent of the essential role uncertainty plays in our lives is Professor Fred Wolf. In his best-seller *Taking the*

Quantum Leap (1989), he says: 'Without uncertainty there is no world' (p. 250). As Wolf explains it, the physical universe is fundamentally paradoxical. It is composed of facts and their opposites at the same time. Our Western upbringing, Wolf goes on, has preconditioned us to think objectively. Yet objectivity is only an illusion (p. 146).

The 'illusion of objectivity' has also helped shield attacks on coincidences which, paradoxically, show us that a belief in certainties is another illusion.

A final word on this subject from Michael Shallis. He points out that statistics, which are so often accepted as the basis of certainty, are inappropriate when dealing with a coincidence. 'How can we quantify or evaluate a unique event?' he asks (p. 136).

An obvious question that arises from much of the material so far is, what are the limits in the probability theory? Emile Borel, in his *Probabilities and Life*, observes that the 'calculus of probabilities is an exact science . . . as long as it confines itself to the numerical evaluation of probabilities' (p. 4). Darrell Huff, in his book *How to Take a Chance* (1959), says more pertinently that the theory of probability isn't simply true or false, but is rather a model of reality – a good model as long as it is useful, a bad model when extended beyond that point (p. 41).

Coincidences, improbable by definition, are forever pushing beyond that point to the boundaries of the impossible. However, in probability the point is reached where the mathematician is no longer dealing with a mathematical problem: it cannot be shown that something is impossible, so mathematicians must use intuitive evidence to make the assertion of impossibility. At this point they must invoke the single law of chance. It is a simple law. It is also, as Borel says, rationally undemonstrable (p. 2): events with a sufficiently small probability never occur.

A classic example of such impossible events is the monkey at the typewriter already mentioned. Borel says that such an event, though its *impossibility* may not be rationally demonstrable, is, however, so unlikely that no sensible person will hesitate to declare it *actually impossible* (p. 3). He adds:

> *It is . . . clearly absurd to imagine experiments whose number would extend to more than a million figures; that is a purely*

*abstract conception, a piece of mathematical juggling of no
consequence, and we must trust our intuition and our common
sense which permit us to assert the absolute impossibility of the
typist's miracle.*

When events occur, as they do, with a sufficiently small
chance of probability, we are left with what – the occurrence of
an impossibility? Or a coincidence?

To summarize, we have Borel talking about the need to trust
our intuition at a certain point in the probability process
and Laplace appealing to the 'instincts' of 'exact minds' as an
explanation of the 'why' of probability 'without being able to
give a reason for it'. Both these comments serve to show that
the probability theory does have its share of ambiguities and
paradoxes.

Take these two examples.

In the late 1980s author Gavin Souter set out on a car journey
which normally took him several hours. On this day the trip was
drastically reduced when he encountered fifty-three green
lights in a row. Anyone who drives a car in the city can picture
Gavin as he gleefully passed through yet another light, feeling
that something was shining for him that day. But on reflection
it is possible to analyse the journey – the speed of the vehicle,
the predetermined programme of the lights, other traffic on the
road at the time, etc. – and come up with a valid probability of
his uninterrupted journey.

In this second account the assessors involved were forced
to admit they were dealing with impossibility rather than
probability.

In 1978 the wife of Spanish hotel executive Jaime Castell
became pregnant. Three months before the baby was due,
Jaime had a warning dream. In it a disembodied voice told him
that he would die before the birth took place. As a result, he
approached an insurance company and took out a policy. The
sum assured was payable only on death.

A few weeks later he was driving on the motorway at 80 km
an hour when a driver travelling at twice that speed in the
opposite direction lost control; his car hit the central barrier,
turned upside down and landed on top of Castell's. Both
drivers were killed instantly. The insurance company paid up

without demur. A company spokesman explained that it was not carrying out an investigation because 'this incredible accident rules out suspicion ... a second either way and he would have escaped'.

The US mathematician and physicist Charles Sanders Peirce says: 'This branch of mathematics [probability] is the only one, I believe, in which good writers frequently get results entirely erroneous.'

Some early work done by the Rand Corporation is an example of the dubious nature of placing probability on a pedestal. The American think-tank had a powerful influence on that country's foreign affairs policies for two decades from the early 1950s. Its view was that the world's problems could all be dealt with scientifically, the future was a matter of plotting and predicting through statistical analysis. That is, all human behaviour and thought were merely systems of probability. The Cold War, for example, could be fought by logic, its outcome calculated by statistical probabilities. Members of the Rand Corporation took to rolling dice to estimate the probabilities of such human problems as birth control and even thought control.

No doubt influenced by such assertions, the US government used probability flows in the Vietnam War to predict its course and outcome. A Pentagon computer was asked in 1968 to predict the year America would win the conflict. Its response: 1964.

Coincidences as an unknown principle

Arthur Koestler says in *The Challenge of Chance* (p. 209) that whether one believes certain highly improbable, meaningful coincidences are manifestations of some ... unknown principle operating beyond physical causality, or are produced by that immortal monkey at the typewriter, is ultimately a matter of inclination and temperament ... no amount of scientific knowledge can help a person to decide which of these alternative beliefs is more reasonable or nearer to the truth. He goes on: 'I have found to my surprise that the majority of my acquaintances – among whom scientists predominate – are inclined towards the first alternative, although some are reluctant to admit it, for fear of ridicule . . .'

When one considers the following string of strange and apparently non-causally linked events, one is entitled to ask, what is going on, is something at work whose principle we have not yet grasped?

The series of events I describe make up what I call the Magic-dial Effect. The first case in this cluster of events left me feeling rather doubtful about its authenticity, although I had no doubts about the person who passed the details on.

Two colleagues work at a booking office of a cross-Channel ferry company in Dover, Jim and Jane (not their real names). One day in 1992 Jane was on duty when the fax machine started playing up. She could not fix it so, reluctantly, decided to disturb Jim, who was having a day off.

Looking down the staff list, Jane found and then rang what she believed was Jim's home number. In fact, she'd read the wrong column and had dialled his six-digit staff payroll number. In the centre of Dover a pay-phone rang and, hearing it as he walked past, a curious young man could not resist picking up the receiver.

'Hallo?'

'Oh, Jim,' a female voice apologized. 'I'm sorry to trouble you, but the fax is on the blink.'

The young man was staggered. 'Jane! How did you know where to find me?'

Jim, out shopping on his free day, had taken the mis-called call.

I at first put the story in the 'iffy' file – that is, until similar stories began to surface. This second story in the cluster came from the opposite side of the world.

A professional gardener was working on a client's lawn in a northern Sydney suburb when a neighbour spotted him and asked if he could do her lawn too. He finished the first lawn and had started on the neighbour's when she came out of the house looking puzzled. There was a call on her phone for him.

He had applied to a bank for a loan and the bank was ringing to tell him it had been approved. The bank employee had by mistake dialled the last four digits of his home number backwards, which had put him through to the neighbour's house, where he had found himself by coincidence.

There was another report of a man buying some goods in a sports store. As the assistant was filling out his purchase slip, the salesperson was interrupted by a phone call. It was for the customer, whose name she was staring at on his credit card. The caller thought she had dialled his office number and had no idea he was at that moment in the large department store.

Next, back to Britain, to an earlier version of the Magic-dial Effect. In 1967 Peter Moscardi was a constable with the Metropolitan Police, based at a suburban station when its telephone number was altered. Moscardi gave what he thought was the new number to a friend – 40166. The following day he realized it was the wrong new number, it should have been 40116, but could not contact the friend to let him know.

Shortly after this he was on night patrol in an industrial estate with a colleague. They noticed a factory appeared to have been broken into – its front door was open and a light was on in the manager's office. As they reached the office the phone on the desk began ringing. Moscardi lifted the receiver and asked, 'What number are you calling?'

In response he heard the voice of his friend asking to be put through to him. Mystified, Moscardi looked at the dial on the set but there was no number shown. He found he had answered the manager's private telephone, the number of which was ex-directory. That number was 40166 – the same as the incorrect number he had given his friend.

Catherine Butler wrote to me that when she and her brother were young in the 1920s, they played a game of talking on the telephone (the telephone in this case being two empty syrup tins connected at their base with a length of string – it actually works!). She gave herself the play number 7605. In 1940 she had her first telephone connected and 'I was amazed when the gentleman from the post office said, "Your number, madam, is 7605."'

A variation on this theme came in a letter from Pamela Biron. She was in her doctor's surgery when their consultation was interrupted by a phone call from an obviously upset woman. The doctor, saying the woman's name a number of times, finally managed to calm her, by which time Pamela had gathered that the woman had heart problems and must have been seriously ill. She went on: 'Not long after this we settled into our new home and within a day or so found out that our next-door neighbour was the same lady who had rung the doctor when I was in his surgery. We became the best of friends in a very short time, and my husband and I were often on hand to help this semi-invalid widow until her death nine years later. Our entire family went to her funeral, which was not gloomy but, as she had planned well before her death, a warm and special occasion, filled with relatives and friends.'

My Magic-dial Effect file had grown by this time to a respectable size. I had the distinct feeling that it was all leading up to something . . .

One Saturday afternoon I was sorting through some papers on my desk when I came across a letter from someone called Glenn Cooper which contained details of an interesting coincidence. With the letter in my hand, I had what I can only describe as a sudden, strong urge to call him and check on a detail. His phone number was not on the letter so I rang directory inquiries, giving the operator the surname and then the address.

After what seemed an overlong pause, the operator asked for the first name. 'Glenn,' I told him. This prompted another pause, a sudden intake of breath and then, 'Who wants him?'

I thought this an unusual question for an operator to ask, and it added to my growing feeling that something odd was going on. I wondered for a moment whether this Cooper had a silent line or there was some other reason why an inquirer had to identify himself. I responded briefly with, 'Why do you want to know?' Yet another pause, a further intake of breath.

'Because I'm Glenn Cooper of that address!'

I had dialled, on a sudden impulse, directory inquiries for the number of a person whom I had never met to have that person answer the call!

When I had finally recovered, I started to explain why I was calling. 'You wrote me a letter – about coincidences.'

'I did,' the Telecom operator broke in, the tone in his voice changing from suspicion to excitement. 'I can't believe what I'm hearing.' He went on excitedly to relate some of the details in his letter, as though I needed proof he was who he said he was. In his letter Cooper had not given any hint of his occupation. He had been one of hundreds of operators on duty that day dealing with inquiries.

As I said earlier, in my Preface, Schopenhauer felt that the real significance of coincidences exists only for the individuals concerned, while others, for whom they have no significance, do not notice them. What Schopenhauer has to say contains the broad truth of the matter, although I can't help feeling life would be richer if we were all able to share that 'real significance' of other people's coincidences. Yet I know that no one can be more impressed than Cooper and I were at our shared coincidence. When we tell others about it, they are intrigued, certainly, but they cannot share that moment of sheer incredulity which enveloped us for that moment in time and will go on doing so whenever we recall the incident.

The phone-call stories cannot simply be dismissed as trivial blips on the telephone lines, accidents of chance. Do they provide evidence for the argument that there is an unexplained theory or hidden principle at work?

In making evaluations such as this, Koestler says, in *The Challenge of Chance*, that intellectual decency demands that somewhere we should draw the line between significant coincidences which we suspect to contain some hidden factors and trivial coincidences due to pure chance (p. 208). He is obviously peeved about the fact that so many sceptics ignore cases such as the phone calls and seize on trivial coincidences to build a case for why they should not be taken as phenomena worthy of serious consideration.

He goes on to admit that just where that line should be drawn is decidedly tricky: 'We are moving in a borderland shrouded in fog which blurs the frontier between chance and design, between coincidence which appears to us meaningful in a numinous way, and others which are merely an insult to the laws of probability.'

Sadly, the question of coincidences as the work of an unknown principle is left in the air, while the anecdotal cases mount.

However, let us not be intimidated by laws that are not explained, or that appear to be explained. Rather, we should encourage the search for an explanation and, at the same time, not be afraid to take from the phenomenon of coincidences what it has to offer in making our own lives more meaningful.

As the nuclear physicist Max Born says, 'Modern physics . . . has given up or modified many traditional ideas but it would cease to be a science if it [gave up] the search for the causes of phenomena.' This is an assertion to be taken seriously. We need a resurgence of interest in research into the unexplained as a new science in search of a believable theoretical explanation for coincidences – and other 'improbable' phenomena. Theoretical physicists and psychologists may even now be burrowing away at their research stations, on their computers and calculators for explanations.

On the other hand, answers may not lie with such professionals as physicists, psychologists or even parapsychologists. They may be looking in the wrong reality. An answer may lie in philosophy – or with you! We all know coincidences are not events beyond our experience. Each of us carries around vivid memories or tales of examples that have influenced or impressed us, or both. Why should it not be somebody undisciplined in the laws of either science or philosophy who comes up with an acceptable theory. Professor Cyril Burt makes this very point in his introduction to Rosalind Heywood's *The Infinite Hive* (1964), arguing that 'too often we forget how much we owe in every branch of science to the inquiring amateur, to the shrewd observer of common things, or uncommon incidents – in short to the snapper-up of unconsidered trifles'.

In the meantime, we do not have to wait for the existence of a coincidence law to take advantage of what the phenomenon has to offer, according to the experts. Psychic Alan Vaughan says that the more we allow coincidence to play a part in our lives, the more we benefit. The way we do this is by letting more people into our lives, taking more responsibility, acting according to our impulses and keeping in mind that coincidences seem to happen when they are needed. Koestler also urges us to act on the coincidence imperative: 'If you have a sudden overwhelming impulse to take some action, do it, provided of course it is legal. You may well be putting yourself in tune with the natural forces of coincidence.' Was it the subconscious memory of his advice that led me to ring Glenn Cooper that Saturday afternoon, leading to the incident described earlier in this chapter?

The relationship between heightened awareness and coincidence is raised by Bernie S. Siegel, MD, in his best-seller *Peace, Love and Healing* (1989). Siegel describes coincidences as 'God's way of remaining anonymous'. He says that he often finds symbols which he believes are coincidence messages:

> *Once you start to become receptive to these messages, you get more and more of them. I can't tell you how many times . . . as we travel around the country, we jump into a taxicab at an airport and find a penny on the carpet, letting us know we're in the right cab in the right city. Brand new pennies in unexpected places, elevators that open without a button being pushed, even a flat tyre – they can all be messages.*
>
> *When you are open and aware, you will have them in your life. They help you get in touch with the schedule of the universe, as opposed to your own personal schedule, which relates only to questions like 'Am I late? How do I look? What do other people think?' They get you to look at the real questions: 'How can I live and understand the moment?' These will occur more often when you are in touch with your intuitive, unconscious awareness.*

Coincidences can stimulate this level of awareness, if we learn to recognize them for what they are, if we do not dismiss them lightly when they happen to us but instead pause to consider what they could be trying to tell us. That is what their 'law' is.

The authors of a *New Scientist* article (5 August 1989), Peter Fenwick, a consultant neuropsychiatrist at the Maudsley hospital in London, and David Lorimer, director of the United Kingdom Scientific and Medical Network, coin the phrase 'new dualism' to describe the world of subjective qualities as opposed to the objective world studied by conventional science. They argue that this secondary world should be studied via a science of subjective experience in which, naturally enough, coincidences fall.

Fenwick and Lorimer go on to say that much of the work of psychology from the turn of the century could regain its validity from this process, although it would be viewed from a different perspective. They are referring, of course, to pre-Einstein research into the non-material world.

The authors advocate a return not only to the anecdotal evidence of such phenomena but also to the pathways followed by those researchers before they succumbed to the new physics of the material world, which promised (but has failed to deliver) an answer to all things. In describing the 'how' of their new discipline, Fenwick and Lorimer appear to echo Jung's cry after his years of frustration in seeking answers in primary scientific research when they say: 'Before we can determine the nature of new dualism we must define the laws of mind and consciousness. This can be done only by the detailed observation of subjective experience.'

Given the subject matter under discussion, the anecdotal material which comprises a major part of this book assumes a growing importance.

Coincidences as non-causal events

Causality is the relation between linked events. In other words, the events are not the cause of coincidences. Max Born says that modern physics has not given up causality as a belief entirely but, in his opinion, an unrestricted belief in causality 'leads necessarily to the idea that the world is an automaton of which we are only small cogs'.

Both Koestler and Lyall Watson are more outspoken about the role of causality. Koestler says it was only in the eighteenth century that, in the wake of the Newtonian revolution, causality was enthroned as the absolute ruler of matter and mind – only to be dethroned in the first decades of the twentieth century, as a consequence of the revolution in physics. Koestler continues the debate by saying that the principle of causality is no longer applicable to modern atomic physics. True. Quantum physicists have long accepted acausality in physical theories. These physicists have even shown that physical bodies can influence each other despite there being no apparent exchange of energy between them – which brings us close to the definition of co-incidence I have postulated of two or more unrelated incidents coming together to create an event.

In *The Gift of Unknown Things* (1976) Lyall Watson says of causality: 'We are so used to [it] that we accept it as a fact of life and have trouble believing that it is not a law of the universe' (p. 66). He goes on to say that theoretical physicists have taught him that the objective world in space and time does not exist and that we are forced to deal now, not in facts, but in possibilities (p. 142). He adds that nobody in quantum physics talks about impossibilities any more.

Conventional researchers and scientists are well and truly living with acausal principles as discussed here, which have long been accepted principles in the field of coincidences. This poses a dilemma, as Michael Shallis observes: 'The inability of instructional science to handle coincidences, combined with their acausal uselessness, is, perhaps, why the notion of coincidence is anathema to so many scientists.' He goes on:

A coincidence is a reminder of the forgotten acausal side of things. That, in one sense only, is its purpose. As there are at least as many unconnected or acausal events as there are causal ones, a coincidence can be seen as pointing to this missing half of reality. If a scientist believes that his work is to explain all of reality ... then a coincidence is not a very encouraging reminder.

[The scientist] can dismiss it quite easily as being anecdotal, etc., his mind can be set at ease and the coincidence has, to all intents and purposes, been explained away. Or has it? (p. 140)

We all experience this 'law' on a daily basis. It provides the logic of much of our existence, but does it provide the logic of our thinking? Any consideration of this question gives the answer 'no', because we are not a logically thinking species, however much we may believe we are in most situations. If we were, logic would tell us not to accept so much of what we put up with in our daily lives – the unwanted stresses, the pollution, jobs we are not happy with, partnerships which result in more suffering than joy. Even such mundane things as shopping are conditioned largely by illogical attitudes – just ask any advertising agency executive.

Physicists argue against logic when they tell us there is no objective way of ordering events in time as a sequence, that time may even be circular and, in theory, we could make journeys into the past. Like the possibilities of that argument, the pattern of our very existence is illogical. We are, after all, not computers; we are emotional and have feelings. So why should we continue to believe that cause and effect has a powerful influence on our lives? It has an influence, but why not allow coincidence to displace it where possible so it can play a greater role, as the experts suggest? Why should we be mere cogs in the mechanics of the causality and ignore the non-causal simply because the theory that might explain it has not yet been formulated? In *Orthodoxy* (1908), G. K. Chesterton says of the law of causation: 'It is the worst chain that ever fettered a human being.' As we shall see in Chapter Six, Chesterton was a man who made the most of coincidences, both in the plots of his stories and in real life. They gave him a more meaningful existence.

A final point: sheer logic tells us not to believe in coincidences or any of the other unexplained wonders of the world!

The Law of Averages

A law linked to the cause and effect principle is the Law of Averages. 'According to the Law of Averages, I've been driving for so long without an accident I'm due for one . . .' Fatalistic comments such as this are commonplace and we hear ourselves murmuring in agreement, stirred no doubt by some primitive instinctual affinities with fate that lie deep in our psyches.

However, there is no valid reason to justify this assertion – or inevitable rendezvous with fate, or fortune. There is no law that can predict anything will happen to any of us. Statistician Dr Manoo Vasholkar agrees: 'There is simply no reason behind the assumption. People who believe in it [the law] are being superstitious.'

The 'Man Who Broke the Bank at Monte Carlo' did not break the bank at all; he increased its income because so many people, blind believers in the Law of Averages, were betting against his run continuing. The book *Stung* (1987) by Gary Ross tells how a bright young bank executive, Brian Molony, carried out the largest single-handed bank fraud in Canadian history, stealing $C10 million over many years to feed his gambling obsession. He lost most of it because of the erroneous belief in the Law of Averages – that his losing 'streak' must change and he would recoup the losses. It didn't and he didn't. Randomness is another strange area in which there can be no certain predictions.

Now consider the way Peter Fairley, at one time science correspondent of Britain's Independent Television News, had a profitable string of wins on the races all because of coincidences. Names seemed to come to him from nowhere. Though not a betting man, he heard the name Blakeney four times on the morning of the 1969 Derby, none of them connected with the horse of that name which duly won, to Fairley's glee, at odds of 15 to 2. He backed a filly called Pia at 100 to 7 after he had received a letter from a woman named Pia and then read a story about a woman called Pia Lindstrom. Prior to this he had never heard the name. After eating at L'Escargot, the restaurant in London, he found there was a horse by that name and he bet on it; it came home at 33 to 12. Then the 'messages' stopped coming. Unlike Molony he shrugged and found something else with which to amuse himself.

To summarize, as with coincidences and probability, and coincidences and unknown principles, we are left with more questions than answers, and also with further indications of just how uncomfortable, even suspicious, many scientists and sceptics feel about a phenomenon that most of us regard as reasonably normal.

Coincidences and the psychic

In her book *The Infinite Hive*, Rosalind Heywood relates an anecdote which is evidence for the argument that supernatural powers may be at work in coincidences.

One day in 1962 her husband handed her a £5 note with the comment that, as she had not bought herself anything lately, she should go out and buy a jumper. The gesture was out of character but still, she decided, it would be fun to indulge in such madness. She was too busy at that exact moment but later that afternoon she felt an urge to go and get the jumper right away. While turning over jumpers in the store, another impression came over her with equal force: 'This is all nonsense, you don't want a jumper. Go home now.'

She left the store and half-way home came across a huddled, quivering man with tears pouring down his cheeks. After some persuasion, he told her his story. Unable to climb stairs he had managed to find, that morning, after much searching, a ground-floor room. But the landlady was demanding the rent in advance and he did not have it. She obediently fished out the £5 note.

Heywood concludes: 'Ought I to look on such a string of coincidences – my husband's unusual gift, my own inconsequential impulses, the apt meeting – as an inner pattern of communication, of relationship, of inner *Gestalt*, or just a random series of chance happenings?'

No aspect of coincidence excites the purists in the scientific community more than linking it with the psychic. Many mathematicians, and others who would legitimize the role of coincidences, assert that there must be a probability of occurrence in every coincidence, otherwise they could never happen. The probability, though it may be minuscule, must exist. One mathematician told me: 'In many cases it is the case that we are unable to see the causes and, therefore, believe that the effects are impossible or most unlikely to happen. If they do happen we call them coincidence and look to the occult for reasons.'

Just how entwined with the occult are coincidences? I may sound dogmatic, but I do not regard the following as a significant coincidence: a person has a profound feeling, or dream, that their great-aunt has died and subsequently finds out that she had, at the precise moment of the feeling or dream. There is a perfectly adequate name for these experiences: premonition.

However, it is not always easy to separate the two phenomena; the similarities keep getting in the way. Like coincidences, premonitions are most significant to those exposed directly to them. Picking up the 'feelings' of another person's trauma at a distance is obviously disturbing and full of non-causality in a physical sense. It is on a par in coincidence with having a long-lost friend appear or make contact after you have inexplicably begun to think constantly about him/her.

I do admit that all this is arguable and can be a matter of personal definition. Often when discussing coincidence on the radio, callers will ring with premonition stories. If people want to regard them as coincidences, that's their personal right – there are, after all, elements of coincidence in premonition ... two seemingly unrelated events that come together in time ...

The following is an example of a coincidence-premonition.

Brilliant young veterinarian Manuela Trueby was feeling emotionally and mentally drained. A long-standing affair had ended and she had also just completed her doctorate. Looking around for some way to relieve the strain, to redirect her life and break free from her past, she answered an advertisement for a short-term international flight attendant. Lufthansa offered the new doctor the job. But she found herself hesitating over whether to change her life in so drastic a fashion.

Still battling with the problem, she wandered into a bakery in Hamburg. As she opened the door she was struck by the strains of an old pop song blaring from the shop's radio, 'Freiheit über den Wolken'. Instantly her doubts cleared and she knew she would accept the airline job.

Dr Trueby told me, 'The song was once a big hit, but I had not heard it for many years and was surprised it was being played. However, the moment I heard it I knew what I should do ...'

The song's title in English is 'Freedom over the Clouds'.

As the above anecdote shows, there can be episodes which contain a mixture of premonition and coincidence. Although

I deal with the subject more fully in Chapter Fourteen, I do want to make the point here that there can be distinctive differences between the two. A major reason for the need to be quite clear about this is that premonitions as coincidence can confuse academics.

A prime example of this was a *New Scientist* article in September 1990 by Dr Susan Blackmore, of the psychology department of the University of Bristol and the University of Bath.

Arguing against belief in the paranormal, Blackmore seizes on what she calls 'amazing coincidences', saying people who experience them are either subject to some totally mysterious new phenomenon or are suffering from an illusion of probability. She then proceeds to analyse the standard I-dreamed-of-great-aunt-at-the-moment-she-died premonition as though it were, unarguably, one of her 'amazing coincidences'.

Blackmore quotes statistician Christopher Scott, who has analysed the great-aunt hypothesis this way (this is serious):

> *There are about 55 million people in Britain and they live about 70 years each; if each has one such dream in a lifetime there should be 2,000 every night. Also about 2,000 people die in each 24 hours [why does Blackmore not acknowledge the coincidence thrown up here of the number of deaths and dreams of death?]. So there will be 4 million coincidences among 55 million people. In others words such an 'amazing coincidence' will be expected about once every two weeks.*

Blackmore does concede that the figures do not mean much if it happens to you personally – in other words, you are deeply impressed by the coincidence, which is one of its intrinsic elements. But why she thinks this simplistic equation debunks coincidences is hard to fathom.

As we have seen, Michael Shallis asserts that the uniqueness of a coincidence is another reason why it cannot be reduced to a probability – as Blackmore seeks to do. By coincidence (it keeps intruding on its own behalf!), to illustrate his argument Shallis comes up with a similar sum to Scott's.

> *At best it can be said that if one notable coincidence is experienced every five years and that an average coincidence takes five*

*minutes and an average lifetime is seventy years, then there
is a one in 525,600 chance of a coincidence occurring in any
five-minute interval of someone's life. (p. 136)*

Professor John Allen Paulos shows he has also given the
problem some thought when he says that he is unimpressed by
the prophetic dream which traditionally comes to light after
some natural disaster that occurs, saying that given the half-
billion hours of dreaming in the US each night – two hours a
night for 250 million people – we should expect as much. Once
again, it is an assertion lacking in detail, a mere sum.

The importance of Scott's, Shallis's and Paulos's sums is
that they show how meaningless probability definitions of coincidence can be and how futile it is to attempt to evaluate
anecdotal material as insubstantial as the content of dreams
as though it were raw data in conventional research, as alike as
white mice.

The point can be made that statistics, properly used, do not
deal with individual cases – these cases are the unpredictable
element in statistics and yet the most significant element in
coincidence.

When they set out to debunk coincidence, scientific
researchers should not take the easy option, as they mostly
do, and ignore the impressive individual anecdotes, even
though it is accepted scientific practice to do so.

Here is an example of the type of coincidence anecdote
scientists find awkward, and which has its psychic elements.
The writer and pioneer of aviation J. W. Dunne, in his book *An
Experiment with Time* (1927), relates how, staying at a hotel in
Sussex in 1899, he dreamed he had an argument with one of the
waiters about what time it was. Dunne insisted it was 4.30 in
the afternoon, while the waiter maintained it was 4.30 in the
morning. In the dream Dunne realized the point behind the
argument was that his watch must have stopped. He took it
from his waistcoat pocket and it had stopped – with the hand at
4.30. At this point he awoke and searched for his watch.

*To my surprise it [the watch] was not, as it usually is, by my
bedside. I got out of bed, hunted round and found it lying on
the chest of drawers. Sure enough it had stopped and the hands
stood at half-past four.*

Dunne goes on to say the solution seemed perfectly obvious. The watch must have stopped the previous afternoon. He had noticed but forgotten the fact and remembered it in his dream. Satisfied with this, he rewound the watch but, not knowing the real time, left the hands as they were.

Next morning, after dressing, he went downstairs and found a clock so he could reset the watch: 'To my absolute amazement I found that the hands had lost only some two or three minutes, *about the amount of time which had elapsed between my waking from the dream and rewinding the watch.*'

Dunne points out that this suggests the watch had stopped at the actual moment of the dream: He adds in a footnote:

> *[The] improbability of my having dreamed of half-past four at half-past four must be multiplied by the improbability of my having been bothered by a stopped watch on the previous afternoon without retaining the faintest recollection of such a fact.*

Dunne's story is what I call a significant coincidence. I can find no record of so-called serious researchers offering an alternative explanation in the ninety-odd years since he first related the story.

Can coincidences foretell events? Well, we have the case of the TV journalist mentioned earlier in this chapter who picked horses by using coincidences and in Chapter Three we discuss the famous case of the *Titanic* predictions. These are cases of non-deliberate prophecy. Deliberate prophecies could not be classified as coincidences.

Perhaps the most notable person who sought to relate coincidences to the psychic was Carl Jung. He formed his synchronicity theory working in conjunction with Nobel Prize winner Wolfgang Pauli, one of this century's greatest physicists, father of the neurino and of the 'Pauli Principle' (that no two electrons can exist in an atom in the same state, i.e. they cannot share the same quantum numbers), to produce an essay on synchronicity, which they defined as 'the simultaneous occurrence of two meaningfully but not causally connected events'.

In a later edition of the essay entitled 'Synchronicity, an Acausal Connecting Principle', Jung said: 'Synchronistic events rest on the simultaneous occurrence of two different psychic states. One of them is the normal, probable state [i.e. the one that is causally explicable], and the other, the critical experience, is the one that cannot be derived causally from the first' (pp. 28–9). This is understandable as an argument but, quite frankly, I find much of the essay incomprehensible and was pleased to read that Koestler thought it 'very vague'. The great Albert Einstein ('God does not play dice with the universe') was cautiously impressed.

Jung had convinced himself early in his medical career that psychic phenomena such as telepathy, precognition, psycho-kinesis and coincidence existed. What he wanted was to be able to understand the 'how' of their existence. To clarify his comments, he makes a crucial distinction between 'chance co-incidence' and 'meaningful coincidence'. The latter he describes as groups of things or events which share some common meaning. To put this into perspective, he believes that the most commonly occurring coincidence – thinking about somebody you have not seen for some time and running into them or hearing from them – is meaningful. Other events – say, for example, a taxi driver getting a concert ticket which is the same number as his licence – are 'mere' chance. Why he makes such a distinction is unclear – as is much of his essay. I would have thought he, a psychiatrist, would relate the significance of an event to the person/patient rather than to an objective category. A run of simultaneous numbers linking unrelated events is a coincidence that could be far more significant, or meaningful, in the mind of the person concerned than running into old friends. Still, it's his theory and up to him to make the arbitrary decisions. One example he gives that is meaningful – to him – is of a theoretical physicist writing a paper on the unity between the observer and what he observes in quantum physics. Browsing through a library with his wife, the physicist randomly selects a volume by an Indian guru of whom neither has heard and the book falls open at a page on which are the words 'there is no distinction between the observer and the observed'.

Perhaps Jung's most-quoted example of a meaningful coinci-dence is his account of a young woman patient who, the night before she saw him, dreamed she had been given a golden scarab. Sitting with his back to the window, listening to the woman talk of her dream, Jung heard a gentle tapping behind his shoulder. He looked around and saw a small insect knocking against the pane. As he opened the window, the insect flew in and he caught it. He realized it was a scarabaeid beetle, the closest equivalent to a golden scarab to be found in Switzerland. Until then the woman had not been progressing in her therapy, but Jung says that showing the woman the beetle had the effect of breaking down her rational defences and led to a new phase in her mental maturity. After admitting that nothing like this had happened to him before, or since, and that the dream of the patient was unique in his experience, he goes on to say: 'Any essential change of attitude signifies a psychic renewal which is usually accompanied by symbols of rebirth in the patient's dreams and fantasies.' The scarab, he points out, is the classic symbol of rebirth in some ancient cultures.

Jung felt compelled by the experiences of his patients and by his own questioning mind to try to come up with a theory for such unexplained phenomena, including his 'meaningful' coincidences. He had grown up with and come to look at the world through the laws of causality, but Einstein's Special Theory of Relativity, published in 1905, and other developments in physics – including the strange behaviour involving subatomic events in quantum physics – had caused something of a rebellion against causality in the mind of the psychiatrist. Indeed, a great many other researchers in the realms of not only psychology but also the psychic and physics from early this century felt the same.

Jung wrote:

> After collecting psychological experiences from many people [including, of course, coincidences] and many countries for fifty years, I doubt whether an exclusively psychological approach can do justice to the phenomena in question. Not only the findings of parapsychology, but my own theoretical reflections . . . have led me to certain postulates which touch on the realms of nuclear physics and the conception of space-time continuum.

The Jung and Pauli essay was published in 1952. In it they argued that in their view there was an absolute spaceless, timeless cosmos in which both the psyche and the material universe existed. Jung, fond of abstract terms, called it a 'transpsychic reality', a realm beyond our conscious in which past, present and future merge and where the psyche (or the soul, if you prefer) and matter are alternative manifestations of a single reality. Synchronicity was, therefore, an 'unexpected parallelism between psychic and physical events'.

With his new-found knowledge of physics he compared his theory with the tendency of fundamental particles (electrons, protons, etc.) to behave sometimes like waves and at other times like particles. He contended that thoughts or events which shared some common meaning were attracted to each other like magnets, without a known causal relationship.

The whole theory of synchronicity is bound up intrinsically with Jung's theory of the collective unconscious and the archetypes. He believed that archetypes structure the shared sense of meaning for mankind as a whole. They come from other times and other parts of the world but are waiting to be used by man dipping into the collective unconscious. The scarab beetle incident is one example he gives.

His ideas led him to another belief in a subject that could not seem further from the world of science – the Chinese *I Ching*, a means of fortune-telling that waxes and wanes in popularity in the Western world but definitely has as its basis coincidence (in Jung's terms, of course, it is meaningful coincidence). His belief is based on the 'odd fact that a reaction that makes sense arises out of a technique seemingly excluding all sense from the outset'.

The *I Ching*, for those who don't know it, involves the tossing of three coins to find one of the sixty-four hexagrams which are supposed to give an appropriate answer to today's problems. The texts accompanying the hexagrams were written thousands of years ago and the words are inscrutable – that is, their *meaning* is rather like those predictions in verse of Nostradamus, although Jung would not have compared the two famous divining references. Nostradamus' messages are so cryptic that the same ones have been interpreted in wildly different ways (see Chapter Six). Jung argues that the *I Ching* hexagrams represent an archetypal situation, with synchronistic links between the moment they were written and the moment the modern-day user looks for an answer.

There is the story of a London couple who in 1978 were involved in buying a house. Like many such purchases, the process became bogged down, what with selling their own house, getting the tenants of the new house to move and organizing their mortgage. They asked the *I Ching*: 'Will our intention to buy the house proceed with success?' After tossing their coins the required number of times, the answer was hexagram twenty-eight, which reads: 'The load is too heavy for the strength of the supports. The ridge pole, on which the whole roof rests, sags to the breaking point because its supporting ends are too weak for the load to bear.'

Within days the couple heard from the building society that their mortgage application had been refused because of the state of the property. Their surveyors had found major cracks in its supporting walls. No doubt regular *I Ching* users can tell similar stories.

Jung stressed the importance of using the *I Ching* in moments of sincerity and with deep concentration. Such advice about Nostradamus' verses is probably wasteful.

Koestler said of Jung's views: 'It is painful to watch how a great mind, trying to disentangle himself from the causal chain of materialistic science, gets entangled in its own verbiage' (he believed Pauli had little influence on the essay). Both Kammerer and Jung, Koestler claimed, were caught up in the logical categories of Greek philosophy, whereas he believed explanations for many coincidences are to be found in terms beyond traditional categories of philosophy, analysis and languages; language can stand as a screen between the mind and reality.

Theories that do not coincide

Despite their arguments, both Jung and Koestler compared the strange laws of physics with the material of parapsychology and found that the disciplines meet in coincidence. But do they? As we can see with Jung, Koestler and others, the reason many psychic researchers – psychiatrists to some extent – have tried to impose on their work and beliefs the theories and concepts of modern physics, especially quantum physics, is that they see in it a world where known laws of nature do not apply. *It is safe to say this comparison has resulted in a singular lack of success.*

Discoveries in physics have helped us understand the mechanical side of the universe, but not the non-physical side, in which our conscious and subconscious are located. Of course, they were never meant to. The change in direction of psychic research from investigations into what were mostly anecdotal cases to this 'scientific' approach came about with Einstein's relativity theory, when many concepts, including the understanding of time as a fixed sequence, were wiped away. Until then, the practical view was that time was an ordered sequence of moments following one upon the other. Einstein said this separation between past, present and future had had the 'value of mere illusion'. It was this removal of the 'time barrier' that seemed to offer one of the most powerful hopes to psychic (parapsychological) researchers, because it was thought to promise a view into the mysterious world which such phenomena as coincidence were believed to inhabit. This hope is now looking more and more futile as the century draws to a close.

Other research in physics also buoyed those who were seeking an explanation of coincidence and, in their mind, related ESP phenomena, such as precognition. The German physicist Werner Heisenberg offered proof that the universe's foundations rest on nothing more solid than unpredictable and wholly random subatomic events. He called this the Uncertainty Principle and in 1931 won the Nobel Prize for his findings.

Another principle, the Principle of Complementarity, established that matter and energy are two sides of the same coin. Therefore, psychic researchers argued, if our consciousness is looked upon as an energy form, part of the mechanical universe, it could have some influence over matter in creating phenomena, including coincidences. Other theories and postulations have also been seized on as tools for explaining psychic phenomena. Certainly, as we have seen, there are principles and theories that do apply to coincidence, such as the theory of probabilities and the Clustering Effect. But in the end even Jung turned back to anecdotal evidence as the most likely source for a 'why' of phenomena, saying that anyone who expected to find a scientific answer to the question of parapsychological truth would be disappointed.

Jung concluded that the most important part of research into the subject *'will be the careful exploration and qualitative description of spontaneous events'* (my italics) – that is, the kind of anecdotal evidence presented in this book, much of it having stood the test of time.

It is difficult to understand why psychic researchers set such store by the new physics discoveries once we realize how science pushed phenomena such as coincidence and other non-mechanical subjects like consciousness out of the picture centuries before Einstein came along, when the first waves of modern scientific discoveries were sweeping the world – at the time of not just Newton but also Copernicus, Kepler, Descartes, Galileo and Bacon. Their science looked at the physical world, at material that could be checked by observation and repetition, as with material used in scientific research today. Anecdotal material, along with once revered subjects such as astrology, ceased to be of scientific interest from that early time, not from the twentieth century, as some would have us believe. The axiom laid down then and still held as valid today was that everything in the universe can be explained in physical terms. As our academics pointed out early in this chapter, Jung's universal or collective unconscious is not seen as worthy of consideration as a means of explanation for the universe and all things in it. Koestler, of course, would trace this separation back many centuries earlier, to a time before Aristotle and other Greek philosophers, when Western thought was, in his terms, 'ensnared with a logic that has permeated our vocabulary and concepts, and decided for us what is thinkable and what is unthinkable'.

CHAPTER TWO

The Clustering Effect

For years now, walking along a busy main road near my home to pass the time, I have counted the number of vehicles driving by with only one occupant and those with more than one. Invariably two-thirds of the vehicles have only the driver. This would more or less confirm official surveys. But what intrigues me is the consistency of this ratio in the space of the three- to four-minute walk during which time I may count anything between thirty and fifty vehicles. If the numbers look like varying, there will always be a cluster of, say, solo-driven vehicles to balance the sudden 'run' of vehicles with two or more occupants. What is going on? What causes such a constant pattern? Obviously the drivers are not consciously sorting themselves out into appropriate categories.

Another odd effect I have begun to notice – and it would take a more serious study to confirm – is a clustering of drivers by sex. Car after car of male drivers, then suddenly a stream of women takes over. There are still more male drivers on the road, but at times it could be assumed from this observation that women predominate behind the wheel.

I walk along the road at different times of the day and wondered if that – time – had anything to do with it – mothers picking up their children from school, for example. Or has it to do with men, being the more aggressive drivers, overtaking or being allowed to pass by the women until women are bunched at the rear of the traffic flow, much in the way that the more aggressive racing drivers tend to lead the field? Or is there a more subtle explanation?

At the basis of all this is the Clustering Effect, as proposed by Austrian biologist Paul Kammerer. Kammerer's concept was set out in his controversial 1919 book *Das Gesetz der Serie* (*The Law of the Series*). He was one of the earliest researchers to draw up a definition of coincidences, which he found to be 'a series of lawful occurrences of the same or similar things or events . . . which are not connected by the same active cause'. Note that he avoids the use of the word 'chance', as I have done (see Chapter One).

He wrote of an image of 'a world mosaic or cosmic kaleido-scope, which in spite of constant shufflings and rearrangements, also takes care of bringing like and like together'. In reality, he said, coincidence was the work of a natural principle.

Kammerer collected examples of coincidences all his life, even the most trivial (although he did not regard them as such) – for example, on 4 November 1910, he records that a relative went to a concert where he had seat number 9 and cloakroom ticket number 9. The same relative went to a concert the next day and had seat number 21 and cloakroom ticket number 21. Kammerer also used to spend days just sitting in public places, noting the number of people passing, the way they dressed and what they carried. His examination of the data collected helped him to his conclusion that things happen in clusters.

The following are further examples. An American mathematician noticed the earlier pages in books of logarithms kept in his university library were dirtier than later ones, indicating that students, for some reason, had more occasion to calculate with numbers beginning with 1 than with any other number. Theoretically each digit from 1 to 9 should occur equally, but he found that 30 per cent of the numbers were 1 and only 5 per cent 9. A newspaper librarian told me that when newspaper clippings were piled together prior to filing, they always went in descending order with the A–G section much higher than the other two piles, I–P and Q–Z. Areas that are covered by more than one telephone directory will generally show more usage for those containing the first letters of the alphabet – say, A–K – than the rest.

But what most interests me is whether these seemingly illogical occurrences are part of a hidden principle that those who take Kammerer's observations seriously believe lies behind many coincidences. In other words, is clustering another facet of coincidence?

Generally, mathematicians view examples cited as proof of the Clustering Effect as no more than occurrences that can be found in any random system. One told me, 'Go through a book of random numbers, a telephone directory, a book with mathematical tables, or take the first 1,000 decimal digits of *pi* or *e*, and everywhere clusters of the same digits may be seen. The phenomena are neither extraordinary nor coincidences, they are merely proofs of randomness. The same applies to the so-called Clustering Effect.'

There is no argument about some remarkable clusters thrown up in random series. But what happens when we apply the Clustering Effect to events and people?

Author William Burroughs asserts that events do appear to be somehow magnetically attracted to one another as a series. For example, we hear of a bus crash and the chances are within the next few days there will be another. Burroughs says that the significance of such a 'run' is to tell us: 'Lightning always strikes twice in the same spot. The first incident is a warning . . .'

Another believer argues: 'I have found that using the Clustering Effect I can almost predict the news before it happens. If I hear of a fatal airline crash somewhere, I can say with a degree of certainty that shortly there will be another. Almost invariably there is. An example, three recent incidents involving planes crashing into houses.'

To find for myself whether there was anything in such claims I decided to keep a close eye on news events over a period. The trial was to be for the interrelated purpose of showing whether events had a predictive quality and whether they occurred in cluster.

At the time, in the early months of 1994, the most unusual story in the news was the case of Loretta Bobbitt, who had cut off the penis of her husband, John Wayne Bobbitt. One obvious reason for its prominence was its rarity, surely. How could there be a clustering of penis-cutters? On the basis of its seeming improbability of recurrence, I decided to use it as a test case.

I cast about for another incident, one that would also suggest itself as unlikely to be repeated. The story that caught my eye in this category was one about the collapse of a concrete supermarket roof in Nice in which at least two people were killed and many injured (reported on 28 January 1994). A cluster of roof collapses? Not with modern building standards and the risk the builders and owners run of being sued. In any case, even allowing for shoddy work, further collapses would have to be of the same dramatic proportions as this one to make the news. This became the second unlikely incident I resolved to watch for evidence of clustering.

First, the Penis Effect. On 28 January 1994, some days after Loretta Bobbitt was found not guilty of malicious wounding, there was a report of a forty-two-year-old South Korean found with his penis cut off, groaning in front of a motel in a provincial city. He died as a result of his injury.

A report of 3 February 1994 told of a Turkish woman severing the penis of her lover on 23 January, claiming he regularly forced her to have 'divergent' sex. The man was reunited with his penis when it was stitched back on in hospital.

The same report belied the copycat nature of the penis-bobbing – that is, women taking their cue from the well-publicized Bobbitt case – in that it also told of a German woman who had attacked her would-be suitor in Frankfurt-on-Oder in 1992. Prosecutors said the woman knocked her victim out by punching him with a chair. She then cut off his penis and tried to burn it. Doctors did attempt to rejoin the severed – and singed organ – but without success. It was, however, useful in evidence.

This was a crime that was beginning to look less than unique.

On 7 February 1994 a TV presenter mentioned on air that ten years before a Brisbane woman had chopped off a man's penis in a *Psycho*-style attack on him in the shower.

All these reports had me recalling that in Thailand in the early 1980s a German married to a local woman confided to me that he did not dare stray because his wife had threatened to cut off his penis if he did. 'And she would do it too,' he added mournfully, sipping at his beer. I had never heard of such a threat and took it as a joke.

It was not until 9 March that the final incident in the cluster occurred, with a twist to it. A Los Angeles woman told a court she had castrated her husband with a pair of scissors after he tried to force sex on her – the complaint made against Bobbitt by his wife. Bobbitt's penis was surgically reattached but in this case the man's testicles were not, although he had become reconciled with his wife at the time of the trial.

So we have five incidents of penis attacks – a cluster?

Now to the roof collapse. This seemed to be a most unlikely subject for clustering and I was reluctant to pursue it, but it had 'caught' my eye and I could not in all conscience go looking for a more likely event. I was stuck with it.

The very next day a TV report said that in West Virginia a large warehouse had collapsed under the weight of snow on its roof.

On 29 January 1994 a newspaper picture showed the collapsed roof of the Olympic Zetrsa stadium in Sarajevo, destroyed by Serbian shelling.

On 30 January 1994 there was a further newspaper report of two people hurt in Nice when the ceiling collapsed in a super-market run by the same French chain that owned the store whose roof had caved in a few days before.

On 7 February 1994 there was a newspaper photo of members of the African National Congress scrambling to safety as the roof of a stadium in Seisoville township in the Orange Free State collapsed.

So, within the space of ten days, there were reports of five roof collapses, not minor incidents, as the photographs that went with the stories showed.

There are, of course, many reasons why a roof would collapse – the weight of snow, shelling, people gathered there. In these cases there was no common denominator to mark the pheno-menon as anything more than a non-causal Clustering Effect. It leaves us with a question whose answer would appear to lie, and then only partly, in the Clustering Effect: why suddenly and without warning for ten days in 1994 did roofs of public buildings in different parts of the world become vulnerable?

As a footnote to the above, on Tuesday, 29 March 1994, a tornado caused the roof of the Goshen Methodist Church in Piedmont, Alabama, to collapse during morning service, killing seventeen worshippers and injuring more than ninety.

In this same period there was a variation on the Clustering Effect of air accidents, as the following details show.

On 15 March 1994 six soldiers died when a US gunship crashed in Kenya. On the same day, six soldiers were injured in an army parachuting exercise about 100 km from Wagga Wagga, Australia. And on 25 March 1994 fifteen paratroopers were killed and more than eighty were injured as a result of a collision between two planes over Pope Air Force base, Florida.

However, the grimmest Clustering Effect I came across during this monitoring period began as the toll of bodies being unearthed from a home in Gloucester, England, rose – three, five, seven, nine . . .

A report from Poland appeared (10 March 1994), saying police were holding a man suspected of killing at least twenty-seven people, mostly women, in towns across the country. The bodies found at the Gloucester home of builder Frederick West were also of women. West, at the time the Polish story broke, had been charged with three murders.

In a further development in this particular cluster, serial killer Jeffrey Dahmer appeared in a TV interview to say he had eaten some of his seventeen victims because he wanted to make them part of himself. The report did not indicate whether his appearance was a result of the Gloucester killings – or, as seems more likely, coincidence.

An Agency France Press report from New York said Ricardo Silvio Caputo, once dubbed 'the most wanted man in America', had turned himself in to police and confessed to murdering four women. He was also suspected of a fifth killing. Caputo had been on the run for twenty years, following the killings, and said he had begun having nightmares about his crimes two years ago.

Why did Caputo choose this point in time in the twenty-year period since the killings to give himself up? Did reports of the Gloucester killings finally tip the scale for Caputo?

On 26 February 1994 reports from Israel told of the slaughter of more than fifty (numbers later amended) Palestinians and the wounding of dozens more by a lone Jewish gunman at a mosque on the occupied West Bank. It is one of the worst mass killings by a lone gunman of modern history.

The same day as the Polish mass killer was revealed there was a further report, this one from Germany, of a man who had killed at least six people in a courtroom in Euskirchen following his conviction for assaulting a woman. The man fired at the judge and then threw a bomb across the courtroom. In addition to the six deaths at least six were injured.

Further, a report from Moscow told of two young border

guards on the Pacific island of Tanfilyev in the southern Kuril Islands who shot dead six other guards and injured more. They claimed they had been harassed by their colleagues.

The cluster killings continued into March. On 15 March a report from Charlotte, North Carolina, said a man police described as a drug addict was charged the previous day with ten counts of murder. This followed the strangulation of young women he knew in North Carolina. The suspect, Henry Wallace, twenty-eight years old, was a drifter who had settled in the town three years earlier. Nine bodies had been recovered and the search was going on for the tenth victim.

There was a variation of the theme in this period. First came the report of 13 March quoted earlier about Ricardo Caputo turning himself in and confessing to a series of murders. The following day, Monday, 14 March, another confession grabbed the headlines around the world. Christian Spurling had revealed before dying the previous November that he had helped fake the famous photograph purporting to show the head and neck of the Loch Ness monster apparently rising from the surface of the lake in 1934.

Spurling had used a small toy submarine and wood to build the neck and head. The photograph was fabricated by a Mr Marmaduke Wetherell, a film-maker and self-styled big game hunter. He had been hired by the UK *Daily Mail* to find the monster. Spurling was his stepson and had been asked by Wetherell to make him a monster. The model was then floated into the shallows of the loch and the photograph taken. The men were so overwhelmed by the huge fuss their trick caused, they had been afraid to confess.

For sixty years the grainy photograph has been touted as positive proof that the Loch Ness monster existed and led to endless scientific probes of the lake.

The following day (15 March) a further report of an owning-up. Ray Jones, a seventy-eight-year-old former prisoner, confessed he had stolen jewels from Italian-born film star Sophia Loren in 1960. It was his most famous crime. He had resold the haul for $90,000 (worth about $395,000 in today's terms).

Meanwhile, the slaughter continued . . .

On 16 March a report from Los Angeles told of a gunman who broke through an elaborate security system in a Los

Angeles computer company and opened fire on staff, killing three and wounding two others. He then turned the gun on himself, dying from a gunshot wound to the head.

On 17 March there was a report from New York of another suspected mass killer, Frank Potts, a paedophile who may have killed fifteen young people from New York to Florida. Police had unearthed one body in a grave near Potts's cabin in Estillfork, Alabama. They believed ten or twelve other bodies might be buried there (presumably the others are buried elsewhere).

With all these killings, the impulse is to look for a link, to try to make some sense of this saturation clustering, both their occurrence and their consequence, if only in the hope of finding a clue that would help prevent further killings. But how can there, for example, be a significant causal link between the killings in a mosque on the West Bank, those in the small town of Euskirchen in northern Germany and those that took place about the same time on a Russian Pacific island thousands of kilometres away?

In the Polish, Gloucester and Charlotte killings, it may emerge that similar urges or mental aberrations drove the three men involved, despite the very different cultures and social systems in which the killers were operating.

The urges may have been the same as those that drove Dahmer, but it is not the task of this chapter to discuss that. It is the occurrence that interests us. When all is said and done, the collection here can be seen only as largely non-causal. In other words, it is more than likely that we are once again faced with a series of coincidences in this chain with no obvious links – a grim Clustering Effect.

Another argument is that such seemingly unrelated behaviour may be an indication of human nature operating in some unknown manner to bring about patterns of similar events in time. Some would see in these unknown 'patterns' not so much a rule of coincidence but British biologist Dr Rupert Sheldrake's 'morphic resonance' theory (which, in any case, has coincidence overtones). For example, it was not until 1954 that Roger Bannister achieved the 'impossible' by breaking the four-minute mile. Once broken, however, many runners followed, consistently improving on the time. However, if there is such an influence behind the material we have dealt with, how do we explain the collapsing roofs, unless we imbue them with a collective memory?

I found some patterns behind the mass killings involving sudden, inexplicable bursts of violence on the part of an individual. For example, three of Australia's four worst mass killings all happened in the month of August! Some more weird statistics emerged from the eight major random killings in different parts of the world between 1986 and 1989. Two of these also happened in the month of August. Then there was the extraordinary fact that in half of the shootings the death toll was the same: fourteen! It was as though some cosmic being had been keeping score and ending proceedings once a certain grim cluster of numbers had been reached.

As for the role of morphic resonance in this, the archetype of such mass killings occurred in 1966, when student Charles Whitman fired randomly from the twenty-seven-storey clock tower at the University of Texas at Austin before being killed by a police marksman. The month: August. The toll: fourteen.

The Clustering Effect of date and number of victims aside, it can be said that the phenomenon of mass killings by a lone assailant had entered the universal psyche from that day in Texas – a process involving action at a distance in space and time, morphic resonance! The Clustering Effect?

Paradoxically, the link between Sheldrake's morphic reso-nance theory and Kammerer's Clustering Effect lies in the increasing frequency of a phenomenon. We only have to look at the best-known example of morphic resonance, the manner in which blue tits got the hang of pecking through the foil tops of milk bottles soon after they were introduced into Britain. Despite the fact that tits seldom venture more than a few kilo-metres from their breeding place, the habit spread throughout Britain and also to other European countries. Sheldrake finds the Dutch records of this phenomenon particularly interesting. Milk bottles practically disappeared during the war and did not reappear in any number until 1947 or 1948. Few if any tits that had learned the habit of piercing the foil caps could have survived this length of time. However, with the reappearance of the tops, attacks on them began again rapidly in many different places. Detailed analysis of the records showed that the spread of the habit accelerated as time went on (J. Fisher and R. A. Hinde, 'The opening of milk bottles by birds', *British Birds*, 1949, 42, pp. 347–57, quoted in Sheldrake, *The Presence of the Past* (1988), pp. 177–8). If the morphic resonance theory has relevance, this evidence of acceleration is ominous news as far as the matters we are considering are concerned – the incidence of mass murders (serial killings or someone going berserk with a gun) – to the extent that from being a rarity they are frequent enough for them to occur in clusters.

Part of the reason for the enduring legend of Jack the Ripper lies in the fact that for many years people had no reason to believe the killings and dismemberings of the five prostitutes in London's East End over a period of time in 1888 were anything other than a unique event. For years it appeared that would be so. Now the crime is remembered more because the perpetrator was never caught and speculation continues as to who the murderer was.

Since the 1970s we have had Pedro Alonso Lopez, the 'Colombian Monster', who admitted in March 1980 to killing more than 300 pre-teen girls; John Wayne Gacy, thirty-three victims, the first body found under his house in Chicago in 1978; Peter Sutcliffe, the Yorkshire Ripper, who killed thirteen women between 1975 and 1980; Dennis Nielsen, who strangled fifteen men between 1978 and 1983; Jeffrey Dahmer, who was jailed for life in 1992, for slaying seventeen men and boys . . .

The current cluster of mass murders draws from criminologists, sociologists and other experts in the field of human behaviour the view that nothing other than accidental patterns are behind them. For example, most of the killers appear to have come from impoverished backgrounds and present to the world a normal face, while inside they are a seething mass of hatred and resentment.

Should we, as a result of such views, approach the mass-killing phenomenon with equanimity, as random quirks which will even themselves out in the long run? Or should we take to heart Burroughs's dictum that lightning strikes twice and the first strike is a warning? After all, we all know it never rains but it pours!

I now come to an even more controversial aspect of the Clustering Effect: its influence on our personal destinies. This is an exercise that involves astrology. The link between the Clustering Effect and astrology may at first glance seem tenuous, but at one level we find an affinity in that both are non-mechanical forces whose energies are said to affect us directly. A further link was forged as a result of research carried out by Michel Gauquelin in the 1950s.

The French mathematician decided to study a basic hypothesis of astrology. This is that the position of the planets at the moment of birth, as opposed to the star sign under which it is born, influences the future of a baby. Gauquelin compiled a list of 1,083 eminent professors of medicine and found that Mars and Saturn formed the ascendant and descendant – that is, separated by 180 degrees – at their moment of birth. This was gigantically beyond chance: 10,000,000 to 1 against. The ascendant is the rising sign on the eastern horizon at the moment of birth and is said to modify the star sign under which you are born and form your true inner nature. Even when he spread his research to other professions and other countries, for a total of 25,000 Gauquelin came up with similar findings. For example, in the charts of 3,305 scientists in the survey the same planets showed up 666 times, against a chance score of 565. The odds against this were 500,000 to 1. With 1,485 athletes in the large test group, the planets were prominent 327 times, against 253 by chance. As with the scientists, the odds against these figures coming up were 500,000 to 1.

He did further tests and found soldiers and politicians were born more frequently under the influence of a rising Jupiter, and no famous French writer was born when Saturn was in the ascendant.

Gauquelin's findings were greeted with scorn in academic circles. However, he did not recant under the ensuing pressure. In fact, the attack on him from the 'scientific' world is a cautionary tale showing that sceptics can be just as devious as those they claim to expose.

Members of a scientific committee in Belgium, set up to demolish Gauquelin's results, found, in fact, that they were confirming his figures. Their deviousness took the form of simply refusing to publish the results. In the US in the 1970s, the Committee for the Scientific Investigation of Claims of the Paranormal (the psycops) thought it had a winner with

Gauquelin. It conducted an inquiry into the French mathematician's findings, specifically those for sports persons – the Mars and Jupiter Effect. To their consternation, the committee members, like the Belgian boffins, were embarrassed by the results. Instead of exposing the findings as wrong, they proved them. Their initial reaction was to deny the results. But they went further . . . Dr Dennis Rawlins, a physicist and member of the committee, showed just how much further by issuing a pamphlet which said in part:

> [the committee members] are a group of would-be debunkers who . . . falsified the results, covered up their errors, and gave the boot to a colleague who threatened to tell the truth . . . I am still sceptical of occult beliefs that CSICOP was created to debunk. But I have changed my mind about the integrity of some of those who make a career of opposing occultism.

Undeterred by all this, I decided to carry out my own modest survey of star signs and careers. It began with the astrological hypothesis that a disproportionate number of doctors 'cluster' beneath the birth sign of Taurus.

From professional directories, I randomly selected the birth dates of 260 doctors born in Australia, the UK, the US, Europe and Asia. Lo and behold, the results showed Taurean doctors (those born between 21 April and 20 May) were easily the largest single group of the twelve signs of the zodiac. They totalled thirty-one (12 per cent), followed by Virgos at twenty-five (9.6 per cent), with Aries, one of the star signs adjoining Taurus, at twenty-four (9.2 per cent). The test showed a low number of Aquarians, seventeen (6.5 per cent), and one of its adjoining star sign, Pisces, with thirteen (5 per cent).

Therefore, first and second signs on the zodiac table, Aries and Taurus, had 21.2 per cent of the doctors, while at the bottom the eleventh and twelfth signs, Aquarius and Pisces, had only 11.5 per cent.

Doctors are possibly the most suitable group for statistical analysis because they tend to follow their occupation throughout their working lives. Nevertheless, encouraged by the clear-cut findings, I decided to enlarge the scope of the research and look for birth-date significance in other groups.

An examination of the birth dates of 130 prominent lawyers and judges showed the highest single group were Aquarians at seventeen (13 per cent), the poorly represented star among doctors. They were followed by Capricorns (23 December–20 January), again an adjoining sign, at fourteen. Together they made up an impressive 23 per cent of the twelve star signs.

A separate analysis found that seven of the thirty-one Federal Court judges (birth dates were not available for five) were Librans (22 per cent). The number was disproportionate, the next highest was three each for Virgos, Aquarians and Leos. Librans had scored badly on the original list of 130 lawyers. However, the lawyers list had included barristers, solicitors and judges. In this case, we were dealing with a much narrower field, judges only. The symbol for Libra is the scales of justice!

Librans, says astrologer Linda Goodman, 'go around mediating and patching up quarrels between others. Still, they enjoy a good argument themselves.' What better description could there be of a judge?

Next analysed were the birth dates of 130 senior armed service officers. Again a clear leader emerged, those whose sign was the goat, Capricorns, with seventeen (13 per cent), while the high-scoring Taureans in the doctors' analysis managed only a lowly seven (5 per cent), the same number as one of its adjoining sign, Gemini. Sagittarians (23 November–22 December) showed the least preference for service life, at four (3 per cent).

An examination of the birth dates of well-known artists (singers, writers, painters, etc.) revealed Sagittarians were equal leader with Capricorn, again an adjoining sign. Each scored fifteen (11.5 per cent) – that is, a disproportionate 23 per cent between them. Two other stars that adjoin one another, Gemini and Cancer, were next, each with fourteen (10.7 per cent). The 'doctor' sign, Taurus, was least represented in the arts, with a total of four.

Of 130 leading business personalities, Taureans headed the list, along with Scorpios and Capricorns, each with seventeen (13 per cent). Numbers here were all close to average – not unexpectedly, considering that the backgrounds of those who have made it in business are likely to be more diverse than those of the professions.

However, adjoining star signs – in this case Aquarius and Pisces – once again were a feature, with the lowest numbers, seven and eight respectively.

It should be apparent by now that throughout this survey one of the major findings has been the Clustering Effect involving *adjoining* star signs. In other words, members of a profession tend to be born not so much under a star sign but at a particular time of the year.

With Taureans scoring high as doctors and businessmen, it is interesting to see what Goodman says about them. In her *Sun Signs* (1970), one of the world's best-selling books on astrology, she remarks that they make 'good doctors'. Goodman goes on to say Taureans are never more at home than when expressing themselves creatively, through their senses, as long as the financial rewards are sound . . .

She again talks business when she says Scorpios belong in any field that allows them to investigate its assets and its liabilities. The third group, Capricorns, are in business because they are happy only when involved in a gold-embossed sure thing. I must emphasize that Goodman does not as a rule talk of specific professions for star signs.

The birth signs of MPs also showed clear preferences, even though MPs come from more divergent backgrounds. Virgo- and Scorpio-born MPs topped the list, each with sixteen (12.3 per cent) out of the 130 birth dates checked. These were followed by three adjoining stars, Capricorn, Aquarius and Pisces, with thirteen, twelve and thirteen respectively. Geminis were the least politically motivated, with only four representatives (3 per cent).

For a definition of the Virgo and Aries characters, we look to another astrologer, Suzanne White, author of *The New Astrology* (1986).

White says that 'people in high positions' often turn out to be born under the sign of Virgo. Virgos, she goes on, tend to think of themselves as separate and not-so-equal beings in relation to the rest of the world.

Aries is the first sign of the zodiac and White confirms that those born under its sign are natural leaders. Curiously, there have been some notable cases of attempts to link histori- cal leaders with the warlike sign of Aries – said, when the astrological sign under which they were born has been the adjoining Taurean, to be symbolic of healers, creators and home-lovers with placid natures.

Antonia Fraser notes in *Cromwell, Our Chief of Men* (1974) that Cromwell was born on 25 April 1599, making him a Taurean, but that a tradition arose that he had been born in the early hours of the 25th, thus producing a rising Aries in his birth sign.

The most famous prediction made about Hitler was also based on the belief in an Arian birth sign. In 1923 Hitler and his followers were looked upon as rabble-rousers, little known outside Bavaria. In that year respected German astrologer Elsbeth Ebertin wrote that a 'man of action' born on 20 April (Hitler's birthday in 1889), with the sun in the twenty-ninth degree of Aries at the time of his birth, 'can expose himself to personal danger by excessively uncautious action and could very likely trigger off an uncontrollable crisis'. She went on to say that his constellations showed he was to be taken very seriously indeed:

> *He is destined to play a Führer-role in future battles. It seems the man I have in mind, with this Arian influence, is destined to* sacrifice himself for the German nation, *also to face up to all circumstances with audacity and courage, even when it is a matter of* life and death, *and to give an impulse, which will burst forth quite suddenly, to a German Freedom Movement. But I will not anticipate destiny. Time will show . . .*

Her prediction was highly accurate, but she did not know until later that Hitler was born in the evening of the 20th, which is a cusp day – in other words, a day when the birth sign changes at midday, in this case from Aries to Taurus. The significance of this is that astrologers believe the minute of birth is critical in drawing up an accurate personal horoscope.

Current world leaders with apparently Arian tendencies include Saddam Hussein of Iraq, also a Taurean, and the fiery Russian political party leader Vladimir Zhirinovsky (born, like Cromwell, on 25 April). What all this hints at is further evidence of the tendency of characteristics attributed to one star sign to spill over into the adjoining sign, as my small survey indicates. This is an area well worth further exploration, as it might provide new, hidden or forgotten insights into the ancient body of knowledge that is astrology.

Suzanne White also reveals another trait demonstrated by the Taurean leaders just mentioned: 'Show Aries chaos and he will jump right in and begin putting things in order.'

A fault with Arians is that they do not make good followers. Three of the four Australian Arian PMs served the shortest terms of all. All three came in, or were called on, to deal with crises ('chaos,' as White says). Having done so, they largely lost interest in further proceedings, a classic Arian trait.

Further evidence of this trait was to be found in the 1992 British general election. Both contenders for the top office were Arians – in fact, both men celebrated their birthdays during the election campaign. Labour leader Neil Kinnock turned fifty on 28 March and Prime Minister John Major was forty-nine the following day. True to their Arian character, both had been chosen to lead their parties as the men for the job in a crisis. Kinnock took his party through the crisis of settling divisions in its ranks to bring it before the electors as a united party. Having lost, he did not argue about departing.

Major had become PM when the long-serving Margaret Thatcher stepped aside under pressure, precipitating a crisis. He was expected to be a short-term leader, as Labour was tipped to win the first election he faced ... Although Major won that election, it is appropriate to ask how long it will be before his Arian temperament asserts itself and Britain has to look for another long-term PM.

A Capricorn who is quite happy with the job the stars foretold for him is the mathematician and astronomer Stephen Hawking. Although largely a sceptic, Hawking is intrigued by the fact that his birth date, 8 January 1942, is the exact date on which, 300 years before, one of the world's greatest scientists, Galileo, died.

The author of the best-seller *A Brief History of Time* (1988) considers himself a rationalist, even an atheist. He would be expected to scoff at what astrologers have to say about his Capricorn personality. Let's look at astrologer Suzanne White's interpretation.

According to her, Capricorns can be bossy and self-confident in the extreme. They are either always on top of the heap or moving – slowly and certainly – towards the summit of their field.

In what amounts to a sad commentary on Hawking's incurable disease, which causes the body to waste away and confines him to a wheelchair, White says: 'Forget Capricorns in areas that call for supple, smooth body movement. Capricorn adults are clumsy and you want to warn them, "Be careful, watch where you are going."'

White also combines Western and Chinese astrology in *The New Astrology*. Under this system Hawking is a Capricorn who was born in the Chinese Year of the Snake. Of Capricorn snakes she says that they are destined for some form of prominence. They sincerely believe that they are the best and greatest at their craft or field. They could 'probably live a very full life just following hunches and answering premonition's call'. They find 'brilliant solutions to problems'.

Hawking's biographers, Michael White and John Gribben, in their 1992 book *A Life of Science*, describe a man who fits the astrological picture so exactly that it is an amazing coincidence. They write of a self-confident young genius, 'an upstart' whose rise to the summit in the field of mathematics was inexorable. Hawking knew at an early age what he wanted to do and that he was destined for prominence in his chosen field. He was not a hard worker and in fact was 'rather lazy'. He relied on his hunches to 'come up with brilliant solutions' to problems.

White and Gribben tell the story of how, on a train journey between London and Cambridge with his colleagues, a thought suddenly struck Hawking. 'I wonder what would happen,' he said, 'if you applied Roger's singularity theory to the entire universe' (colleague Roger Penrose was a young applied mathematician who was working on 'singularity theory' in relation to black holes).

The authors say: 'This flash of inspiration turned the final chapter of [Hawking's] Ph.D. thesis into a brilliant piece of work and set him on the road to science superstardom.'

The similarity between the astrological and biographical descriptions is too close to be accidental: the single-minded, arrogant person who relies on flashes of inspiration for breakthroughs.

Professional statisticians will be critical of my star-sign–job survey and the findings of clear occupation choices by star signs. However, in my defence, I can argue that it serves the purpose of hinting at outside influences in picking one's occupation. A further point is that the findings in some way parallel what has been written by astrologers about the character of these star types. If coincidence is involved in these parallel findings, then it's significantly so.

As we have seen, the survey also shows a twist to the single-star-sign influence in that there is the Clustering Effect around not the one sign but adjoining signs. This occurs in the analysis of doctors, lawyers, artists, the services and business. This finding appears to indicate that a period of the year, rather than the specific star sign, may have some influence on one's career. If so, it emphasizes the belief that an unknown principle is at work.

Of course, people of all occupations and talents are found under each of the star signs. But how many people secretly wish they were doing something else and curse the causes that led them to do what they are currently doing?

In all this clustering of births and jobs, harder evidence than mine has been produced. For example, Harold Burr, who was Emeritus Professor of Anatomy at Yale Medical School, found that a complex magnetic field not only establishes the patterns of the brain at birth but continues to regulate and control it throughout life.

Tantalizing clues of an influence of heavenly bodies on our lives and events continue to surface. At the twenty-ninth annual meeting of the American Association of Suicidology in April 1986, Loren Coleman, director of a suicide prevention project at the University of Southern Maine, pointed to the fact that a wave of teenage suicides and plane crashes in 1985 had coincided with the appearance of Halley's Comet. Coleman went on: 'Comets and mass suicides are also associated for the years 1506, 1528–9, 1582, 1666, 1823 and 1910 . . . When two comets appeared in 1347–8 the Black Death first appeared in Europe, eventually killing 25 million, a series of mass suicides occurred.' Coleman said the appearance of the comet Kohoutek in 1973–4 coincided with the Watergate scandal, the assassination of the Spanish premier Luis Carrero Blanco, earthquakes in Mexico and Pakistan that killed 5,500 and droughts in Africa and India. 'These kinds of association between comets and disasters are still around.'

A recent study by Dr Steven Stack, a sociologist from Auburn University in Alabama, and Dr David Lester, a psychologist from Stockton State College in New Jersey, provides evidence that it is possible to be born under a 'bad' star sign which has a bearing on behaviour and attitude. Specifically, their study shows that a person's astrological sign can predict his or her inclination towards suicide – especially the sign of Pisces, which, they say, is 'significantly associated with suicide ideation'. The two academics claim that in the Greek and Indian interpretations of astrology, 'persons born under Pisces will have lives characterized by various kinds of losses'. They say that people who believe they are more or less predestined to such a life may, indeed, feel more depressed and hopeless. If this were the case, it could be anticipated that those in such a depressed mood would be more likely to commit suicide. Another statistical quirk, a random anomaly? I should hasten to add that astrology, or indeed other philosophies, believe that we do have free will to overcome obstacles of birth or circumstance foretold by destiny.

Before science insisted on verification with observation and experiment, astrology was regarded as not a superstition but a learned profession whose proof was its consistency. Liz Greene says in the Foreword to *Nostradamus: Countdown to Apocalypse* (1983):

> *The great conjunctions of the major planets known in the sixteenth century – Mars, Jupiter and Saturn – were always believed to herald certain types of upheavals and changes in the world and among its spiritual and temporal rulers. If Jupiter and Saturn conjoined – as they did when Anwar Sadat of Egypt was assassinated and attempts were made on the lives of President Reagan and Pope John Paul II – then for the sixteenth-century astrologer, a king or head of state would die. If Mars and Saturn conjoined – as they did when Argentina invaded the British sovereign territory of the Falkland Islands – then for the sixteenth-century astrologer, war loomed on the horizon.*

Maybe researchers should have begun, as a result of Gauquelin's findings, a re-examination of astrology on the basis that, like the Clustering Effect, it may contain unrecognized knowledge. It is a question whose answer in scientific circles has changed little since French scientist Edmond Rostand said that if his compatriot (Gauquelin, a professionally qualified statistician) had proved astrology from statistics, as to some extent he has, then he (Rostand) no longer believed in statistics. Nobel Prize winner Max Born, in his earlier published work *Natural Philosophy of Cause and Chance*, reasons: 'Science accepts only relations of dependence if they can be verified by observation and experiment, and we are convinced astrology has not stood this test.'

What are we to make of the evidence of the Clustering Effect on careers as revealed by the position of planets and birth dates, the validity of astrological character readings, the ancient wisdom of the significance on human affairs of the positions of the planets – Gauquelin's 'embarrassing' findings? Should we do what the 'psycops' and the Belgian scientists did and try to deny, or hide, the evidence? Should we ask ourselves whether, under pressure from sceptics and other conformist thinkers, we have lost some subtle instinct that helped our ancestors forecast accurately the future and gave them reasons for the ways of the world? The answers should depend on which approach advances the cause of human knowledge. But that is being idealistic.

However, even without having to weigh the probable influence of astrology on births, we are still faced with some interesting figures that show yet another aspect of the Clustering Effect. For example, official statistics show a baby is least likely to be born on a Sunday. Thereafter, its chances increase day by day until Thursday, the peak day of the week for births. This is followed by a slight drop in numbers on Friday, a bigger drop on Saturday and a further drop on Sunday. In other words, there is a weekly pattern, a charting of birth days, that rises progressively during the week, then falls abruptly, to be repeated the following week . . . a Clustering Effect.

In one Australian study the highest number of births in that country on record occurred on 12 April 1990 – it was Easter

Thursday. The following day, Good Friday, the births dropped to below average and remained that way over Easter. Instinctively, it appears, the mums-to-be did not want to have an Easter child.

Here is another odd statistic which was revealed by an earlier survey. On leap years there are fewer births on the extra day in the year, 29 February, than on the average for that same day of the week in a non-leap year. In one case it was more than 15 per cent below the average.

That research, although done in the late 1960s, is still regarded as valid. It shows also that the average number of births that occur on public holidays is only 82 per cent of that on other days. Christmas Days can be as much as 36 per cent below the respective daily averages for the days concerned.

Are the seemingly strange birth patterns noted above not evidence of natural clustering? Are modern surgical techniques, together with a supposed reluctance of gynaecologists to work at the weekends or over the holidays, the real causes of these patterns of birth? Not guilty, said gynaecologist spokesman Dr David Woodhouse; just over one-quarter of births were artificial. Dr Woodhouse puts the birth patterns down to what he calls the 'mystery of women generally'. He says gynae-cologists and obstetricians are as much in the dark as anyone else about the timing of births – and always have been. He speculates that labour pains could be started by any number of things, psychological, cultural and physical – for example, lightning could set off a reaction of births. The doctor did not mention another cause – the Clustering Effect.

If mothers do have any control over the timing of their baby's birth, they may do well to go against the tendency to avoid a Christmas Day birth. Research shows that children born on that day have above average chances of becoming successful. A disproportionate forty-two of the 620 US congressmen have 25 December birthdays, while a check of the birth dates of 9,000 people listed in *Who's Who* shows 600 such birthdays. This is fifteen times above the expected rate.

Intriguingly, a study of leading clergymen, such as bishops, suggests that they are four times more likely to have been born on Christmas Day than on any other. Clergy who were not as successful were as likely to be born on this day as any other.

The *Guardian*, commenting on the findings, offers the suggestion that the perceived importance of birth dates may explain the Christmas Day Effect. The newspaper says that people who regard themselves and others as unique because of special birthdays may acquire the confidence to achieve things they might not otherwise have attempted. It adds that if this theory is correct, there may be a simple way for parents of children not born on Christmas Day to replicate the effect – seek particularly positive historical and biographical associations with their children's birthdays to enhance self-esteem.

In one experiment, subjects who were led to believe that they shared a birthday with Rasputin responded by softening their view of Russia's 'mad monk'.

▶ Merry Birthday ▼

Isaac Newton, Humphrey Bogart and Princess Alexandra were all born on Christmas Day.

▶ Last Laugh ▼

Two famous comedians, W. C. Fields and Charlie Chaplin, died on Christmas Day.

▶ Star Choice ▼

Peter Anderson is a member of an astronomical society whose members, he assures me, regard astrology as bunkum. Nevertheless, one day he glanced at a newspaper lying on his desk. It was open at the horoscopes and he found himself doing what most people, believers or sceptics, would normally do, glancing at them. He told me: 'I read my so-called sign, Capricorn. It said I would be offered two jobs in the next week. I had a good laugh. The next day I was offered two jobs . . .'

CHAPTER THREE

Predictions

Non-deliberate predictions manifesting themselves through coincidence are another intriguing aspect of this phenomenon. They generally involve the creative process, as we shall see.

In this chapter we look at some of the most remarkable cases of non-deliberate predictions in the annals of coincidence cases. One concerns the still unexplained publication of top-secret codenames before the D-Day invasion in the Second World War. Another concerns the stories that foretold the sinking of the 'unsinkable' *Titanic*.

But, first, some other examples of non-deliberate predictions, all of which, by coincidence, concern tragedies involving water and life imitating art.

▶ Drowning Pool ▼

Film star Julie Christie appeared in the movie *Don't Look Now*, in which she and her screen husband (Donald Sutherland) are haunted by the spirit of their young child, who has drowned in a shallow pond at their English country house.

Some years later Christie was visiting her farmhouse in Wales, looked after by a married couple, when the husband found the body of their twenty-two-month-old son floating in the large duckpond near the house. Christie waded in to recover the body from the shallow pond, just as the father (Sutherland) had done in the film.

▶ Playwright's Prediction ▼

In the 1880s, Arthur Law had written a play in which the sole survivor of a shipwrecked vessel, the *Caroline*, was called Robert Golding. Within days of the play's first performance he read a newspaper story about a real shipwreck in which there had been only one survivor. The name of the ship, the *Caroline*; the name of the survivor, Robert Golding.

▶ Cabin-boy Fodder ▼

The circumstances of the above incident only add to the bizarre nature of a similar story which began with Arthur Koestler when he wrote an article on coincidences for the *Sunday Times*. As a follow-up the newspaper offered a £100 prize for the reader who submitted the best coincidence.

The winner was Nigel Parker, aged twelve, who told a story that demands comparison with the story told by Law all those years before. Parker's story was of his great-grandfather's cousin, a cabin boy on a yawl, the *Mignonette*, which foundered in 1884. The boy and three senior crew members managed to launch an open boat. They were the only survivors. The three men eventually ate the boy, whose name was Richard Parker.

The case was reported in *The Times* of 28 October 1884. In 1838 Edgar Allan Poe had written a story called 'The Narrative of Arthur Gordon Pym of Nantucket'. Poe tells a similar story of shipwreck and a cabin boy survivor who is also eaten by the other survivors. His name, Richard Parker!

▶ *Titanic* Tales ▼

Several works of fiction relate to the *Titanic* tragedy. The best known concerns Morgan Robertson, a writer of stories about the sea.

In 1898 he began working on a new novel, allowing his imagination to guide him. In his mind – like an animated panorama – he saw a ship moving through fog in the mid-Atlantic, at a rate of twenty-three knots. As it came closer, he saw it was a large luxury liner, 880 feet (268 metres) in length, driven by three propellers and, he estimated, 75,000 tons deadweight. People strolled on its long, broad decks. There were more than 2,000 on board, more people than any ship had ever before carried.

As the panorama became more focused, the name of the ship stood out: *Titan*. The word 'unsinkable' came to him. He counted the lifeboats. There were twenty-four – not enough for the number of passengers and crew on board, which Robertson was to explain away as due to her unsinkability.

Then, ahead of the ship, he saw an iceberg . . .

He leant forward and started working feverishly. The writer's block that had troubled him had vanished with the vision:

> *She was the largest craft afloat and the greatest of the works of men, spacious cabins . . . decks like broad promenades . . . Unsinkable, indestructible, she carried as few lifeboats as would satisfy the laws . . . Seventy-five thousand tons . . . rushing through the fog at the rate of fifty feet a second . . . hurled itself at an iceberg . . . nearly 3,000 human voices, raised in agonized screams.*

Robertson called his work of fiction *The Wreck of the Titan or Futility*.

In the issue that hit the newsstands on 7 April 1912, *Popular Mechanics* carried another fictitious story about the maiden voyage of the largest ocean liner in the world. As she nears Newfoundland, an iceberg rips through her hull, sinking her.

The 'unsinkable' *Titanic* was not built until 1911. It was the largest craft afloat and went down on its first voyage on the night of 14 April 1912, with up to 2,207 people on board, after hitting an iceberg.

Some years before the 1898 novel was written, the *Pall Mall Gazette* had run a story about a ship as large as the *Titan/Titanic* which also sank in mid-Atlantic. Its author, W. T. Stead, wrote another article in 1892, about a steamship colliding with an iceberg in the Atlantic in which its only surviving passenger is rescued by the White Star liner *Majestic*, a ship that actually existed at the time and was captained by Edward Smith (who later captained the *Titanic*).

Stead sailed on the *Titanic*, despite his own predictions and despite warnings from psychics that it could sink, and he perished along with 1,502 other passengers. Like many authors, he had not seen what he was writing as a prediction or a fatal coincidence.

Morgan Robertson's story has interested Noel Prentis for many years. He explained why in a letter to me:

> On 3 April 1945, toward the end of my air force service in World War II, I sailed from the port of Brisbane aboard a troopship, the US Liberty ship Morgan Robertson.
>
> Late that night, heading north in very rough conditions, we were wakened by a frightening crash. We thought it was 'The End'. However, the cause was a bulldozer which had broken loose from its ties and crashed from one side to the other as the ship rolled. Fortunately, our army colleagues and crew managed to constrain it by dumping a large number of tires into the hold. During this scare, we recalled the rumours to the effect that Liberty ships' welded construction was relatively vulnerable.
>
> Having drafted this letter last night, I was amazed to see in today's newspapers and TV programs the report that US marine experts now blame the loss of the Titanic on low-grade steel construction.
>
> The Morgan Robertson eventually delivered us to Morotai in the Halmaheras. There, our radar unit boarded a landing craft in the invasion fleet of about seventy ships which took us to Japanese-occupied Tarakan . . .
>
> We arrived in the harbor on the night of 30 April for the landing operation commencing the next morning, on which 'all hell broke loose'.
>
> The army decided to 'borrow' our landing craft and put us aboard a US troopship on which we remained until our 'turn' came to move into the beach-head. The ship's name Titania!

Prentis passed on the details as a bemusing incident and this might well have been the end of the matter, However, his interest piqued, he rang his son, an academic, to tell him he had written to me and to ask whether his son might be able to help in tracking down Morgan Robertson's book.

'No problems,' said the son. His own son, aged twelve, was

at that very moment reading Robertson's book; he had for some time been interested in the history of the *Titanic* and was currently building a model of it.

Some doubts about the authenticity of the Robertson story were raised with its republication in 1986 by the Ayer publishing company of Salem, New Hampshire. Bibliographical details show the book as having been 'first published in 1912'.

For obvious reasons, the point of the work as a piece of non-predictive coincidence would be lost if this were the original publication date, even had it been published shortly before the sinking, when the name and other details were by then general knowledge. However, the British Library catalogue gives the lie to the 1912 date; it shows *Titan* was published *c*. 1900 by Stone & Mackenzie of New York. In fact, according to its listings, all Robertson's five novels were published between 1899 and 1901.

Doubts about the predictive basis of Robertson's story have been raised elsewhere. It must be kept in mind he was an ex-mariner with a detailed knowledge of ships, and as a writer on the subject he kept himself in touch with the latest developments. Planning for the building of the *Titanic* was going on years before the keel was even laid and among the worst-case scenarios considered were its collision with an iceberg – it was, after all, due to sail a route where that was of concern, even though icebergs rarely drifted that far south.

Dr Ian Stevenson, Professor of Psychiatry at the University of Virginia, argues that even the name Robertson chose for his ship may have had some logic in it. 'Titan has connoted power and security for several thousand years,' he says. Other facts in Robertson's story which foretold the *Titanic* disaster, such as insufficient lifeboats, the time of year the tragedy happened and the belief that the ship was unsinkable, amount, Stevenson feels, to a case of *inference* on the author's part rather than to coincidence or precognition.

Against that is the fact that Robertson was not the only one who put pen to paper . . .

▶ *Achtung* **Pearl Harbor!** ▼

On 2 November 1941 – sixteen days before the Japanese attack on Pearl Harbor – *The New Yorker* ran two advertisements for a new dice game called the Deadly Double.

A boxed advertisement, carrying the name Monarch Publishing Co., New York (with no further address), appears as a pointer to the main advertisement on page 86. This pointer has long been held to contain clues to the 7 December raid on Pearl Harbor. It is headed: *'Achtung, Warning, Alerte!'* In it are two dice, one black, one white, each with three faces showing. The white dice faces carry the numbers 12 and 24 and XX (twenty in Roman numerals), while on the black dice faces are the numbers 0, 5, 7.

The figures are supposed to represent a cryptic 'message' which has been interpreted a number of ways. In the authoritative *The Pacific War* (1981), author John Costello says the numbers on the faces appear to spell out '0 hour for a "double cross" on the 7th day of the 12th month at the 5th hour out of 24'.

Another interpretation of the numbers' message is to be found in the Reader's Digest book *Mysteries of the Unexplained* (1982). It says there was speculation that 12 and 7 could have referred to the date of the attack, while 5 and 0 indicated the planned time of the attack and the XX stood for the approximate latitude of the target; the significance of the 24 was unknown.

The main advertisement on page 86 shows a mixed group of people tossing dice at a table in an air-raid shelter, while outside searchlights probe the night sky. A ground explosion and flak also feature. Under the same heading – *Achtung, Warning, Alerte!* – the copy begins: 'We hope you'll never have to spend a long winter's night in an air-raid shelter, but we were just thinking . . .' At the foot of the main advertisement is a crest similar to that of the German double-headed eagle.

The overall impression given may explain the suspicion that the advertisements had been placed by the Axis powers to alert their agents to the forthcoming attack which was to precipitate America into the Second World War.

There is general agreement that the FBI investigated the advertisement. However, Costello adds fuel to the mystery by saying that FBI agents found that the game was in fact non-existent and the Monarch Publishing Company (he calls it the Monarch Trading Company) a dummy corporation. The agents further discovered that the advertisements had been placed by a 'white [*sic*] Caucasian' who had delivered the printing plates and paid in cash. Still more curious was the fact that the man identified as the suspect died suddenly a few weeks later in a manner similar to that used by British secret agents to dispose of Nazi operatives in New York.

Costello asks: 'Was *The New Yorker* warning genuine and were the Germans responsible for trying to raise the alarm?' He concludes that the fascination of the Pearl Harbor story lies in questions like these that still remain to be answered.

However, *Mysteries* writers on this episode say the game of Deadly Double was legitimate and was being sold by several New York department stores in 1941. They add, however, that suspicions about the advertisement were so strong that FBI agents visited the people who had placed them, a Mr and Mrs Roger Craig – apparently not a mysterious Caucasian with his own printing plates and a wad of cash.

Mysteries adds that the story of the FBI investigation did not break until 1967, when Ladislas Farago, formerly of the US Naval Intelligence Department, revealed details in the media release for his book *The Broken Seal*, published that year. Interviewed by a reporter following up the release, Craig's widow said any connection between the advertisements and Pearl Harbor was simply 'one big coincidence' (*Mysteries* gives as its source *Scientific American*, October 1972, 227, pp. 111–12).

As you can see from the above, the incident is still very much a mystery and is full of contradictions. Did *The New Yorker* carry out its own investigation? If so, what did it find? Was the advertisement run in more than one issue? I put these questions to *The New Yorker* in a letter, but did not receive a reply.

▶ Secret Clues ▼

If an air of doubt hangs over the significance or otherwise of the cryptic media message discussed above, no such doubt exists about what was revealed by some strange process in the story that follows concerning the codewords for the Allied invasion of Europe in the Second World War.

This story involves not a magazine but a newspaper, the *Daily Telegraph*, and its crossword answers to clues just before the invasion on 6 June 1944.

The codewords hid the invasion plans, which were the best-kept secrets of the Second World War in Europe. The codename for the total plan was *Overlord*, the naval operation was named *Neptune* and the two Normandy beaches on which members of the American forces would land were *Utah* and *Omaha*. The artificial harbour which was to be placed off the beaches was named *Mulberry*.

On 3 May, the first codeword appeared in the *Telegraph*'s crossword solution – *Utah*; the second on 3 May – *Omaha*; the third on 31 May – *Mulberry*; the fourth and fifth, the major codewords, appeared together on 2 June, four days before D-Day – *Neptune* and *Overlord*. The series created near-panic among the military. As with *The New Yorker* advertisements, security officers (MI5) mounted an investigation, convinced that there was a highly placed spy with access to the plans who was using the puzzle as a cunning means of communicating the most vital secrets to the enemy.

Instead they found schoolmaster Leonard Dawe, the newspaper's senior crossword compiler for the previous twenty years, who was as baffled as the military. Dawe had no idea the answers were codewords and could give no explanation as to why they came into his mind when he was compiling the puzzles.

The mystery remained seemingly beyond rational explanation for many years. Various references to it over the years since are offered without any logical explanation. However, in 1984 a letter from a Ronald French was published in the *Daily Telegraph* which appeared to offer a solution. French said that he had been a student at Dawe's school in 1944 and had become friendly with some American and Canadian service people who were camped near by. He had learned the codewords from the soldiers and had contributed them to Dawe as answers to puzzles. Dawe would often use his class to provide words and he would then devise the clues.

In his 1990 book *Coincidences: A Matter of Chance – or Synchronicity?*, author Brian Inglis cast doubts on French's explanation. French's account was made into a BBC TV programme in 1989 and the implication was that the matter was now settled. However, Inglis argues that the programme trivialized the story and that French's claim that he had kept silent because of a promise to Dawe sounds too glib. French was unable to produce satisfactory corroboration. Inglis goes on to say that French's further claim that he recalled laughing at Koestler's explanation of telepathy did not promote trust in his memory, for Koestler gave no such explanation (Koestler, in fact, presents the story without any substantial comment).

Even if French's story is correct, there remains the timing coincidence. As with some other regular features in a news-paper – comic strips, astrology guides, etc. – the puzzles are prepared months in advance. Yet the crosswords appeared within days of the invasion, which had also been twice post-poned late in the day. Had the invasion gone ahead on either of the earlier occasions, the puzzles would have been seen as containing words that were on everybody's lips.

Anthony Ralph, Dawe's nephew, subsequently suggested to *Sunday Times* columnist Godfrey Smith another explanation. Dawe had been sharing a house at the time with a deputy director of naval construction who worked on the artificial harbour and therefore should have been aware of its codename, *Mulberry*. Smith explains that the words would have been in open use at the time: 'After all, that's what codenames are for. It is the things and places they describe which are really secret.'

Against this, it can be argued that while a deputy director of naval construction may well have known the codename *Mulberry*, was security so lax that the other top-secret names – which did not directly concern him – were also bandied about? A prime rule in security is need-to-know.

On balance, the mystery of the codewords in the crossword puzzles remains. I contacted the *Daily Telegraph* in 1993 to go over the details of the mystery. I asked whether there had been any developments in recent years. There had not and, added a senior executive, 'We probably won't know the truth until MI5 opens its files.'

The Mystery of Numbers

'Both [number and synchronicity] possess numinosity and mystery as their common characteristics.'
CARL JUNG, in his essay on synchronicity

Coincidence investigators find their coincidences in unlikely places. While being interviewed on TV some years ago, the presenter told me one of the crew had something I should hear.

► Lennon's 'Nine' Lives ▼

I expected to be told after the show, but the presenter pointed at one of the cameras focused on us and I heard, although I could not see past the studio lights, the voice of its operator. Another camera swung around and picked him up so I was able to see the man behind the voice on the monitor. Still operating his camera and with other crew members' good-naturedly heckling his performance, he mentioned some details of John Lennon's involvement with the number 9 – the Beatle was born on 9 October 1940 and Sean, his and Yoko's son, was also born on 9 October. It was an intriguing anecdote.

Anecdote?

As a result of hearing it, I spent the next few months immersed in research into the mystery of numbers, which is revealed so often through coincidence – synchronicity, as Jung preferred to call it.

Among the things the research revealed was that, like Lennon, most of us have a specific number that dogs our lives to a greater or lesser degree. Depending on your temperament, it can mean a little – one of life's little eccentricities – or it can mean a lot – a marker of significant events in your life. In Lennon's case, it was the latter.

For those who do take it seriously, their number can serve as a useful guide to the future. That this is so is one of the mysteries of numbers and their numinous – that is, supernatural – qualities.

Back to Lennon, whose life was a prime example of the one-number rule, as well as numbers' numinosity and synchronicity. It all began with his conception, at 9 Newcastle Road, Penny Lane, Liverpool. (The number 9 is considered to have more than its share of those numinous elements, one reason being that if you add it to itself it reproduces itself: e.g. $9 + 9 = 18$, $1 + 8 = 9$. Further, if you multiply 9 by *any* number, it always reduces to a number 9: e.g. $9 \times 6 = 54$, $5 + 4 = 9$. In numerology, groups of numbers are generally reduced in this way to a single digit to reveal various meanings.) Anyway, John's mum, Julia, gave birth to him when she was twenty-seven: $2 + 7 = 9$. On 9 February 1944 (add those figures together and reduce to a single digit), his father, Freddie, set out on a sea voyage which resulted in a lengthy absence and the breakup of his and Julia's marriage.

The Beatles' first album, *Please Please Me*, went to No. 1 exactly nineteen years later, 9 February 1963. Their second tour, which put them on the map, began on 9 March 1963. Lennon and his first wife, Cynthia, had a son, Julian, who was born on 8 April 1963 – one day premature. Yoko Ono had a miscarriage of Lennon's child on his birthday, 9 October 1969. The Beatles signed an important agreement on 29 December 1974, basically dissolving their partnership, after Lennon had refused to sign it on 19 December.

Now for some final intriguing nine influences: Lennon's last home, the Dakota building, was on the corner of 72nd Street, Manhattan ($7 + 2 = 9$). The number of his and Ono's apartment in that building was also 72.

Sam, the son of Marlene Hair, Yoko's only close friend and confidante while living at the Dakota, was also born on 9 October. Lennon released a record called *Revolution 9*.

Lennon did not die on a ninth day – officially. He was declared dead at 11.15 p.m. on 8 December 1980. This last point puzzled me. If numinosity had worked in such a way that so much of his life was predicated on the number 9, why the irrational lapse which left Lennon dead less than an hour away from a ninth day? Did it have some unfathomable connection with the birth of his son, Julian, a few hours before the 9th?

Lennon's assassin, Mark Chapman, shot the Beatle outside the Dakota building at 10.50 p.m. on the 8th. The doorman at the apartment took one look at Lennon, who was gurgling blood and vomiting, and dialled the emergency number for an ambulance: 911, the number that had for many years been 999.

The ambulance raced Lennon across town to the Roosevelt hospital, where a team of surgeons fought to save him. Lennon had virtually no pulse. He had three bullet holes in his chest, two in his back and two in his left shoulder. He had lost nearly 80 per cent of his blood.

The Beatle was in wretched physical condition. He should have died instantly. But he survived, almost perversely, until after 11 p.m. that night.

One day I happened to be discussing the story with numerologist Eileen Whittaker. 'Why,' I concluded frustratedly, 'should Lennon not have been killed on the 9th in the first place and if not, why did he seem to linger?' Whittaker asked me exactly what time Lennon had died.

'At 11.15 p.m. on the 8th.'

She smiled. 'In numerology the influence of the following day begins at 11 p.m. the previous night.'

On the Beatles' Australian tour in 1964, John Lennon was asked if the hysterical crowds that mobbed them in every city worried him. 'You could get shot,' he responded. Everybody thought it was another example of his quick wit.

▶ 7onald 7eagan ▼

According to Robert Ripley in *The Book of Chances* (1989), ex-President Ronald Reagan saved seventy-seven people from drowning during his seven years as a lifeguard at a resort near Dixon, Illinois. The book uses this as a starting point to show how the number 7 kept cropping up in Reagan's life. He celebrated his seventieth birthday seventeen days after his first inauguration; he was wounded by would-be assassin John Hinckley on his seventieth day in office, the bullet fired by Hinckley ricocheting off Reagan's seventh rib.

Reagan made his film début in 1937 and became president of the Screen Actors' Guild in 1947. He began his term as Governor of California in 1967 and was re-elected in 1970. His formal acceptance speech for the Republican presidential nomination was made on the seventeenth day of the seventh month 1980. At the end of his second term in the White House he was seventy-seven.

► 7incoln 7oo ▼

Significant '7' has long been attributed to Abraham Lincoln – the sixteenth (1 + 6 = 7) president of the US. Even if the following does stretch credulity, it shows one way of tracing a pattern of a personal number. Each of Lincoln's names contains seven letters. He lived seven years in Kentucky and seven years in Salem. In the army he was a private (seven letters) and a captain (seven).

Lincoln was elected seven times, sworn into Congress on 7 December 1847, held seven offices in succession. His ancestors came from Hingham (seven letters), in Norfolk (seven letters), England (seven letters). He served seven years in the state legislature. He appointed seven cabinet ministers, watched seven states secede and died a few minutes after seven on the seventh day.

► The Third President ▼

The third US president was dogged by a number: 3. Thomas Jefferson was born 13 April 1743, the third child and the third Thomas in the family. He became the third president, but not before he largely wrote the Declaration of Independence at the age of thirty-three. And not before he lost the 1796 election by three votes.

Jefferson died at the age of eighty-three, on 4 July 1826, the fiftieth anniversary of American Independence Day. Another American president also died on that date: John Adams, the second president. Incidentally, 4 July was significant for yet another president, Calvin Coolidge, the thirtieth president, who was born on 4 July 1872.

▶ *Drei* Guy ▼

Not only American presidents are dogged by a particular number or numbers. Count Otto von Bismarck, the first German chancellor, studied at three schools, was ambassador to three countries, served three kings, fought in three wars, signed three peace treaties, fathered three children . . . His coat of arms consisted of a three-leaved clover and three oak leaves.

▶ For Those with Titles ▼

To assess character and predict a person's future, numerologists generally use birth dates and/or the sum of a person's name made up from numbers given to each letter of the alphabet.

However, some numerologists work on the basis that it is not always the given name that can be 'counted' to provide character and prediction readings. One reason for this is that some people are better known by their title. In such cases, the name and title are used for numerological calculations.

Yet another factor is that some numerologists look for further insights into a person's character by using the consonants and/or vowels to calculate a person's significant number. The consonants are generally accepted as a guide to personality, while the vowels represent the 'hidden' you.

Any good book on numerology will explain this in far more detail. My purpose here is to test such things on the basis of their application to coincidence. I returned to my 'model', Lennon, for an example of the use of both title and consonants under what is known as the Chaldean system:

$$
\begin{array}{cccccc}
\text{B} & \text{E} & \text{A} & \text{T} & \text{L} & \text{E} \qquad \text{L} & \text{E} & \text{N} & \text{N} & \text{O} & \text{N} \\
2 & 5 & 1 & 4 & 3 & 5 \qquad 3 & 5 & 5 & 5 & 7 & 5
\end{array}
$$

Using only the consonants of Beatle, the number comes to 'his' number, 9. Using only the consonants from Lennon, the number comes to 18, 1 + 8 = 9. Add the two – 9 + 9 = 18, 1 + 8 = 9 – and we have the numinous power of 9 reproducing itself and just as supernaturally returning us to Lennon's birth number.

► Louis XVI's Other Number ▼

The eighteenth-century adventurer Cagliostro is said to have used the Chaldean system of numerology to forecast the deaths of both Louis XVI and his wife, Marie Antoinette. The prediction was made at a gathering in Paris (some accounts say it was a dinner party of aristocrats, others a meeting of Freemasons). Having found the king's number, Cagliostro said it showed that the king would lose his head on the scaffold before his thirty-ninth year (he was guillotined with his wife in 1793, aged thirty-nine). Cagliostro further correctly predicted that Marie Antoinette's 'number' showed she would meet a premature death through beheading following a term in prison and starvation.

Louis XIV came to the throne in 1643, which equals 14 (1 + 6 + 4 + 3), single digit 5 (1 + 4). He died in 1715, another 14, or 5, at the age of seventy-seven . . .

► Change Your Fortune ▼

Being dogged by a particular number is not as inevitable as it sounds; changing your name can change your circumstances. This can be either deliberately or inadvertently done, such as a person becoming known by a title, as we have seen. The Bible has a number of examples of name changes which led to a change in circumstances in a person's life: Abram to Abraham, Sarai to Sarah (God promised Abraham that she would have a son after her name was changed: Genesis 17: 15–16), Simon to Peter.

Eileen Whittaker says that in the courses she runs on numerology at least half the class change their name once they have gained sufficient insights into the power of the subject.

How many times do people accept, or find themselves pushed into, a major job or task which others believe to be beyond their abilities? Harry Truman is a perfect example. He did not want to be US president. He did not believe he was capable of doing the job. As Roy Jenkins says in his biography of Truman, he had none of the style of his predecessor, Roosevelt, none of his prestige, none of his grandeur . . . yet, as 'President' Truman, among his achievements was the more difficult feat of being the leader of the free world at peace . . . Once he got into his stride, Truman's emerging abilities were found to be remarkable and many observers believe he ended up a better president than Roosevelt.

▶ Character Readings ▼

To return to our 'test case' John Lennon, let's see what numerologists say about the broad character of 'nines', as opposed to the more specific assessments based on vowel or consonant numbers.

The following comments are compiled from five separate numerologists.

Nines are struggling to hold the lid on a volcano of anger and irritation . . . Often the life-pattern consists of stretches of smooth self-control, broken by fits of rage and anger . . . Very few live and die in the same place they were born . . . A leaning towards philosophy and teaching . . . Greatest danger comes from their impulsiveness and foolhardiness . . . Good at organizing large functions . . . Make good leaders . . . Often involved in events that are larger than life . . . Have an important message to give the world . . . Respond to people, atmosphere, environment, colour and music . . . In some capacity nines are in the public eye . . . An entertainer . . . Know love is too great an experience to be limited to one person or one family or group . . . A high degree of creativity (the nine Muses) and spiritual achievement . . . Visionaries and poets at their best, wildly volatile at their worst, given to intense romanticism . . .

Even those with a passing interest in the man who was such a phenomenal presence in twentieth-century music would recognize the descriptions above as forming an accurate portrayal of the complex character that was John Lennon. Yet the marvel is that they were not specifically written as such, but as descriptions of a 'nine' character in numerological terms.

▶ Sandberg's 11 ▼

Poet Carl Sandberg had a thing about the number 11. He told *The New York Times* in a 1967 interview that he would die at an age that would be a multiple of this number. 'I had two great-grandfathers and a grandfather who died in years divisible by eleven and if I don't die at eighty-eight, I'll go on to ninety-nine,' he said. At the time he was eighty.

Like John Lennon, and relatively speaking, he just missed out on what he believed the fates had in store for him. He reached eighty-nine years, then died a few months later.

▶ Schoenberg's 13 ▼

Another artist who believed his death was predetermined by his birth date was the Austrian composer Arnold Schoenberg.

Born on 13 September 1874, he believed he would die on the thirteenth day of a month. Schoenberg, noted for his originating of the twelve-note technique, further believed that, as the numbers 7 and 6 make 13, he would die at the age of seventy-six. He died thirteen minutes before midnight on Friday, 13 July 1951. His age: seventy-six.

▶ Number 17, Your Time is up ▼

King John III of Poland was born on 17 June. It was also the date on which he ascended the throne, the date on which he married and the date on which he died.

▶ Birth dates ▼

There are many cases of whole families who seem dogged by a number persistently weaving itself into their lives, often involving a birth date – that is, brothers, sisters, cousins, parents all born on the same date over the generations, although there are variations.

Some examples.

Julie, a caller to a radio programme, said her mother was born on 2/2/22 and is a twin. The mother and her husband bought a block of land, Lot No. 22. When it was given a house number, it was again No. 22. They lived there for twenty-two years. The telephone number added up to twenty-two. After many years of calling lottery tickets by her two daughters' names, she decided one day to name one 'No. 2' and she won first prize.

Allan, another caller, said he and his wife lived in house No. 22, the second house from the corner. They were married for two years, she died at the age of twenty-two, on 22 August in Ward 22 of a hospital on the second floor.

Mrs L. Rea writes that her husband cannot get away from the number 5. He was born on 5/5/55, the fifth child of a family whose address was No. 5. Further, the house he now lives in is also No. 5 and his clockcard at work is No. 5.

Margaret Huxley found that when her daughter married in 1986 both mothers-in-law had the same birth date (13 August), as did the fathers (6 September).

Bruce Wilson joined the police force in 1940 and was given the collar number 2465. After retiring from the force, he joined the police club and received badge 2465.

Let's move away from the personal for the time being to broaden our investigation and look at the significance of number on events.

▶ Six Too Many ▼

Seven Toronto stockbrokers worked at a building whose street address was 777. Their offices were on its seventh floor. On 7/7/77 they decided to take a gamble on a horse. They bet $777 on the seventh horse in the seventh race (over seven furlongs). The horse ran seventh.

▶ It's Time ▼

Three of the longest-serving leaders of the Australian Labor Party were Gough Whitlam, who served ten years and ten months, John Curtin, nine years and nine months, and Herbert 'Doc' Evatt, eight years and eight months.

▶ A Day for Politics ▼

On 19 December 1991, Paul Keating took over from Bob Hawke as Australian Prime Minister. On 19 December 1931, the Labor Party, led by James Scullin, lost government in a landslide to the Conservatives. On 19 December 1949, Sir Robert Menzies was sworn in as Prime Minister. On 19 December 1967, John 'Black Jack' McEwen was sworn in as temporary Prime Minister. On 19 December 1972, the first Labor government since 1949 was sworn in. In 1992, Mr Keating came within a whisker of calling a snap 19 December poll.

The circumstances leading up to these six significant events so widely separated in time were all unrelated and the date has no other significance in Australia.

▶ Quitting to Time ▼

On 5 April 1955, Sir Winston Churchill resigned as British Prime Minister. On 5 April 1976, James Callaghan became British Prime Minister.

▶ Resignations and Royal Divorces ▼

While we are on the subject of resignations, on 1 March 1976, British Prime Minister Harold Wilson announced his resignation. On the same day Buckingham Palace announced that Princess Margaret and Lord Snowdon were seeking a divorce.

On 14 April 1992, British Labour Party leader Neil Kinnock resigned as party leader after failing to become Prime Minister in the general election. On the same day Buckingham Palace announced that Princess Anne was seeking a divorce from Captain Mark Phillips.

▶ Another Royal Number ▼

Buckingham Palace announced the separation of the Duke and Duchess of York on 19 March 1992. On the same day six years before they had announced their engagement.

▶ Princess Eight ▼

Princess Beatrice, the first child of the Duke and Duchess of York, was born at eight minutes past 8 p.m. on 8/8/88.

▶ August End ▼

Actress Ingrid Bergman died on 29 August 1982, her birth date.

▶ Date with Death ▼

From Australia, more unrelated but significant events on the same date.

On 24 July 1979 a gas explosion killed fourteen miners in the Appin coal mine. On 24 July 1980, as the townspeople of Appin were mourning the first anniversary of the disaster, a rock fall killed two more miners. On 24 July 1991, three more miners died accidentally.

Australia's worst mining disaster was on 31 July 1902, when an explosion killed ninety-six miners. On 31 July 1972, seventy years to the day later, an underground explosion killed seventeen men.

▶ A Living Death ▼

On 8 August 1991, the British hostage John McCarthy was released by his Lebanese captors. The date was the second anniversary of the death of his mother, who had died of cancer in 1989 after begging those who held McCarthy to free him so they could be reunited before her impending death. Her poignant wish was not fulfilled.

It would be hard to imagine that the date of her death had preyed on the minds of the desperate men who held McCarthy and influenced their decision as to when to release him. Or did it, in a warped way?

Later in the year, just two days before Dr Thomas Sutherland was released by his Lebanese captors (November 1991), his father-in-law died from cancer. 'We don't know whether to celebrate or mourn,' was the way Ms Kit Sutherland, the daughter of the freed doctor, summed up the diabolical situation.

▶ Aiming for the Hole ▼

In December 1991 in England, golfer Tony Wright died on the fourteenth green of his local golf course fourteen months after his father, Les, collapsed and died at the same spot. Both men had been lining up for putts when they suffered heart attacks.

▶ Reaching the Score ▼

Swiss statesman Niklaus von der Flue was fond of saying he would live exactly three score and ten years. On his seventieth birthday he died of natural causes.

▶ Pelé scores Ten ▼

Pelé, one of the world's most famous soccer players, was obsessed with the number 10. Playing for Brazil, he drew the number 10 jersey both times he played for that country's successful World Cup winning teams. When touring he stayed in room number 10 on the tenth floor and made sure the numberplate of one of his cars added up to 10.

▶ Numbers 'Rule the Universe' ▼

Humans have always used numbers as something more than simple figures for maths. The Chinese, for example, consider that odd numbers connote day, white, heat, fire and sun; even numbers signify night, black, cold, water and earth. This symbolism points to myths and the numinous aura that Jung speaks of in his famous essay on synchronicity. Jung asserts in that essay that numbers have an unpredictable quality.

However, he also calls them 'the predestined instrument' for creating order, or for understanding an already existing but still unknown arrangement of 'orderedness'. In this chapter we have seen evidence of these attributes and further evidence for his assertion that there is a link between numinosity and coincidence. As a result we can understand how he came to believe in the same mysterious quality in other aspects of coincidence.

▶ Odd Numbers ▼

If the numbers of pop star David Bowie's real name, David Jones, are calculated then he is a '1'. This suggests the private Bowie is much the same as the public Bowie.

Ex-Romanian President Ceauşescu's number is '8', which can be indicative of a dramatic fall from power.

Marilyn Monroe's key number is '2', the number of femininity.

▶ Cab Number ▼

Colin Archer drove a taxi cab for fifteen years with the numberplate T390. His private car numberplate was CRA 390, and when he wrote away for a ticket for a senior citizens' week concert, he was sent a ticket numbered 390. The following year when he received his ticket to the concert it was again 390.

CHAPTER FIVE

The Fish-stomach Effect

Any researcher in the field of coincidences soon comes across examples of what I have come to call the Fish-stomach Effect.

An example. Norwegian fisherman Waldemar Andersen found the gold earring his wife had lost in the North Sea one week earlier – in the stomach of a cod he caught while fishing in the place where the earring had been lost. His wife, Ragnhild, said: 'Think of all the fish swimming around and that the same cod which swallowed my earring should bite on my husband's fishing hook a week later.' Andersen had not realized he was fishing in the same spot.

The source for this story is a reputable world-wide wire service. It appeals as a classic case of a significant coincidence, especially to Mr and Mrs Andersen, who were obviously awestruck by its impact in Schopenhauerian terms – that is, the real significance of coincidence is for the individual who experiences it.

Initially, it struck me as a case beyond probability, a rational impossibility, a resounding example of a significant coincidence's other causes. But I soon came across a surprising – even disturbing – number of similar stories.

Some examples:

• In the summer of 1979 fifteen-year-old Robert Johansen caught a 10-lb cod in a Norwegian fiord and proudly presented it to his grandmother for a family meal. Preparing the fish, Thekla Aanen opened its stomach and found inside a valuable diamond ring, a family heirloom she had lost while fishing in the fiord ten years earlier.

• A 1980 report says Joseph Cross of Newport News, Virginia, lost his ring when it fell into floodwaters during a storm. In February 1982, a restaurateur in Charlottesville, Virginia, found the ring – inside a fish.

• In Britain on 28 March 1982, the *Sunday Express* and *News of the World* both reported that two years after farmer Ferdi Parker lost an antique wedding ring, a vet found it in a cow's stomach while performing an autopsy.

• Robert Ripley's *Believe It or Not* says the wife of Howard Ramage lost her wedding ring in a drain in 1918 and a Vancouver man found it thirty-six years later in the stomach of a fish and returned it to Mr Ramage.

• A variation on the above items concerns Wallace Williams of Charlottte, North Carolina, who accidentally dropped his watch from a plane at 2,000 feet and found it in his own backyard, still running.

Are these stories true, merely apocryphal or mythological?

Certainly the miraculous Fish-stomach Effect can be traced back to mythology. There is the story of the Pharaoh Amasis (*circa* 550 BC) and Polycrates, the tyrant of the island of Samos. Amasis advised Polycrates to test his luck by throwing a valuable ring into the sea. A few days later a fisherman brought him a fish as a gift and, on opening it, the ring was found inside.

Bishop Mungo, who was to become the patron saint of Glasgow, is reputed to have relied on the Fish-stomach Effect to save the reputation of a married woman. She had reported her wedding ring lost, but was suspected of having given it to her lover. The bishop asked that the first fish caught in the morning in the Clyde be brought to him. He spent that night praying. When the fish was placed on his table and opened, it was found to contain the lost ring.

Another bishop, Gerbold, threw his ring into the sea in anger having been driven from his palace at Bayeux. Shortly afterwards a fisherman caught a fish which contained the episcopal ring in its stomach and his flock were so impressed they promptly restored Gerbold to his bishopric.

I have come across similar anecdotes widely circulated as valid coincidences, leading me to believe that a number of tales

– not necessarily those mentioned here – must be apocryphal. For example, there is the story of the Canadian postcode number for a farmer named McDonald: EIEIO. There are a number of variations in circulation, all claimed as fact, such as EIEIO being a vehicle's numberplate.

It may be that these coincidences are significant, whether they be apocryphal, mythological, true, or a mixture, because they serve to fulfil one of our deepest desires, for security. This is manifested in our concern at loss – of valued personal possessions, of friends, relatives and, indeed, the worse loss of all, our own lives.

The singular theme of these Fish-stomach Effect anecdotes is that nothing is lost for ever, however hopeless the chance of recovery may seem. This reasoning appeals to our basic belief in miracles and the widely held further belief of reincarnation. There is, too, the symbolism of fish as the representations of motherhood and the womb, life-giving rather life-losing.

My colleague Helen Chryssides, who has come across many similar stories, began wondering whether they were true happenings or urban myths, and how much they had been checked before being published.

One day she heard a most unlikely variation on the Fish-stomach Effect: an American had lost his thumb in a boating accident; the thumb turned up inside a fish.

Chryssides set to work to track the story to it source, determined to expose it if necessary and thereby cast doubts on the other fishy tales. Finally she found the man concerned, Robert Lindsey, a thirty-two-year-old welder with the Union Pacific railroad. Lindsey was most forthcoming and spoke willingly about the accident that led to the loss of his thumb.

He had been on an outing on a friend's boat at the Flaming Gorge Reservoir, a popular recreation spot in south-west Wyoming. 'Some cabin cruisers came by and their wake swamped our boat,' Lindsey said. 'I leant forward to grab a child, but another wave washed me overboard.' He was swept under the boat and towards the propeller. 'I was trying to get away, but my hand and leg got caught in the blades. My leg got messed up, my thumb was taken off completely and my index and middle fingers on my right hand were cut so badly that they were only attached by a strip of skin.' As more waves came in, the boat sank and all on board were thrown into the water. 'Only the driver and I didn't have life-jackets on,' said Lindsey. 'We were hollering for help. A friend in a life-jacket saved me, and then other boats gave help. I'm lucky to be alive.'

Lindsey was taken by helicopter to a Utah hospital, where surgeons reconstructed his right hand, reattaching the two fingers, and fixed his badly injured leg. He concluded the story this way: 'I was sitting home recovering and waiting to go back to work when my wife showed me an article in the local paper. The story was about a man out fishing who'd found a human thumb inside a fish he had caught, five miles from where I had my accident. I figured it was probably my thumb, so I called up the coroner, who thought I was joking at first. But then I went to see him and the thumb. From what I could tell, it looked like my thumb. It was in really good shape for having been inside a fish for six months.'

Chryssides says further checking brought to light that when Lindsey's hand X-rays were checked out alongside the thumb, there was no doubt. The bone structure matched perfectly and the cut was at the same angle.

Lindsey was given the thumb and keeps it in a jar of preserving fluid in his closet. As a final clincher to the story's authenticity, Chryssides organized a press photographer to photograph Lindsey at home with his gruesome trophy.

Chryssides now keeps an open mind about the Fish-stomach Effect and counts it as the strangest coincidence she has come across.

▶ Good Bait ▼

Andrew White, thirteen, was fishing with his family on Smiths Lake in Australia one day in January 1994 and dropped his green-coloured chewing gum overboard when it lost its taste. Within minutes his brother Greg caught a fish and when it was gutted back on shore they found inside the discarded wad of chewing gum.

CHAPTER SIX

Literary Coincidences

Coincidences in the literary world give us insight into some extraordinary powers at work in the creative processes.

► Rejection Slip ▼

On a Friday night early in 1992, a London publisher was dining in a Notting Hill Gate restaurant when thieves broke into her car. Among the things stolen was a manuscript she had big hopes for, although she had not yet told its author. Its loss was what most upset her about the incident.

The thieves, however, obviously didn't think as highly of the manuscript and, unknown to her, had thrown it over a wall before driving away.

She spent a nervous weekend and in her office on Monday morning was trying to decide how she should deal with the problem when a call came from the author of the manuscript. In a voice tinged more with sorrow than anger, he asked the publisher: 'Why did you have my manuscript thrown over my front fence?'

► Apt Authors ▼

Motorcyling for Beginners, Geoff Carless (East Ardsley EP Publishing, 1980).
The Boy's Own Aquarium, Frank Finn (Country Life and George Newnes, 1922).

▶ Overshadowed ▼

The pleasure of browsing through a bookshop was disturbed for me one winter's afternoon when I came across a novel called *Walking Shadows*. With a gasp that had heads turning in the otherwise silent atmosphere, I snatched the book from the shelf.

The title had barely had a chance to sink in before I began turning the pages, looking for the quotation from *Macbeth* that had to be in there somewhere. Sure enough:

> *Life's but a walking shadow, a poor player,*
> *That struts and frets his hour upon the stage,*
> *And then is heard no more . . .*

For more than eighteen months I had been working on various drafts of a book and screenplay both entitled *Walking Shadows*. I too had used the Shakespearian passage as an inspiration, having come across it at some stage of the creative process and realizing how perfectly it wove itself into my plot.

Some days after this encounter I had calmed down enough to realize I should have bought the 'other' *Walking Shadows* to discover how far the coincidence extended. When I did return to the shop, the book had lived up to its title and 'walked'. Nobody there seemed to have heard of it.

Having been too upset to note the name of the publisher or author, or any other details, at the time, I toyed with the idea that I had imagined it . . .

▶ Unwelcome Coincidences ▼

One likes to have allies in adversity, souls who have suffered similar ill-fortune. So I was perversely pleased when I read an article by British author Susan Hill in the *Spectator* (18 January 1992), which was headed 'Novel and unwelcome coincidences'.

She had written a novel about the love of two young soldiers in the trenches of Flanders in the First World War called *Strange Meeting*, which was published in 1971. She said:

In that ultra-sensitive state immediately following on the completion and publication of a novel, I was plunged into depression when another about the love of two young soldiers in the trenches of Flanders, Jennifer Johnston's How Many Miles to Babylon?, *came out shortly after mine.*

Still, she consoled herself, at least hers had come out first and in the two decades since has not been out of print.

Years later, she had an idea for a story which came to her all at once and so completely it did not alter in essential details from the first notes she made. It was to be some years before she turned the idea into a novel which she called *Air and Angels*. It was finished and sent to her publisher in May 1990. Set in Cambridge, *circa* 1912, the principal male character is a don and cleric who falls unexpectedly and passionately in love with a sixteen-year-old girl. As well as being a theology tutor, he has a strong leaning towards the biological sciences and is a serious ornithologist and naturalist.

Hill writes:

One fine Sunday morning – I remember everything about it with astonishing clarity – we were having coffee at a café table overlooking the Royal Shakespeare Theatre and the River Avon at Stratford, each reading a newspaper, when my husband looked up from his Observer *and said quietly, 'There is an interview with Penelope Fitzgerald here that you had better read.' Alerted, though somewhat puzzled by the seriousness of his tone, I set aside my own paper and did so. I discovered that Mrs Fitzgerald was about to publish a new novel called the* Gate of Angels *[note the similarity of titles], its hero was a clergyman with a scientific bent, who falls passionately in love with a very young girl. Its setting, Cambridge,* circa 1912.

Hill points out the 'complete and absolute coincidence' of the bizarre event. She and Fitzgerald had met only once, briefly, years before. They had never spoken or corresponded about their work, they have different publishers and neither had spoken publicly about their current work in progress. Again, both novels were published and did well.

Even with the hand of coincidence touching her First World War novel, then another novel, Hill was still not prepared for a third 'and far more grievous blow'.

She had always been fascinated by the Antarctic and in 1989 finally decided to write a novel about British explorer Captain Scott and his companions, who perished on a journey to the South Pole in 1912. Her notes took shape and she made plans to begin writing. Then,

> *just before Christmas on the 8.50 from Oxford to Paddington I opened my copy of* The Bookseller *and saw an advertisement for a new novel by Beryl Bainbridge, called* The Birthday Boys, *based on the last voyage of Scott and his companions to the Antarctic.*

As with the previous incident, she had never met the author or corresponded with her and as far as she knows neither had made public details of their work in progress.

She asks: 'The moral? Well there isn't one, I suppose. Two years' work gone down the tube . . .' She resolves, all you can do is grin and bear it, and adds: 'I haven't read her book – I couldn't.'

▶ Apt Author ▼

Round the Bend in the Stream, Sir Wilmot Hudson Fysh (Angus & Robertson, 1968).

▶ Title Search ▼

Do we set out unconsciously to find things that are significant to us, led by coincidence? Is that what I did when I came across the 'other' *Walking Shadows* on a random browse through a bookshop, allowing the chance of coincidence to lead me on? There are variations on this. The other day I was doing some editing work and came across the phrase 'demilitarized zone' in relation to Vietnam. I needed to know whether 'demilitarized' was unhyphenated and whether the words were treated as proper nouns. I checked with two books I thought would contain the phrase without finding it mentioned in either of their indexes. Then I took the large-format *Chronicle of 20th Century History* from the bookshelf, lay it on the desk and randomly opened it on a page in the final third of the book. The first item that caught my eye was: '5 April 1968, Vietnam War. In Operation Pegasus a 30,000-man US and South Vietnamese force lifted the 76-day siege of the 6000-man US Marine garrison at Khe Sanh . . . near the demilitarized zone . . .'

▶ Eccentric Search ▼

Discussing random literary searches with Audrey Best prompted her to recall an incident which began when a cousin suggested she read a book, *The Last of the Eccentrics*, a life of Rosslyn Bruce, who was at one time the vicar of a small village near her childhood home.

Best says she tried libraries everywhere for a copy without success. One Saturday morning, on leaving her local library she crossed the road and entered a large store. In the book department was a cardboard box full of cut-price books. Something prompted her to take out every book and the final one she unearthed was *The Last of the Eccentrics*.

▶ Apt Author ▼

The Encyclopaedia of Association Football, Maurice Golesworthy (Robert Hale, 1967).

▶ Double Cover – I ▼

In December 1990, two books released within a week of each other carried as a cover illustration *The Man in Black* (1925) by Napier Waller (1893–1972). The books were Frank Moorehouse's *Lateshows* (Picador) and Margaret Scott's *The Baby-Farmer* (Collins A&R).

There was a further coincidence. One of the stories in *Lateshows*, 'The Disciplining of Other People's Children', tells of the author's efforts at babysitting. In Moorehouse's case the illustration is clearly meant to represent a debonair man about town, with his black suit, hat and white silk scarf. Scott's novel is set in the 1870s and concerns a murderous trade in babies in Victorian London, thus giving the illustration a very different meaning.

▶ Double Cover – II ▼

In 1988, two books were published whose contents were very different yet whose covers were remarkably similar. The cover for Marianne Wiggins's novel *John Dollar* features a blue dolphin, black and white compass and a map. The cover for Tim Robinson's guide to Ireland's Aran Isles, *Stones of Aran*, features a blue dolphin, a black and white compass and a map. The colour motif in each is reddish-brown with a grey background. Both are collages created with the help of Canon colour copiers. Publishers brought out both books almost simultaneously. Oh, and the artists are different! Neither saw the work of the other. Peter Dyer, Secker and Warburg's art director, made the point that the *Dollar* cover had been widely published within the trade months before the book was released. 'I was annoyed and upset,' he said. 'We'd had our jacket for eight months before publication – it had appeared in three catalogues and in a design magazine. The idea grew from a very lovely scene in *Dollar* featuring dolphins, and the map came from the author herself.'

Viking's artist John Caple said all the elements in his design were mentioned in the brief he had been given, which grew from the contents of the book. 'I was told to include the dolphins, the compass and, obviously, the stones of Aran, and interpreted those in my own style.' He strenuously denied having seen Secker's cover before completing his work.

Fiona Carpenter, art director of Viking, said it was 'just completely accidental', one of the miracles of our time. 'Ours was finished long before we first saw the Secker book and the fact they were so similar came as a complete shock,' she went on, adding, 'I agree it is extraordinary but it's just a *very unfortunate coincidence*' (my italics).

▶ Little League of Nations ▼

Following the *Man in Black* business, Frank Moorehouse (see above) spent most of 1991 working on a novel about the old League of Nations, living in Geneva and France to do his research and writing.

Moorehouse chose as his central character Edith, a young Australian who joins the League's secretariat in the 1920s. He wanted a model for Edith to give him an underpinning career path on how League people worked, lived, played and whatever else they did in Geneva from 1920 to 1946. An archivist directed him to the files of a Canadian woman in the secretariat, Mary Craig McGeachy, and he went through all her letters, records, expenses claims and other documents until he felt he knew her personally.

Towards the end of his research Moorehouse moved to live in Besançon, a French town midway between Paris and Geneva. One day he was talking to Canadian visitors about his book and happened to mention McGeachy. This is when the 'small world' coincidence came into play. The Canadians said they used to live next door to a McGeachy, but the chances of there being any connection, surely not . . .

Weeks later he received a letter from them saying they had actually tracked down 'his' Mary McGeachy and, a further surprise, she was alive and living in New York state. Moorehouse couldn't resist hopping on a plane to meet his heroine, then aged ninety-two. A case of life creating art?

▶ Apt Author ▼

Grace of God, A. Lord (Truro, James R. Netherton, 1859).

▶ Mirror Death in Reflection ▼

London scriptwriter Steven Moffat completed the first episode of a new fictional series, *Press Gang*, early in 1991. It concerned a media mogul dying suddenly and leaving his family to take over his business, which has a financial crisis looming.

Nine months later the UK Mirror Group media mogul

Robert Maxwell died suddenly and surprisingly, in strange circumstances, and his family were left holding the reins in the midst of a huge financial scandal.

▶ Penned in Pen ▼

Oscar Wilde, Adolf Hitler and Cervantes all wrote major works while in jail.

▶ Is This a Record ▼

Colin Wilson, in his book *Strange Powers* (1973), tells an odd tale of artistic timing.

He was reading a review of a recording of Verdi's opera *Attila* in which he saw a reference to a ballet called *The Lady and the Fool*, put together from an early Verdi opera. To his surprise, he found the *Lady* record on his shelves. He did not know he had it and had certainly never played it. From the details on the jacket he found the ballet had been arranged by John Cranko.

The record notes mentioned that Cranko's other most popular ballet was *Pineapple Poll*, arranged from the music of Arthur Sullivan. He had the *Poll* disc, so took it out and played it after he had played *The Lady and the Fool*.

Immediately after playing both records, he turned on his radio to get a programme he had planned to listen to at 8.30 p.m. It was 8.25 and the radio happened to be tuned to the wrong station. A newsreader was announcing the death that day of John Cranko, whose best-known ballets were *The Lady and the Fool* and *Pineapple Poll*.

He had never played *The Lady* and had not played *Pineapple Poll* for years. Furthermore, he did not know *Poll* was by Cranko. They had been the only two records he had played during the evening before hearing the news of his death.

▶ Apt Author ▼

Landscape Painting was written by William Splatt.

▶ The Twain Shall Meet ▼

A cluster of literary comings and goings occurred between 21 and 24 April.

American author Mark Twain, who was born on 30 November 1835, a year in which Halley's Comet appeared, died on 21 April 1910, when the comet next made its appearance.

Another literary figure, Vladimir Nabokov, was born on 22 April 1899.

The death date of two of the world's greatest literary geniuses, William Shakespeare and Miguel de Cervantes (author of *Don Quixote*), is 23 April 1616.

Shakespeare was baptized on 26 April 1564 – his actual birth date is unknown.

Finally, on 24 April 1815, English novelist Anthony Trollope was born.

▶ For Whom They Tolled the Bell ▼

Ernest Hemingway, Somerset Maugham and Walt Disney all did their bit in the First World War – as ambulance drivers.

▶ Apt Author ▼

Electronics for Schools, R. A. Sparkes (Hutchinson Educational, 1972).
The book *Sunrise* (Arrow, Sydney, 1991) is a work of fiction by Sylvia Story.

▶ Ode to Eighteen ▼

Henry Longfellow (1807–82) wrote eighteen volumes of poetry, graduated from Bowdoin College at eighteen, married his second wife eighteen years later, was a professor at Harvard for eighteen years and died on 18 March.

▶ On the Side of the Angels ▼

Sophy Burnham, author of the best-seller *A Book of Angels*, relates in an *HQ* magazine interview how, in her research for a four-line quote from the Koran one afternoon, on a sudden whim she wandered into a bookshop, sure that she would find the quote there. As she picked up a copy of the Koran, she suddenly realized just how huge the book is. Also, she had no idea where the quote was; she could have been searching for ever to find it. So she offered up a brief prayer, then allowed the book to fall open – and looked down. On the page before her was the four-line quote.

▶ Apt Author ▼

Australian Freshwater Fish was written by John Lake.

▶ Coming Clean ▼

An editorial assistant on the staff of *Inside Soap*, the magazine with all the stories about the TV soaps, is called Melissa Bath.

▶ Junko Food ▼

Co-author of a book on health food – Junko Lambert.

▶ Same Titles ▼

Journalist Peter Watson went undercover for a book he wrote that resulted in this coincidence. He posed as an art dealer called John Blake in order to recover a stolen Caravaggio painting. The book of his experiences he called *The Caravaggio Conspiracy*. In the week it was published, a novel by Oliver Banks also came out, called *The Caravaggio Obsession*, a fictional account of an art dealer trying to locate a stolen Caravaggio. In it the fictional dealer's name is Richard Blake. Watson had had some dealings with coincidences before this: he had written a book about the coincidences in the lives of identical twins.

▶ The Hanging Man ▼

Matthew Manning, the psychic, notes a coincidence in his book *In the Minds of Millions* (1978). Among his psychic claims is that of automatic drawing and writing. One of these drawings was used on a London Weekend TV programme. He called it the *Hanging Man*. It shows a figure in long dress-like clothes, pointed shoes and a skull cap, with his hands evidently tied behind his back, suspended by his neck from a rope.

Many of Manning's works have been identified as those of long-dead artists, but all attempts by art experts to source the *Hanging Man* failed. Then, out of the blue and more than two years later, he heard from a woman who sent him a copy of a book, *Lorenzo the Magnificent*, by Hugh Ross Williamson (1974). She had been reading about his picture one day and the next, by 'sheer coincidence', she had bought *Lorenzo* and there was the *Hanging Man*, a sketch by Leonardo da Vinci of the hanging on 8 December 1478 of Bernardo Bandini, a Pazzi conspirator who had murdered Giuliano de Medici. 'The details of his clothes, the position of the feet, the inclination of the head, I had got these almost exactly,' writes Manning.

He goes on to say that when doing the drawing some wording which had appeared at the top left-hand corner of it trailed off in the fifth line. 'I knew I couldn't go on, although at a glance there would be no reason to think the writing was unfinished, because it was illegible and unintelligible.' Now, seeing the original, he noted: 'The writing went on for another six lines. It is mirror writing in medieval Italian.'

▶ Swiss Twist ▼

To add to the notion of the literary 'universal mind' as opposed to the mind-set of the plagiarist, Sir Arthur Conan Doyle tells of a literary coincidence in his *Through the Magic Door* (Doyle, famed for his creation of the character Sherlock Holmes, was also a spiritualist). He was staying in Switzerland and had visited the Gemini Pass, where a high cliff separates a French from a German canton. On the summit of the cliff was a small inn which used to be isolated in winter for three months as it became inaccessible during heavy snowfalls. His imagination was stirred and he began to build a short story of strong antagonistic characters being stuck at the inn, loathing each other yet utterly unable to get away from each other's company, each day bringing them nearer to tragedy . . .

On his way back to Britain, in France, he came across a volume of Maupassant's *Tales*. The first story was called 'L'Auberge'. The scene was set in the very inn he had visited and the plot was the same as he had imagined, except that Maupassant brought in a savage hound. Doyle's initial reaction was relief that he had avoided a charge of plagiarism. He believed the coincidence was spiritually inspired, a psychic coincidence.

▶ Battle Fact ▼

Robert Hutchenson had been working for two years on a fictional story about the Israelis attacking an Iraqi nuclear reactor. In 1981, while he was still completing the novel, it actually happened.

▶ Vision of *Vision* ▼

The *International Journal of Parapsychology* reported the following eerie experience, which began when Dr Lawrence LeShan met Dr Nina Ridenour to discuss his manuscript, which dealt largely with mysticism. Dr Ridenour is an expert on the subject. As they talked, LeShan took careful notes of her advice and comments, including making a list of the books she recommended he read. One of the eight books on his list was Crammer-Bing's *The Vision of Asia*. He mentally noted her comment on it: 'Until you read this, you won't understand the difference between Eastern and Western mysticism.'

It was significant for him, because the difference between the mysticism of East and West was vital to the idea he was exploring.

Shortly after their meeting, he checked at two specialized libraries but was unable to find a copy of the book. Later, on his way home, an impulse made him change his usual route, even though he was in a hurry, and he found himself standing at traffic lights in an unfamiliar spot. He glanced down and his eye was caught by a book lying on the ground. A further impulse made him pick it up: the title leapt from the cover – *The Vision of Asia*. by L. Crammer-Bing. The following day he rang Dr Ridenour and told her of the strange coincidence that had led to his coming into possession of the book she had so highly recommended.

Her response was to ask: 'Which book?'

'*The Vision of Asia* by Crammer-Bing.'

'I've never heard of it,' said Dr Ridenour. This serious and responsible scholar was not joking.

▶ Kidnapping Forecast ▼

A book foretold the kidnapping and brainwashing of American heiress Patty Hearst. The novel, *Black Abductor* by James Rusk, was published in 1973 and related the events of 1974 with stunning accuracy. Both the kidnapping and the novel share the following features: a young college student named Patricia, daughter of a wealthy and prominent right-wing figure, is kidnapped near her university campus while she is with her boyfriend, who is severely beaten. Initially, the boyfriend is a suspect in the case. The kidnappers, led by an angry young black man, are members of a terrorist revolutionary group. At first the girl is an unwilling captive but later she adopts their ideology and joins the group. In what is termed 'America's first political kidnapping', the group sent Polaroid pictures of the young woman, along with messages to her father.

The fictional abductors predict – as happened in the real abduction – that they will ultimately be surrounded by police, tear-gassed and killed.

Four weeks after the Hearst kidnapping, author Rusk was visited by the FBI. They suspected that either he was in on the planning of the kidnapping or that the kidnappers had got the idea from his book. They had difficulty accepting it for the coincidence it was.

► Apt Authors ▼

The Abel Coincidence, J. N. Chance (Robert Hale, 1969).
The authors of *The Imperial Animal*, an analysis of human nature, are Lionel Tiger and Robin Fox.
Shady Gardens was written by Virginia Reed.

► Book of the Year ▼

When Arthur Koestler's *The Roots of Coincidence* came out in 1972, Kay Dick, a *Times* critic, voted it her book of the year, giving the following explanation:

> *I stood at my gate after midnight, looking out to sea, and at a clear starful sky. Suddenly I had a strong feeling that, to use words shaping in my mind, some rays from outer space were streaming through my skull. I wrote this down, so impressed was I.*
>
> *The next day I bought . . . Roots . . . just published, with no prior intention. I read it at once, and came across the description of neutrinos (to me then unknown) and the following quotation by a scientist: 'As you read this sentence, billions of neutrinos coming from the sun and other stars, perhaps even from other galaxies, are streaming through your skull and brain.' After that who can doubt which is my book of the year.*

► Active Authors ▼

Illustrated History of Gymnastics, John Goodbody (Stanley Paul, 1983).
Your Morning Broadcast Physical Exercises by Frank Punchard (U.P. London, 1943).

► A Tale of Two Plots ▼

This case involves the furore that broke out over two books which were published fifty years apart and in different parts of the world yet have so many points in common that claims of plagiarism were levelled, claims hotly denied by one of the authors involved, Colleen McCullough.

The books in question are McCullough's *The Ladies of Missalonghi* and the earlier *The Blue Castle* by Canada's Lucy Maud Montgomery, author of *Anne of Green Gables*. Consider the plots. The heroine of *The Ladies* is Miss Hurlingford, a plain thirty-three-year-old spinster who lives with her mother and elderly aunt in a small pre-First World War town in the Blue Mountains, west of Sydney. Throughout her life she has been afraid of offending the Hurlingford clan's opinions and prejudices. Her only pleasure in life is her visits to the local lending library, where she borrows romantic novels. She suffers from pains around her heart and is sent to see a specialist. He tells her the pains are not serious, but she finds an unaddressed letter on his desk, telling a patient she has no more than a year to live. Missy decides that she will live her life as though she had received the letter. It liberates her, ridding her of her inhibitions. She begins to speak her mind. She also falls in love with the mysterious John Smith, a local recluse with a shady past, a rugged red-haired man She shows him the letter and asks him to marry her for the short time she has left. Startled, he nevertheless agrees.

Now the plot of *The Blue Castle*. The heroine is Valancy Stirling, a 'homely' twenty-nine-year-old spinster who lives with her domineering mother and an elderly cousin in a small Ontario town. She has spent her life being patronized by the Stirling clan's opinions and prejudices. She is totally without status or independence. Her mother is even reluctant to let her walk to the library alone. She consults a doctor about pains around the heart. He treats her in an off-hand manner and later informs her by letter she has severe angina and no more than a year to live. This news liberates her and she decides to live for herself and to have some fun. She falls in love with a mysterious reclusive bachelor, Barney Snaith, a rugged red-haired man with a bad reputation. Valancy shows him the letter and proposes to him. Startled, he agrees to marry her. When Valancy discovers the letter was a mistake, she tells all.

Both men turn out to be other than they appear. Smith is, in fact, a wealthy landowner, Snaith the son of a millionaire. In both stories the couples live happily ever after.

Canadian journalist Maureen Garvie broke the story of the two plots, but did not raise the possibility of coincidence. Yet it seems incredible that McCullough, a highly successful and imaginative author, would copy somebody else's work. 'I'm not that stupid. It hurts that people would say I was that bloody 'stupid,' she told the Sydney *Sunday Telegraph* on 21 February 1988. 'It might have been subconsciously there, but it's not plagiarism. I am not a thief and I have never been a thief.' Later that year she told the *Weekend Australian*: 'It is something I thought would never happen to me. I remember reading *The Blue Castle* when I was 10 years old and I definitely didn't take anything from it – and if there were any similarities between the two books it was from my subconscious.' In a further interview with the *Sydney Morning Herald* Miss McCullough also admitted she had based the novel on her own experience. 'I'm no Miss Australia to look at, I never was, and it was because of my own personal experience that I have had a particular fascination with the old maid,' she said. Four or five of her novels have featured unmarried women as heroines or villains. 'The life I gave Missy is based on my own experiences and those of my mother, who really had a tough time of it – if you look inside the cover you'll see that the book is devoted to her.' She also said that the idea of a woman trying to catch a man on the basis that she was dying had come to her 'a long time ago because I met yet another woman who did just that'.

The key would seem to lie in the fact that McCullough had read the other novel, even though it was forty years earlier. The brain and its abilities remain a largely unknown quantity, and her belief that it was her imagination and her own personal experiences and feelings providing those details, even the plot, is quite acceptable.

Consider some more details. Both heroines work at useless tasks, Valancy piecing quilts, Missy hemming linen. Both must eat porridge daily for breakfast and dress only in brown, which they both hate. Both also have to wear unfashionable sailor hats. Each has an identical high-necked, long-sleeved, sexless nightgown . . . And so it goes on.

Nancy Seitz, who has co-edited McCullough's work in America, says: 'Yes, it is puzzling and worrying. I have to admit that there are striking similarities.' Her British editor, Rosemary

Cheetham, says: 'Of all the writers I know, Colleen McCullough is the one I would least suspect of any sort of plagiarism. The nature of the woman is so fiercely independent and formidable, it would be complete anathema to her. She is extraordinarily original and bubbling over with ideas.'

A final point on this: during an argument about whether this McCullough incident could even be considered a coincidence, my attention was drawn to the case of the Scottish poet Christopher Murray Grieve, who wrote under the pseudonym Hugh MacDiarmid. His most anthologized poem does not appear in his *Collected Poems*, published in 1962, since it was revealed that it is a 'versification' of another writer's prose.

▶ Collective Thinking ▼

Jung, with his interest in synchronicity, would have loved all this. As we saw in Chapter One, he believed many coincidences were the work of a universal force seeking to impose some kind of order. One part of that force was what he called the collective unconscious – that is, in addition to our individual unconscious we are all tuned into a collective unconscious. He wrote:

> We may think we are following our noses and may never discover that we are, for the most part, supernumaries on the stage of the world theatre. There are factors which, although we do not know them, nevertheless influence our lives, the more so if they are unconscious.

Of this collective unconscious, economist John Maynard Keynes said, 'Practical men who believe themselves to be quite exempt from any intellectual influences are usually the slaves of some defunct economist.' 'Economist' can be substituted by any other occupation – such as 'author'.

It must be evident by now that the creative process stirs coincidences in the most unexpected ways. It may be through such experiences that those who have to use their imaginations to create attempt to harness the phenomenon to aid that process.

To begin my research into the relevance to writers of coincidences, I selected a work at random from my bookshelves. My intention was to study it closely for any hint of coincidence causing a major breakthrough in the development of the plot. After dithering for some minutes – I did not want to waste my time with a dull book – I chose John Buchan's novel *The Power-House*. It was first published in 1916 and republished in 1984 by Dent & Sons.

I was barely into it when bingo!, the hero, Sir Edward Leithen, a barrister and MP, runs across his first villain and finds himself examining him in a court case on a matter unrelated to the plot. In pondering this incident the hero says:

> *Have you ever noticed that when you hear a name that strikes you, you seem to be constantly hearing it for a bit? Once I had a case in which one of the parties was called Jubber, a name I had never met before, but I ran across two other Jubbers before the case was over.*

In invoking the 'everything happens in threes' coincidence, entrenched in many societies, Buchan is working on the empathy of his readers by reminding us of something we believe we have experienced or witnessed. The 'threes' assumption arises largely from the Clustering Effect, which itself is a rich source for coincidences (see Chapter Two).

Leithen's coincidences are only just beginning. His car breaks down in the English countryside, in an area that is unfamiliar to him, and he goes in search of accommodation for the night suitable to one of his status. He finds it offered at the first gentleman's house he comes to. Its occupant turns out to be the arch villain. Until then the two men had not met.

Buchan has Leithen roundly endorse coincidences:

> *The amazing and almost incredible thing about this story of mine is the way clues kept rolling in unsolicited . . . I suppose the explanation is that the world is full of clues to everything and that if a man's mind is sharp-set on any quest, he happens to notice and take advantage of what otherwise he would miss.*

All those who have ever conducted any rigorous study would entirely endorse the sentiments.

Buchan was writing in 1913 and I wondered how his plot compared with the plots of today's authors. I soon had a chance to find out when I happened to see the movie *High Tide*. In it a woman drifter books herself into a caravan park of a small town, where she finds herself stranded and, lo and behold, her long-lost daughter and her mother-in-law are residents of the park – not of the town, mind you, but the caravan park itself. When I checked the critics to see what they made of this contrivance, all I found was praise for the film and nothing about the coincidence of the plot.

Let's look at two more examples.

The film *Return to the Blue Lagoon* opens in the late nineteenth century, when a ship's crew discovers a boat adrift in the Pacific containing the bodies of two young people – the couple from the original *Blue Lagoon*! Their baby son is alive. A recently widowed passenger on the rescue ship decides she will adopt the son as a brother to her young daughter. But soon she and the children are forced to abandon ship when cholera breaks out on board. Their boat is washed up on the *same* tropical island on which the son was born! Here the widow dies, when the two are teenagers, leaving them to fend for themselves, as the boy's parents had done in the original . . . The reaction when I read the review was, 'Come off it!'

The new *Blue Lagoon* hit the screen shortly after another film with a coincidence plot, *Doc Hollywood*, featuring Michael J. Fox as brash Dr Benjamin Stone, whose Porsche breaks down outside a small town called Grady, which just happens to be in need of a doctor . . .

One is inevitably reminded of the words, 'Of all the gin joints in all the world she had to come into mine,' the immortal lines from *Casablanca*, spoken by Rick (Humphrey Bogart) about his ex-lover Ilse Lund (Ingrid Bergman), who has arrived in the town by chance and then, in an extension of the coincidence, gone to Rick's Bar with her current lover. This coincidental meeting is, of course, central to the plot of the 1943 film, described in Leslie Halliwell's *Film Guide* as 'cinema par excellence'. Significantly he goes on (in a strange turn of phrase) to say: 'After various chances [it] just fell together impeccably into one of the outstanding entertainment experiences of cinema history.' Veteran film critic Walter Sullivan explained this observation by saying that 'they never knew from one day to the next what they were going to do. One of its writers refused to have his name on the credits as a result.' A hallmark in cinema history relied on coincidence for its outcome, its creation! This kind of evidence contradicts that old two-liner by John Gay:

> *Lest men suspect your tale untrue*
> *Keep probability in view.*

Sir Arthur Conan Doyle, whose interest in the psychic and other unnatural phenomena was well known, did not always observe Gay's dictum in his Sherlock Holmes stories. In one passage, however, he has Holmes string a series of guesses together to reconstruct the life of Dr Watson's brother, by looking at the brother's watch. But then he confesses that he 'could only say what was the balance of probability. I did not at all expect to be so accurate.'

This comment by the great detective is an attempt to provide consistent behaviour as expected of other characters in fiction (as it is, of course, of real people). What character would succeed in fiction if he or she were shown to rely solely on coincidence for their motivation and behaviour? Doyle, Agatha Christie, G. K. Chesterton and other greats of the mystery tale tend to be enormously 'improbable' in their plots. All of which leads to an observation that occurred to me while working on this section: as readers and viewers, we can accept coincidence in plot but not in character, within limits. How many times have you heard the comment about a true-life situation, 'If they put this in a novel no one would believe it'?

G. K. Chesterton, creator of the immensely popular Father Brown series, came up with plots that tended to be more improbable than most, plots that were strong on coincidence, as he was, so he is worth looking at a bit more closely. Part of Chesterton's philosophy was that 'life was full of a ceaseless shower of small coincidences, too small to be worth mentioning except for a special purpose, often too trifling to be noticed, any more than we notice one snowflake falling on another'. G. K. illustrates this viewpoint in one of his most famous short stories, 'The Blue Cross', when he has a character say:

The most incredible thing about miracles is that they happen.
A few clouds in heaven do come together into the staring shape
of a human eye. A tree does stand up in the landscape of a
doubtful journey in the exact shape of a note of interrogation.
Nelson does die in the instant of victory and a man named
Williams does quite accidentally [walk into a randomly chosen
house] and murder a man named Willliamson ... In short
there is in life an element of elfin coincidence which people
reckoning on the prosaic may perpetually miss ... wisdom
should reckon on the unforeseen.

Chesterton himself allowed chance to break the monotony
of planned behaviour. He would enter a railway station, buy
a ticket to an unfamiliar place with a name that appealed to
him, then wander home from that place as circumstances
permitted. He tells in his autobiography how he and his
wife 'planned' their second honeymoon. First they boarded a
passing bus, alighted when they saw a railway station and
bought tickets on the next departing train. The journey took
them to the English town of Slough.

From Slough they wandered through the countryside until
they reached an inn in the town of Beaconsfield, a place they
liked so much they later bought a house there. Martin Gardner,
who edited *The Annotated Innocence of Father Brown*, described
Chesterton's world as one of 'bizarre semi-fantasy where improbable events are as commonplace as improbable characters'.
Making the characters improbable is really stepping out of
the bounds set by literary licence!

Christopher Hollis, in his *The Mind of Chesterton*, points a
finger at the gruesome 'The Secret Garden' as the most
improbable of all Father Brown stories. After questioning
the impossibility of a madman becoming chief of police, an
atheist who hates religion enough to kill a man because he
intended to become a Catholic, then taking his hat off in
deference to a priest, Hollis continues:

Then there is the miraculous coincidence of a criminal having
an identical twin brother, and the impossibility of borrowing
the freshly severed head without that fact becoming known.
G. K. has here pushed the detective-puzzle story to its outer
limits of the absurd.

Gardner defends G. K.'s literary excesses, saying that the hard-boiled novel of today has been pushed to extremes of improbability even greater than those of Chesterton's tales. He points out that contemporary TV or film mysteries are likely to include at least some, if not all, of the following tired motifs: the (male) detective goes to bed with a buxom young woman; there is a wild car chase; the detective engages in a fist fight; faced with a locked door, the detective takes a small tool from his pocket and jiggles the lock so it opens in two seconds. 'This is reality?' queries Gardner.

It may very well not be, but it is evidence of my earlier observation about the way we have come to accept coincidence in plot, even a series of look and sound alike yet seemingly unrelated plots, if not in the characters who inhabit that plot.

As a final note on the detective coincidence, the American crime writer Frances Crane has her fictional private detective say, when wrapping up a case, that we are all 'the servants of chance. The little unthought-of thing, the accidental happening, unravels the whole scheme.'

Author Doris Lessing wrote: 'Life is always much more lavish with coincidence and drama than a fiction writer dares to be.' From what we have seen so far, that is an arguable statement. In Lessing's *The Story of a Non-Marrying Man*, she has one of her characters tell a tale steeped in coincidence. Wherever he went, he heard people speak of the succulent plant black aloes. It becomes such a dominant force that he ponders:

> *most people enjoy coincidence, it gives them something to talk about. But when there are too many, it makes an unpleasant feeling that the long arm of coincidence is pointing to a region where a rational person is likely to feel uncomfortable.*

A final mystery plot before we move on. In Alison Lurie's *The Truth about Lorin Jones*, the heroine, Polly Alter, is working on a biography of Jones, an underrated artist who died some years before. Alter, an artist herself, feels the grant she has been given to do the biography has a certain 'supernatural appropriateness'. Which is not surprising, as the reader discovers. Though they had never met, she had been following in Lorin's path all her life. Both were Jewish, had grown up in the same New York suburb, though Alter was born twenty years later. Both had gone to the same school and after graduation lived in the same street in West Village. The coincidences mount as Alter continues her research. She comes across a work by Jones entitled *Princess Elinore of the White Meadows* and realizes with a shock that when she was a child she and her best friend had made up fairy-tale names for themselves; the friend called herself Princess Elinore of the White Meadows. Polly discovers that Lorin was known as Lolly; a character who knew the dead artist says Polly Alter reminds him of her; Lorin, like Polly, had a half-brother she did not get on with ... And so the coincidences help build an exciting mystery without there being any feeling of questioning the acceptance of such a deliberate plot.

If there is a problem with coincidence in plot, it is not one of avoiding coincidence under any circumstances; rather it is making sure that when coincidence is used it is done unobtrusively.

The prolific American horror thriller writer William Schoell goes further on the subject by saying that the writer should learn to make coincidences work *for* the plot, or not use them at all. In 'Making Coincidences Convincing', an article that appeared in *The Writer* magazine, Schoell says:

> *Sometimes a coincidence can add just that touch of drama that your story needs. If a detective happens to see the felon he's just been assigned to look for as he crosses the street, it might be pretty boring, but if a weary detective takes the commuter train home because his car broke down and at the station sees the fugitive he's been hunting down for months, you have not only another believable situation, but an ironic and exciting one . . . it* could *happen.*

(Could happen? In Chapter Nine there is the true-life account of a detective who boards a plane as he is leaving for his annual holidays and finds a man he had arrested several weeks before about to leave the country, and has to break off his holidays to rearrest the man.)

To summarize, the trick is to make coincidences not only plausible but non-irritating. Once a critic is angered by coincidence, he can only pass it on, as Walter Sullivan did when reviewing the 1992 movie *Voyager*, starring Sam Shepard, Julie Delpy and Deborah-Lee Furness: '. . . We are dealing here with a plot that piles coincidence on coincidence.' The veteran reviewer had been *irritated*!

▶ Cut-up Coincidences ▼

You may think the examples such as those we have dealt with amount to literary trickery. But consider the case of William Burroughs, who went beyond plot to allow coincidence to become a major factor in his composition, a central device in his very writing.

It began in 1959, when the American author was introduced to what is known as the cut-up method of writing, as discovered by his friend Brion Gysin, the poet and painter. Gysin made accidental cuts through several sheets of newspaper, rearranged the fragments at random and produced the cut-up texts which appeared 'unchanged and unedited' in *Minutes to Go*.

Burroughs believed he had been unconsciously working towards the device when rearranging the material which became *Naked Lunch*. Burroughs experimented widely, cutting (for example) verse with scientific tracts, and even using tape recorders and film. Robin Lydenberg, in *Word Cultures*, says:

> In his theoretical explorations of the nature of cut-up writing, Burroughs comes to assert finally that all literature is cut-up [coincidence!] in which we receive subliminally and simultaneously much more than the conscious mind registers.

One method used by Burroughs was to take a page of text, fold it down the middle and place it on another page. The deliberate joining of unrelated incidents, together with random selection, achieved for him the effects of a film flashback (and, I might add, a hint of the theory of relativity), enabling 'the writer to move backward and forward on his time track'.

Another method involves taking a page of text and cutting it into quarters. The top left-hand quarter is moved to the bottom right-hand, and vice versa, to create a text with new meaning, if any. Film dubbing is another application, and record producers cut up snippets from existing records to create new ones.

A side-effect of Burroughs's experiment is that it leaves the copyright laws looking a little superfluous. However, he did not believe that words belonged to anybody anyway. Robin Lydenberg, in *Word Cultures*, says Burroughs's use of coincidence in the writing process was a deliberate and conscious abdication of controls which aimed at an escape from controls – controls posed from within or without. Talking of controls, his random indeterminacy offended more critics than the alleged pornographic nature of his works, which others sought to control through censorship.

Burroughs also railed against another control which concerns us in this discussion: the 'monumental fraud of cause and effect'. In a mid-1980s interview Burroughs said:

> *I was coming around the corner thinking of New Mexico; I get around the corner and there's* New Mexico – Land of Enchantment *on a license plate . . . It's synchronicity . . . the whole concept of synchronicity is much more in accord with the actual facts of perception.*

He argued that 'rationalism just isn't rational', adding that one scientist was quoted as saying he would never believe in ESP, no matter what evidence was brought forward. More pertinent to the argument that coincidences are useless for research because they are merely anecdotal, and so cannot be repeated, he said that some magic rituals can be performed only once.

Burroughs urged people to try the cut-up method for themselves. I know a number of writers who have become hooked on it, finding that it gives their writing insights and perspectives they are unable to achieve with normal prose. It can become addictive, as I was to find when I cut up a number of unsuccessful novels I had written, dividing a page into quarters, as outlined above. This is a sample:

> *Executive decisions and stained fingers which reassure her with sales. In a chair that throbs with power. It was late at night alone and it was so good to mock her with memories that were not exactly creatures.*

Her son growing and somewhere her job shone. Memories and decisions and a creator and a camelhair coat.

As he stood he said breathlessly: 'Women see men as characters of certain outcomes.'

Absorbed, she felt Dawkins's eyes could understand, absorbed sleeve, gasped, sobbed better than most. The silence completed assignment. The paper on which it was, what had she written? But only if it were emotion. She had tried light that seemed to mother, sister best itself. She could not stay, shimmering slightly. The paper told things the power to glow held in her hand before they finish her. Hair pulled to a doll. If I do what she do, do you know they want me to do?

I must confess that to achieve the level of coherence in cut-ups illustrated here, I had to edit in some cases quite considerably, but not rewrite. I felt that somehow the exercise had helped me get further inside the minds of my fictional characters and I enjoyed the imagery of some of the phrases created – for example, the woman executive's 'chair that throbs with power', 'women see men as characters of certain outcomes', 'hair pulled to a doll'.

In a further experiment I used Shirley MacLaine's *Out on a Limb*, which I selected randomly. Without looking, I opened it at a page, folded it down the middle and placed it on another blindly selected page. I did not edit the result. Here is a sample:

When Peter finished/and of its purpose in the/matter-of-fact, Yes,' I said/explosive such a concept/Kubler Ross's stuff and/ within the Church pursue/accounts of so many people/many people who, while/but apparently it wasn't/precepts?

One line – 'the Church pursue accounts of so many people' – caught the eye of Glenn Cooper, a student of Burroughs's works. Cooper said that given the hatred Burroughs had for Christianity, he would have regarded my exercise as a success, because it did provide an insight.

Cooper finds Burroughs's cut-up trilogy the most difficult

works he has encountered, as difficult as Joyce's *Finnegans Wake* and of equal literary importance). He says that cut-up works can have a 'skewed logic of their own whose meaning may not be apparent at the time, but when returned to, weeks or months later, they show a meaning'.

For example?

'The future is glimpsed,' he replied.

Burroughs is on record as saying: 'If you cut into the present the future sometimes leaks out.'

Personally, apart from the coincidence created – the repetition of 'many people' – I did not feel I had gained any more insights into MacLaine's philosophy as a result. Still, I recommend it as an exercise.

Burroughs pointed out that he did not simply use the resulting material from a cut-up. He selected and edited it. The method is creative, contrary to arguments from other literary figures. For example, if two people cut up the same material, the results will be quite different.

Burroughs's final words on the subject: 'I think the writer stands or falls on the actual writing. I'm not just talking about style. I'm talking about the whole process of creation. Good writing remains.'

One critic, sympathetic to experimental writing, wondered if 'perhaps someone else ... [could] make more sense of [Burroughs's books] than I can'.

The psychic Alan Vaughan (also the author of one of the few other books on coincidence) may have unconsciously used the cut-up method when describing a personal anecdote. He says he 'read' of Robert Kennedy's assassination in the Paris edition of the *Herald-Tribune* on 19 April 1968. It was shortly after the assassination of civil rights leader Martin Luther King, and the main story on the front page was about the FBI's hunt for the man believed to have been the assassin. The adjoining story was about two victims of violence. Vaughan's eyes travelled across the eight columns of the stories to read consecutively:

Dr King, killed by a single bullet. Both were hit. Kennedy believed dead. Two more Americans and the former president from the north. Ten weeks.

Vaughan interpreted that to mean that Robert Kennedy would be shot in about ten weeks, at the end of June or early July. The actual date was 5 June 1968.

A final note on this subject: a classic example of the cut-up approach and deliberate attempts at elusiveness in writing is the work of Nostradamus. When he had finished writing his quatrains, the sixteenth-century seer tossed them in the air and gathered them at random. In her Preface to de Fontbrune's book *Nostradamus: Countdown to Apocalypse* (1983), Liz Greene says: 'This has made a dog's breakfast of most efforts to interpret him. The prophet leaps about from one time frame to another with no apparent order or continuity.' This, of course, has not stopped would-be interpreters over the centuries from trying. Most attempts have resulted in either mistranslation or misinterpretation, or both, with a touch of wishful thinking. Nostradamus also made the job harder by writing in gallicized Greek and Latin, dropping letters from some words and adding or transposing others and using wrong place-names.

However, believers in Nostradamus through the ages have seized upon what they regard as significant coincidences in his quatrains as valid indicators of predictive power.

Up to, during and following the Second World War some of the quatrains are said by certain modern interpreters to forecast the rise and fall of Hitler. This claim is based on the fact that the word 'Hister' appears in some interpretations.

The first:

> *Liberty shall be recovered,*
> *A black fierce, villainous, evil man shall occupy it,*
> *When the ties of his alliance are wrought.*
> *Venice shall be vexed by Hister.*

However, Hister is said to be an old name for the River Danube, which would appear to be more appropriate in the circumstances.

Another quatrain is said by some to be the most astonishing and can refer only to an event during the Second World War:

> *The assembly will go out from the castle of Franco,*
> *The ambassador not satisfied will make a schism;*

Those of the Riviera will be involved,
And they will deny the entry to the great gulf.

Stewart Robb, in his *Prophecies on World Events by Nostradamus* (1961), interprets it thus. The Spanish dictator Franco held a meeting with Hitler and the Italian dictator Mussolini in 1941 on the Riviera. When the other two asked Franco for permission to pass through Spain to attack the British fortress of Gibraltar, Franco refused – 'deny the entry to the great gulf'.

Michael FitzGerald, in his *Storm Troopers of Satan* (1990), enthuses that the quatrain concerns the Spanish Fascist leader General Franco: 'The odds against the name Franco, a meeting of ambassadors on the Riviera and the denial of "the entry to the great gulf" all occurring together by chance are more than one in a million, and this prophecy originates in 1550!'

However, Jean-Charles de Fontbrune, the son of Max the historian and noted Nostradamus interpreter, says the quatrain refers mainly to Franco being named as head of government at Burgos in 1938, although he does agree with Robb on the final line.

The de Fontbrune version of the quatrain is as follows:

Franco will emerge from a junta in a strong place in Castile.
The representative who has not pleased will make fa(scism)
Those with (Primo) de Rivera will be with him;
They will refuse to enter into the great gulf of misfortunes
    (Germany).

In *Countdown to Apocalypse*, de Fontbrune explains that Primo de Rivera was not a geographical place but the name of another Spanish leader who had united two right-wing parties. Further, Nostradamus, being full of puns and other cryptic word-plays, could of course have used Franco for France.

Even when the meanings seem clear, there is the problem with interpretation.

Robb's version:

An old man with the title of chief will arise, of doddering
    sense,
Degenerating in knowledge and arms;

Head of France feared by his sister,
The country divided, conceded to gendarmes.

De Fontbrune version:

The good sense of an old leader will be rendered stupid,
Losing the glory of his wisdom and feats of arms;
The chief of France will be suspected by his sister.
Then the land will be divided and abandoned to the soldiers.

Both agree that this refers to the aged Field-Marshal Pétain signing the armistice with Germany in June 1940.

FitzGerald seizes on the word 'gendarmes' in the Robb translation as a sign of precognition, pointing out that there were no gendarmes in the sixteenth century, so it obviously had to refer to an event occurring in a later era. De Fontbrune simply calls them soldiers.

FitzGerald believes the reference to 'his sister' refers to a sister-in-law who expressed fears that Pétain was too old to be head of France. De Fontbrune says 'sister' is a reference to France's Latin sister, Italy.

It soon becomes obvious that nearly all the quatrains can be argued about in such a manner.

▶ Chance Encounters ▼

I turned from my random efforts in the world of literature to a random experiment in non-fiction books, this time picking up *The Monocled Mutineer*, the story of the 1917 British Army mutiny, using the same method, randomly selecting a book from a shelf. It describes how tension had been building for some time among the war-weary troops in a holding camp when the mutiny broke out. Discipline at the camp was harsh, even cruel, and conditions so deplorable that many soldiers said they preferred the front line. But the actual mutiny was sparked by a simple coincidence.

Corporal Wood from the Gordon Highlanders happened to be strolling outside the camp when he ran into a WAAC he had known in Aberdeen. Naturally he stopped to talk to her. They were interrupted by a military policeman, Private Harry

Reeve, who ordered Wood to move on – talking to WAACs was not allowed. Wood objected and a scuffle started which ended when Reeve drew his revolver and shot Wood. 'Quickly the news filtered round the Scots regiment,' wrote authors William Alison and John Fairley. 'It came for them as the final straw, the . . . mutiny was on.'

Of course, there are better examples than this, but to come across one chosen at random!

Let us look at the details again, for it began as one of those small-world coincidences which usually have a very different outcome. Like all such meetings, the one between the NCO and the WAAC was unplanned. It is unlikely that Wood, a self-disciplined NCO, would have broken regulations by talking to the WAAC if he had not already known her. In the second unrelated event Reeve happened to appear on the scene and these two events came together to create the coincidence. Of course, a related cause-and-effect incident may have sparked the mutiny, some deliberate act, but the fact remains it was *not* a deliberate act. It was a coincidence that was the straw that broke the camel's back.

Finally, I picked at random Barbara W. Tuchman's acclaimed work *The March of Folly* and soon found some passages that told of how 'circumstances' turned Vietnamese leader Ngo Dinh Diem into a dictator, with devastating effects for his country. Diem had been living in exile in Japan and no one thought him a likely candidate to lead his country. Then coincidence took a hand. He visited the United States in 1950 with no particular aims in mind. But because his brother was a Catholic bishop, Diem made contact with Cardinal Spellman. The cardinal introduced him to a number of important people, including Catholic politicians, among them John F. Kennedy, then a senator. 'Thereafter Diem was on his way,' says Tuchman – propelled by a series of chances.

▶ Dial-a-Plot ▼

Paul Auster, the author of seven novels and a volume of poetry, is no stranger to coincidence in the creative process. In a recent issue of *Harper's* magazine, he recalls how he was led to write his first novel, a story that had an eerie aftermath. He was at home alone in his Brooklyn apartment when the phone rang. The caller asked if he was talking to the Pinkerton detective agency. When Auster said he wasn't, the caller hung up. Next afternoon the same person rang again, asking for the agency. After Auster again told the caller he had the wrong number, his creative juices began to stir. What, he wondered, would have been the outcome had he said it was the agency? He waited for a third call, but it never came.

A year later, when he sat down to write *City of Glass*, the wrong number incident became a crucial event in the plot. A character named Quinn receives a phone call from someone who wants to talk to a private detective; after the third night Quinn pretends to be the detective . . .

Ten years later, Auster says a strange coincidence shows that it is 'possible for stories to go on writing themselves without an author'. He was again alone in his apartment in Brooklyn when the phone rang. The caller asked to speak to a Mr Quinn. Auster thought someone was pulling his leg and asked the man to spell the name out, Q-U-I-N-N. Auster suddenly grew scared and could not speak for a moment or two. When he did manage to say there was no Quinn there, the man apologized and hung up. He never rang back.

CHAPTER SEVEN

Random Anecdotes: I

The anecdotal material in the next few chapters is in no particular order, either of merit, similarity or subject. In other words, it is presented the way coincidences occur in life.

▶ Policeman Arrests Himself ▼

In early March 1987, Constable Douglas McKenzie was sent with his partner, Constable Gary Thomas, to arrest a man being held in a central Sydney chemist's for using false prescriptions. At the shop, Constable McKenzie asked the accused man to identify himself. 'Douglas McKenzie,' said the man, who produced a birth certificate, university card, two bank books and a Health Care card, all in the name of McKenzie.

'I said to him, you can't be Douglas McKenzie – because that's me,' *the* McKenzie recalled.

The identifying items had disappeared from the constable's car about two years before, while it was parked in Sydney's night-life district, King's Cross, a haunt of criminals, addicts and pushers, prostitutes and pimps.

'When I said the items were mine, he knew he was gone,' said Constable McKenzie. His face went stone cold and his jaw almost hit the ground. Finding someone who has taken over your identity leaves you with a pretty strange feeling. It's the strangest arrest I have ever made.' At the time of the incident the constable had been stationed in Central police station, the busiest in New South Wales, with hundreds of police on duty at any one time.

▶ A Life-saving Coincidence ▼

This case was reported in the American *National Tattler* 'Amazing but True' column, written by Doug Storer. It concerns two Texans, one Allen Falby, an El Paso County highway patrolman, the other Alfred Smith, a businessman. They met for the first time on a hot June night when Falby crashed his motor bike. He had been racing down the road, chasing a speeding truck, when the vehicle slowed to turn. Unaware of the change of pace, Falby slammed full throttle into the rear of the truck. The motor bike was demolished and Falby's body was badly battered. One leg had been nearly amputated. As he lay in agony on the road, a pool of blood began to form beneath the shattered limb. He had ruptured an artery in his leg and was bleeding to death.

It was then that fate brought Falby and Smith together, writes Storer. Smith had been driving home along the road when he saw the accident. Shaken but alert, he was out of his car and bending over the badly injured man almost before the sound of the impact died on the night air. Smith wasn't a doctor but could see what had to be done for the dying patrolman. Whipping off his tie, Smith quickly bound Falby's leg in a crude tourniquet. It worked. The flow of blood slackened to a trickle and then stopped entirely. When the ambulance arrived a few minutes later, Smith learned for the first time that he had saved Falby's life.

Falby spent several months in hospital. After surgery, he eventually returned to police work. Five years later, around Christmas, Falby was on highway night patrol when he received a radio call from headquarters to investigate a bad accident. A car had smashed into a tree. A man was in a serious condition and an ambulance was on the way. Falby reached the wreck well before the ambulance. Pushing his way past a group of frightened bystanders, he found the injured man slumped unconscious across the torn car seat. The man's right trouser leg was saturated with blood. He had severed a major artery and was bleeding to death. Well trained in first aid, Falby quickly applied a tourniquet above the ruptured artery. When the bleeding stopped, he pulled the man from the car and made him comfortable on the ground. That's when Falby recognized the victim – Alfred Smith, the man who had saved his own life five years earlier.

▶ The Berlitz Mystery ▼

Arthur C. Clarke, scientist, best-selling author – and a connoisseur of the curious – tells his personal favourite coincidence in *World of Strange Powers*. In December 1969 he flew into Paris to address a Unesco conference. The aircraft doors had just been opened and he was shuffling down the cabin when he noticed a Berlitz guidebook lying on one of the seats. Instantly the thought flashed through his mind: I wonder what's happened to Charlie Berlitz? I haven't seen him for years (this, incidentally, was long before he'd struck gold in the Bermuda Triangle).

> *I took another three or four steps, and a voice behind me said: 'Hello, Arthur. Guess who? Charlie Berlitz!' This incident still astonishes me – yet it shouldn't. In the course of a busy lifetime many similar events must occur, purely by coincidence. Nevertheless they give one an odd sensation somewhere at the top of the spine and tend to induce a semi-mystical belief that there's a lot going on in the universe that we . . . don't . . . understand . . .*

▶ Another Plane Tale ▼

This case concerns a small-world story involving actor Gordon Chater. He was flying from London to New York after a twenty-week tour as one of the leading actors in the play *The Dresser*.

On Concorde Chater chatted with the woman sitting next to him, who said it was her first trip to New York. 'And why are you going?' asked the actor. 'Well,' she replied 'my husband is

Ronald Harwood and he has written a play that you probably haven't heard of. It's called *The Dresser* and it's opening in New York . . .'

▶ Homely Judge ▼

In 1949 a man from Chester, Pennsylvania, was picked up on a vagrancy charge (no lawful means of support). He insisted that he was innocent and did have means of support; in fact he had a home, 714 McIlvain Street. When he came before Judge Lowry, he told the same story. 'Where did you get that address?' the judge asked. 'It's just an address,' said the defendant. 'I'll say it is, that's where I live. Ninety days.'

▶ Holey Tale ▼

In the early 1980s Scott Palmer created the Everest of golf stories. In fact, he got so used to not being believed, he rounded up affidavits from sixty-five witnesses to provide verification of the story. They show he has hit a hole in one eighteen times. Not only that, his drives hit the pin fifty other times. The US *Golf Digest* says this is a clear record; the previous one was set in 1962 by a Californian doctor with eleven in a single year. The *Digest* says the chances of an ordinary human being hitting the hole from the tee are 33,616 to 1. Scott, a Californian, is an author and able to play on most days at the Balboa Park course in San Diego. Four of his holes in one came on consecutive days in October 1983, seven have been on par-four holes and the average length of the eighteen is 209 metres. Scott started taking lessons half-way through this streak, so instead of hooking holes in one he got them in straight. He has hit all but one of his aces with the same apparently indestructible ball, a Spalding Top Flite XL No. 2. He has been offered more than $14,000 for it. Palmer says the way he does it is by getting a mental image of a faceless woman pouring a glass of milk the moment he hits the drive. The imagery is rather obtuse.

▶ Hole in One ▼

In July 1989 golfer Oliver Anthony, sixty-one, of Memphis, Tennessee, placed a golf ball in his pocket while playing a round. On the course a man approached him, brandishing a gun and demanding money. When Anthony refused the gunman started shooting. One shot hit the ball in Anthony's pocket, leaving him with a bruised leg. The other shots missed and the gunman fled.

▶ Same Name, Different Brides ▼

At noon on Saturday, 11 August 1985, Karen Dawn Southwick, twenty-two, married in a church at Tettenhall, Wolverhampton, England. She was given away by her father, Alfred. Three hours later, Karen Dawn Southwick, twenty-two, married in the same church and was given away by her father, Alfred.

It was not bigamy, just two brides with the same full names whose fathers had the same names, who happened to marry on the same day in the same church (the grooms' names were unalike).

The brides' families are not related and neither bride had met until the local vicar introduced them at a pre-wedding get-together for marrying couples. Noon-wedding Karen said: 'I almost fell over. I didn't even know I had a namesake living just a few miles from me.'

I am writing the above item on my wife's computer because I have just come from taking mine to the small company I bought it from to have it repaired. Before they issued me a docket, they found my name on their computer and read out the wrong address. Another person by my name lives a mile away from me.

▶ Two up ▼

Barbara Mercier, who turned fifty late in 1991, was given a 1942 penny by her brother to mark the occasion. She placed the penny on top of the family video.

The following day Mrs Mercier took her young grand-daughter, Cassie, to the doctor's. In the waiting room she noticed the child playing with a 1942 penny and admonished her for taking it from the video. Cassie insisted she had not, she had found the coin there in the waiting room.

When they returned home, the other 1942 penny was still sitting on top of the video.

▶ Lifting the Roof ▼

Life magazine carried a story which told how all fifteen people who were to attend choir practice in Beatrice, Nebraska, due to start at 7.15 p.m. on 1 March 1950, were late. Each had a different reason: a car would not start, a radio programme was not over, ironing wasn't finished, a conversation dragged on, etc. The church was destroyed by an explosion at 7.25 p.m. The chances of them *all* being late were later estimated at one in a million. The choir members did not attribute their lateness to probability but to a more obvious source.

▶ Penmanship ▼

Ms Patricia Weston was deputy principal of a large high school in the town of Bunbury, Western Australia, in 1977. She asked a friend, Barry Smith, down from Perth, the state capital, to partner her at the school's annual ball. They attended a local restaurant for dinner before the dance. Afterwards, as he changed from his dinner jacket, he noticed he had lost his gold pen.

Next morning they went back to the ballroom. Failing to locate the pen there, they tried the restaurant, where its owner was pleased to return the gold Schaeffer, which was easily identified as it had 'B. Smith' inscribed on it.

That evening Barry was packing his case to return to Perth when he came across his pen in the bag. Somewhat wonder-ingly, he went to his jacket pocket, where he had put it that morning.

Another pen. He now had two, both inscribed 'B. Smith'!

Barry left the 'returned' pen with Patricia just in case some-body claimed it, but nobody ever did.

A similar case: in 1953, Boone Aiken lost his pen in Florence, South Carolina. Like Barry Smith's pen, it was engraved with his name. Three years later, Boone and his wife were in New York. As Mrs Aiken left their hotel she saw lying in the street a pen that looked familiar. It was her husband's, as the engraving clearly showed.

▶ Drinkall Doesn't Drink at All ▼

Pastor George Drinkall is in charge of a Seventh Day Adventist church's temperance programme.

▶ Getting Her Man ▼

As a young girl Mrs C. L. Watt of Adelaide, South Australia, had always wanted to meet 'one of those glamorous Canadian Mounties'.

As an adult she went to Canada, but after nearly three years there she still had not fulfilled her wish. Then she had to travel from Vancouver to Toronto and took the Canadian Pacific railway. One evening, in the crowded dining car, she was shown to the only vacant seat at a table for four. The other three were men, one in army uniform, the other a civilian and the third, a fair-haired young man looking resplendent in full Mountie uniform, scarlet jacket, etc.

The other two men struck up a conversation with her but the tall, handsome Mountie at first just sat and listened. Then he spoke, his voice firm: 'You *are* an Australian?' Mrs Watt said she was. 'So am I!'

A Royal Canadian Mounted Police officer who was an Australian! The coincidence grew when he asked what part of Australia she was from. He too came from Adelaide, and not only that but the same suburb, Semaphore.

'Of the many members of the Canadian Mounted Police the only one I had met in three years happened to be from my own home town,' she recalls. 'I am a very elderly citizen but I have often thought of that long-ago meeting with my Mountie.'

▶ Programme Dropped ▼

A TV station sent out an amendment to its programme guide for a 10.50 p.m. movie slot: *Hang 'em High* was replaced by *Vertigo*, starring Jimmy Stewart.

▶ The Killing Hill ▼

The New York Herald reported on 26 November 1911 that Sir Edmundbury Godfrey had been savagely done to death at a place called Greenberry Hill. The three men convicted of the crime and subsequently hanged for it were called Green, Berry and Hill.

▶ Big Noting Himself ▼

A woman responded to a newspaper advertisement from a handwriting expert offering to do character readings from samples sent to her. The woman sent a note written by her boyfriend and asked if he would make a good husband. The graphologist replied with a firm 'no', adding that he had been a pretty rotten husband to her for the past three years. She added a PS: Thanks for the evidence.

▶Travelling Companions ▼

Sara Roberts hitched a ride from the south coast of England back to London and was dropped off in an area she was not familiar with.

She was standing on the street trying to get her bearings when a door opened behind her and out came a good friend. The friend had moved flat a few weeks before and she had had no idea where he had gone.

Talking of friends . . . another one of Sara's booked into a hotel in Ireland and, as he was unpacking, found in one of the drawers a briefcase belonging to his brother (who had stayed in the room the previous night). The brothers live more than 300 kilometres apart and rarely meet.

▶ Good at Her Job ▼

Bertha Tugwell is a midwife.

▶ Lovers Fall out ▼

Gyles Brandreth, in his *The Bedside Book of Great Sexual Disasters* (1984), tells of a Vera Czermak of Prague who discovered her husband had been unfaithful. In despair, she threw herself from her third-floor balcony, only to land on the husband, who happened to be walking directly below. She killed him but escaped herself with minor injuries.

▶ Joker Does Dallas ▼

Another story from *Great Sexual Disasters* details how violently life can imitate art. It appears that a couple became involved in a violent argument over who shot JR while watching an episode of the TV series *Dallas*. During a commercial break, the wife left the room and returned with a shotgun, which she used to kill her husband. The scene of the tragedy? In the real-life city of Dallas, Texas.

▶ Up in Smoke ▼

On 31 December 1968, an Australian television news service reported the crash of a Viscount propeller-powered plane at Port Hedland in Western Australia with the loss of twenty-six lives. At the end of the report there was a commercial break and on came the well-known jingle for a popular brand of cigarettes: 'Light up a Viscount, a Viscount, a Viscount . . .'

▶ Wordsmith ▼

William Caxton, who introduced printing to Britain had an assistant, Wynkyn de Worde.

▶ The Final Act ▼

Canadian actor Charles Coghlan became ill and died in Galveston, Texas, during a tour of the American state in 1899. He was buried in a lead coffin which was sealed inside a vault.

In September 1900, less than a year after his burial, a hurricane hit Galveston, flooding the cemetery and breaking open the vault. Coghlan's coffin floated away, into the Gulf of Mexico, then drifted along the Florida coastline and into the Atlantic, where the Gulf Stream took over and carried it north.

One day in 1908, some fishermen on Prince Edward Island, Canada, saw a long, weather-beaten box floating ashore – Coghlan's coffin. The actor's body had floated more than 5,600 kilometres – to his home. His fellow islanders reburied him in the graveyard of the church where he had been baptized.

▶ Flight Staff ▼

The *Daily Telegraph* reported on 3 June 1982 that a farmer in Lincolnshire had on his staff two people named Crow, four called Robbins, one Sparrow, a Gosling and a 'Dickie' Bird.

▶ Hot Goods ▼

Apart from the incredible coincidence in the following tale, I also like it because it is a story with a moral, although I am not sure who or what was responsible for the moral.

Peter, a young retail store assistant, was told by his boss to go to the store's car park and collect a heater from his car, a white Mazda. The heater, said the boss, handing Peter the car keys, was sitting in its box on the driver's seat.

Peter went to the parking lot, found the car as described

and the heater in its box on the driver's seat. The only odd thing was that the door was not locked. He removed the heater, then made a point of locking the door.

He returned to his boss, who took one look and said the heater was not his, his had been unpacked. This one, although the same brand, was new and in a box that had not been opened.

So far, an amazing coincidence, two cars in the parking lot, on the same level, same make, model and colour, both with a heater of the same brand sitting in a box on the driver's seats.

Peter went back to the parking lot, where he found all the doors of the car from which he had taken the box locked. By then, a bit worried, he approached a store security officer and explained what had happened. Security relieved him of the problem.

Then came the twist. 'The owner of the second car,' said Peter, 'also worked in the store, and he was charged with stealing the heater. He'd been stealing from the store for quite some time and this is how he got caught for it.'

▶ Fancy That! ▼

A 'pleasure palace' in Melbourne is in Horne Street, Elsternwick.

▶ Laughter the Best Medicine ▼

A medical partnership: Payne and Kilmore.

▶ A Fare Cop ▼

A common complaint the world over is that taxi drivers do not know how to find the address you want. An Athenian taxi driver had no such problem. The fare he picked up one day gave the driver's own address as his destination. Once there, the driver watched as the man took out a key and let himself in.

Using his own key, the driver followed and interrupted the man as he was about to make love to the driver's wife. Said the driver later: 'It must have been his unlucky day. Athens has 70,000 taxis.'

▶ Shakespeare Puzzle Solved ▼

Audrey Best was visiting a cousin in New Zealand some years ago. The cousin, a district nurse, took her to meet some of her 'flock' in a small community on the South Island. They included a gentleman who was well over seventy, who lived in a self-built wooden house.

As Miss Best wrote:

He had a considerable collection of books and I mentioned that I too was an avid reader. He said his particular interest, indeed mania, was the theory that the plays of Shakespeare had been written by Bacon. He had been trying for years, all over the world, to get a copy of a book published in 1913 called Is Bacon Shakespeare? *I asked him to write down the name of the author and said I would contact my librarian cousin in England to see if he could help.*

I duly wrote to him and by return of post received the book. It seems that my cousin had visited a dealer in second-hand books, with whom he was very friendly, to find that the previous day (the day on which my cousin received my letter) a man had walked into the shop offering the very book for sale. The book dealer had not seen a copy for years and years.

▶ Table for Four ▼

Geoff Kenihan and his wife, travel-writer Kerry, entered the Hotel Leningrad dining room by one door as an elderly couple, Roger and Alice, entered from another on 2 August 1971. Both couples zeroed in on the one empty table in the room and ended up sharing it. They enjoyed the meal and one another's company, and departed never expecting to meet again.

On 2 August 1972 (note the date), Geoff and Kerry entered

the Indian restaurant of the Hotel Oberoi in Singapore and headed for the one empty table as another couple, who had simultaneously entered through another door, were doing the same – Roger and Alice from Leningrad.

▶ Violent Deaths 100 Years Apart ▼

In January 1889, Elizabeth Bromfield was walking home from church along Adelaide Street, in the New South Wales town of Blayney, when she was killed by lightning.

In January 1989, a man was charged in the town with the murder of a woman in that month. Her name, Elizabeth Bromfield!

Now for an eerily similar story. Two girls of the same age were murdered on the same day and in the same place, 157 years apart. The details:

On 27 May 1817, Mary Ashford, twenty, was found dead at Erdington, then a village about eight kilometres from Birmingham. On 27 May 1974 the strangled body of Barbara Forrest, twenty, was found at Erdington, by then a suburb of Birmingham.

Forrest's body was found in long grass near the Erdington children's home where she worked as a nurse, about 350 metres from the spot where Ashford's body had been dumped. And 26 May in both 1817 and 1974 was not only a Monday but a Whit Monday.

The pattern of the girls' movements just before their deaths was similar. Both had visited a friend earlier in the evening where they had (both) changed their dress to go on to a dance. Both women had been raped before being murdered. They had died at about the same time.

The man arrested for each murder was named Thornton! Both were acquitted. So both cases remain unsolved.

▶ Missing the Dead Line ▼

The Alton (Illinois) *Evening Telegraph* reported in September 1946 that when its normally busy obituary writer Mildred

West – she reported an average of ten deaths a week – took a week's holiday, the people of Alton obligingly stopped dying. Once back on the job, the death rate of ten or so a week immediately resumed.

▶ Le Victim ▼

In November 1991, the *Guardian* told the story of Mr Alain Basseux and his misadventure on an English road. The Frenchman, who worked in Wiggington, near York, was cut up at a roundabout and lost his temper. He overtook the offending vehicle, then lurked in a lay-by until it passed him, whereupon he gave chase and forced it over to the side of the road.

Leaping from his car, Basseux ran to the other vehicle, forced its door open and grabbed the driver by his shirt front. 'Do that again and you're dead,' he roared. Then he recognized the man he was accosting: his boss.

His counsel told the magistrate in so many words that Basseux's behaviour was the French way – at least, until he found himself assaulting his boss. His mood then became one of 'fear, trepidation and fright'.

The *Guardian* said that Basseux did not lose his job, which must have had something to do with the English way.

▶ Experts Fooled ▼

Eighteen senior Health Department bureaucrats attended a conference dinner early in 1992 – and were all struck down with food poisoning!

▶ Pooling the Memories ▼

Melbourne has a memorial to Australian Prime Minister Harold Holt, who drowned while swimming off Portsea, Victoria, on 17 December 1968. The memorial: the Harold Holt Swimming Pool.

▶ Keen by Name ▼

A surgeon is named Mr Gillette.

▶ Truro Stories ▼

Between February and March 1969, the bodies of four young women were unearthed from shallow graves on the northerly hook of Cape Cod in Massachusetts. Each had been brutally murdered; the scene of the crimes was near the village of Truro.

Between March and May 1979, the bodies of four young women were unearthed from shallow graves north of Adelaide, the South Australian capital. All had been murdered. The crime scene was near another village, also named Truro. Later the bodies of three more girl victims were uncovered in the area.

▶ Who Said Synchronicity? ▼

Geoffrey Crooke was in a bookshop scanning page 112 of Jean Houston's *Godseed*. He had just come to the passage, '. . . the pattern of fortunate coincidences around her was astonishing. Synchronicities just seemed to flourish in her presence . . .', when he overheard a snatch of conversation between two women at the counter in which the word 'synchronicity' was emphasized.

His finger on the passage, he approached the counter and asked, 'Did someone just say "synchronicity"?'

As he held the page towards the women, one responded with: 'Don't tell me . . .' Apparently a coincidence had just occurred at the counter. Geoffrey says he was in such a state that, to his eternal regret, he left the bookshop without finding out what the coincidence was.

▶ Forgotten Advice ▼

A librarian sent out a reminder notice when a book became a month overdue. The book's title: *Improve your Memory*.

▶ Bit Wit ▼

The magazine *Dental Advisor*, published in Ann Arbor, Michigan, has as one of its clinical consultants Dr Randall W. Toothaker of Alabama.

▶ Concorde Cousins ▼

Mr W. L. Clark writes that in his seventy-three eventful years he has experienced a number of memorable coincidences. One incident began a few years ago, when he was flying into Britain on a British Airways jet.

An aviation enthusiast, he avidly read an article in the airline's in-flight magazine titled 'A Day in the Life of a Concorde Pilot'. The most intriguing thing about the article was the name of its author, Christopher Orlebar. It brought back vivid memories of his boyhood heroes, the members of the British Schneider Trophy team, one of them Flight-Lieutenant Orlebar. The team itself, he recalled, had been skippered by Squadron Leader Stainforth.

Upon landing he wrote to the author. In reply the author told him that Flight-Lieutenant Orlebar was a first cousin who had died before he (Christopher) was born. He also sent Mr Clark his book, *The Concorde Story*.

In 1993, Mr Clark took a trip around the world which included a stopover with a cousin of his wife's, Gordon, on Hermans Island, about 100 kilometres from Halifax, Nova Scotia.

One pleasant afternoon they were sitting drinking whisky on the veranda, enjoying the peace and tranquillity and the view, when the scene was disturbed by a 'boom, boom' noise, causing Clark to ask if there was a shooting range near by. Gordon said no, the noise occurred twice daily, when Concorde took off from Kennedy airport.

The incident naturally led Mr Clark to mention his story of the cousins who were pilots and the involvement of one of them in the Schneider Trophy team led by Stainforth. As a result of this, Gordon went to his library and returned with a thick bound volume, explaining that it was a book of his mother's family history. He scanned through the pages, found what he was looking for and held it out for Mr Clark to read:

*A letter from cousin Ermytrude in England enclosing a news-
paper cutting announcing that Wing Commander Stainforth
had been killed in action in North Africa. He was the oldest
flying member of the Royal Air Force and in his earlier years
had led the British Schneider Trophy team to complete success.*

Gordon's mother's maiden name was Stainforth and they
had been first cousins.

▶ How They Found Their Husbands ▼

Story I:

Clairvoyant Margaret Dent relates that as a teenager for some
reason she joked with her friend Janis that one day they would
be sisters and have the same surname. They would puzzle over
this comment and thought it may be some sort of carry-over
from a previous life.

In any case, Margaret was due to marry her long-time friend
Paul, even though she was having serious doubts about it. One
day Margaret met a man called Bob by accident. She went out
with him that night but felt so guilty about Paul and was such
miserable company she felt sure she would not see him again.

She decided to break her engagement. To her surprise, Bob
did ask her out again and she had several dates with him. She
told Janis about Bob and Janis asked what his surname was.
Margaret realized with a start she did not know. She would
find out that night.

It was late when Margaret returned home that night, but she
did not wait until morning to ring her friend. 'Guess what his
surname is . . .' she began. The well-known clairvoyant adds:

*I married Bob when I was twenty-two years old, sharing Janis's
surname as we had joked I would all that time ago. We have
already celebrated our twenty-fifth wedding anniversary, so the
name Dent has been with me for more than half my life.*

Story II:

As a child Jean Felkner played a game in which she was a
grown-up called Mrs Mitchell. Looking back, she would often

wonder why she had chosen the play-name of Mitchell. Then one day she met a man who impressed her deeply, even more when he said his name – Billy Mitchell.

A few years later, now married, they went with Billy's mother on a trip to Texas and stopped at the farmhouse where Jean had been born. When Jean pointed to a corner of a room and said that a bed had stood there in which she had been born, Billy and his mother looked stunned. 'But Billy was born there,' said the mother. True, he had been born in the same house in a bed in the same position six years before Jean.

▶ Random Celebration ▼

George Paciullo, the former New South Wales government minister who introduced random breath-testing to the Australian state, was stopped for a test while on his way home from a party to celebrate the tenth anniversary of its introduction. He tested negative.

▶ Pirate Copy ▼

Joan Rodenhuis decided to watch a TV programme while taping another going on air at the same time. She decided to tape over the film *The Crimson Pirate* and set the video in the lounge before going into the bedroom to watch the other show.

When she turned on the bedroom TV she saw *The Crimson Pirate* on the screen. 'I am not very good at taping, so I was stunned that I could pick up the picture of a tape I was trying to erase on a different set,' said Joan.

However, the problem was solved a few minutes later when Jeremy Irons came into the picture. His two screen children were watching the *Pirate* in the film *Reversal of Fortune*.

▶ Where Else? ▼

In 1994, water was found in a galaxy 200 million light-years away. Scientists say the galaxy is in the constellation of Pisces – the fish.

▶ Result Posted ▼

When Sydney successfully campaigned to stage the Olympic Games its long-time postcode became its campaign slogan – Sydney 2000.

▶ Cannonball Curse ▼

Keith Pritchard, thirty-one, an accredited racing-car driver and official in the world's first legal Cannonball Run, was a worried man a few days before the event in early 1994.

He told his parents that Japanese entrant Akihiro Kabe, a millionaire dentist from Tokyo, was absolutely crazy and was going to kill somebody, according to Pritchard's mother.

As he was coming into a checkpoint 150 kilometres south of Alice Springs, Kabe's Ferrari spun out of control and into an official car, killing himself and three others, including the man who had predicted tragedy, Keith Pritchard.

▶ Fiery Stories ▼

In the California fires of 1993, British film director Duncan Gibbins died from burns while trying to rescue his Siamese cat. Gibbins had credits for three hit movies. He co-wrote *Third Degree Burns* (1989), directed *Fire with Fire* (1986) and co-wrote and directed *Eve of Destruction* (1991). As their titles suggest, all had to do with fire and destruction.

The cat was later found safe but singed.

▶ Classic Reunion ▼

Andrew Milton was rummaging through a box of books in a second-hand store when he came across a copy of *Moby-Dick*. He had not read the classic since his school days, so decided to buy it. When he opened the cover looking for its price, he saw his own name and classroom number from twenty years before.

▶ Last Puff ▼

A group of smokers trying to kick the habit went on a nicotine-banned holiday to Lundy Island in the Bristol Channel. The island is famous for its resident puffin colony.

▶ Timed Run ▼

On a visit to his mother, Wayne Jones decided to do something about the clock which had been sitting on her mantelpiece for months not working. Heading for a watchmaker with the clock under his arm, he broke into a jog – and the movement jolted the clock into action at exactly the same time it had stopped.

▶ All's Well ▼

Dr Ian Brighthope believes in the importance of meditation and nutrition in managing cancer.

▶ Apt Name ▼

The membership officer of a Toyota four-wheel-drive club is Mr John Skidmore.

▶ Monkey's Money Tricks ▼

The Stockholm *Expressen* newspaper gave five stock-market analysts 10,000 kronor each to make as large a profit as they could playing the market. They also gave the same amount to a chimpanzee called Ola. After one month the chimp was declared the winner – his stock rose by 1,541 kronor. The runner-up made 1,050 kronor. Ona made his investments by random selection – throwing darts at the finance page.

▶ In Lieu ▼

Ex-pilot Wal Bowles invented a device that converts an ordinary toilet into a squatting one, which he called 'In Lieu'. The squatting loo is considered better for bowel movements.

▶ Sharp Joke ▼

Lindsay Hackforth was waiting nervously to donate a pint of blood to the Red Cross Blood Bank when there came over the sound system the song 'I've got you under my skin'. She was laughing as the needle she had feared slid effortlessly into her arm.

▶ Water That Works ▼

Tour-bus driver David Colley took a party to Lourdes. Before leaving he checked the bus, topping up the radiator with some of the local miracle water. An hour later he noticed the right-hand-turn indicator, which had not operated for weeks, was working, and continued to do so for the rest of the trip.

▶ One Man's Ink ▼

The name of a well-known fountain pen is Waterman.

▶ Bough Wow ▼

A homoeopathic remedy for barking dogs is made from the Bach flower.

▶ Watching Him ▼

TV presenter Larry Emdur, who hosted a show about coincidences, has his own incredible story to tell. It began with his father, who, on his twenty-first birthday, had received a beautiful antique watch from his parents. Unfortunately, Larry's father lost it.

On Larry's twenty-first birthday, his friends at work clubbed together and bought him a grey suit. He had only ever worn navy or black suits. Searching in his father's sock drawer for a grey pair to go with the suit, he discovered – under a grey pair at the back of the drawer – the watch.

'It was my twenty-first birthday, he hadn't seen it for ten years and he got it on his twenty-first birthday,' said Larry, who has not taken it off since – the watch, that is.

▶ Double Booking ▼

In Bermuda two brothers were killed by the same taxi and driver. The brothers were riding on the same moped and the taxi had the same passengers. The only difference was that the deaths occurred a year apart.

▶ One-way Trip ▼

Two advertisements appeared, one directly following the other, on a TV channel in March 1994. The first was a trailer for a current affairs show to be shown later that evening on the death penalty by hanging in Singapore. The second for 'once in a lifetime holidays' in Singapore.

▶ Why Keys Should be Kept ▼

Before author/journalist Malcolm Andrews and his wife, Helen, moved to another town to live, they stayed temporarily in a house where they found an old key that did not fit any of the house's locks.

Andrews wanted to get rid of it, but Helen said it was bad luck to throw keys away. So they took it with them when they moved. They had new keys made for the various doors, cupboards and windows in their new house, but could not get one for the old lock on the rear door which was of unusual design. Finally, almost as a joke, they tried the old key Helen had insisted they keep – and it fitted.

▶ Supermac! ▼

On 13 October 1986, a greyhound owned by Murray McCracken had what punters call a miracle win. About the same time his daughter gave birth to a baby girl. The name of the greyhound was Superkid!

▶ Birthday Coincidences ▼

As he bravely faced the fiery West Indian bowling attack, Australian cricketer Tim May had every reason to believe the coincidences surrounding him were a portent of victory.

It had been four years since May last played for Australia and his recall came for the Fourth Test of the 1992–3 series at the Adelaide Oval, his home ground.

On 25 January, May had taken an amazing five wickets for only nine runs – reason enough for him and his team-mates to celebrate. With the West Indies all out for a lowly 185, victory looked certain.

May had another reason to celebrate: he had managed the amazing bowling feat on the eve of his thirty-first birthday. Now it was his birthday. By coincidence, it was also Australia's birthday, 26 January. However, fortune had taken a turn for the worst. The runs required to win were beginning to seem more and more elusive as Australian wickets fell cheaply.

In fact, the responsibility for winning the Test had fallen on Tim May, as on the previous day. As the other batsmen failed against the desperate West Indians (a defeat for them meant they would lose the series), May held out, his score gradually climbing.

Finally, with Craig McDermott joining May, Australia was down to its last wicket. Each ball bowled could see the end of the match.

May and McDermott stuck to their task of closing the gap. They were cool under fire, as an anxious nation watched.

Would the national day bring the appropriate victory? Could May celebrate his birthday as a national hero?

With tension almost unbearable, Australia reached 184, one run behind. The West Indians were rattled. Fortune had swung Australia's way.

However, a ball brushed past McDermott's gloves and the wicketkeeper caught it. The West Indies had won the narrowest victory in the long history of Test cricket.

Talking of Australia Day, a woman born on its fifteenth anniversary was named Leonore Australia Mullampy. In 1939 she married Lyndon Day. Since then she's been Mrs Australia Day.

CHAPTER EIGHT

Random Anecdotes: II

Coincidences occur at unexpected moments; they are as likely to do so at this moment as in a thousand years' time. If there is a pattern or order to them, its significance remains a tantalizing mystery. It could be said that coincidences underline the fact that our lives are full of uncertainties.

▶ Valentine, Valentine, Valentine, etc. ▼

Judy Valentine gave birth to triplet sons, Rowan, Michael and Mark, on Valentine's Day, 1981. One hundred years to the day before this, the grandfather of the triplets, on the father, Steven's, side, was born. His name: Valentine Valentine.

The parents had not planned the triplets' birth day. In fact, the three were born by Caesarean section weeks before they were due.

▶ Two-way Streets ▼

At a junction in the Sydney suburb of Haberfield the two streets that meet are palindromes of each other, Ramsay Street and Yasmar Avenue.

▶ Wise after the Event ▼

The British Royal Society for the Prevention of Accidents staged an exhibition at which the entire display collapsed. It was an accident, society members concluded.

▶ Barry's Deal ▼

In mid-1989 Barry Smith took over a car dealership. On the first day of trading his first customer was a man who walked in off the street. A deal was made. Now, some new car owners don't like the name of the dealer on their new vehicle, but the customer did not object – his name was also Barry Smith.

▶ Pestered by Flies ▼

When Rod Annets was at school in 1978, the book *Lord of the Flies* was part of his English course. He said: 'I liked the story very much and the teacher told me a movie based on the book had been made, but it was an old movie. Recently I had a strong urge to think about the story. This went on for days until I forgot about it.

'Then I went to a trash and treasure sale. I browsed through a collection of books, something I never do, and there was the book *Lord of the Flies*. I bought it and read it again.

'Two days later I did something else I hardly ever do, looked at the late-night TV guide, and there for the next Sunday movie was *Lord of the Flies*.'

▶And in the Morning ▼

Gladys Vandenberg was a young trainee nurse on night duty. In a room with a balcony facing east a young man lay dying. He was his widowed mother's only child and her whole world revolved round him. He died at about 10.30 p.m., with his mother, the ward sister and Gladys present.

'What will you do with him now?' asked the mother.

'Nurse and I will lay him out and his body will be taken to the hospital mortuary,' Sister replied.

'Please, please,' begged the mother, 'do not take him to the mortuary tonight. Say you will leave him here until the morning and I will watch the dawn and think of him with the sun shining on him for the last time.' Sister agreed.

'Later,' Gladys goes on, 'after the mother had left and we had finished laying out the body, I was told to get the trolley from the mortuary. I was astounded. "Sister, you promised his mother you would not move him tonight," I protested. "Nurse," replied Sister, "when you are older and have more experience, you will learn there are many things one has to say to relatives for their peace of mind which may not be strictly correct. You must realize we could not leave a body in the ward overnight – it would be completely wrong."

'I used the lift and brought up the trolley. We placed the young man's body on it and wheeled it into the lift. The lift would not budge.

'At dawn Sister called me. I watched as she gently moved the sheet down from the young man's face and chest. We stood there silently as the sun grew stronger and shone into the room. We were both thinking of the mother at home also watching the sun. As we left the room, Sister turned to me and said: "Nurse, you will never forget this." And I never have.

'We heard later that the repairman had not been able to get the lift working before 10 a.m. By that time the sun had moved from the room. So a mother's last request for her dead son was granted.'

▶ Yarmouth Trail ▼

A traveller's tale comes from ex-RAF man David Furlonger, who runs David's Seafood Kitchen, in Coffs Harbour, New South Wales. One night in August 1986, he was chef on duty at his restaurant. It was a cold and miserable night, raining heavily. 'We had only a commercial traveller and a couple in the restaurant,' he recalled. 'My wife, who was doing the wait-ressing, came into the kitchen and said, "The couple out there have an unusual English accent."

'I went out to have a chat with them. They were from Great Yarmouth in Norfolk and were on an eight-week holiday in Australia. I said to the man, "I served with a man from Great Yarmouth for four and a half years in Burma in the RAF and we kept in touch from 1946 to 1950. I then came to live in Australia and have not heard of him since. It is just on the off-chance that I mention this to you."

'He said: "What was his name?" I said he was chief officer in the Yarmouth fire brigade and his name was Cyril Aldred. His reply astounded me. "I have recently retired from the Yarmouth fire brigade and I worked with Cyril for the past twenty-six years!"'

David says he was able to tell the story personally to Cyril, now in his seventies, when he and his wife had a two-month holiday of their own. Consider the circumstances. If the restaurant had been busy, David would not have spoken to the couple, his wife may not have even bothered commenting on the 'unusual accent', or had time to do so until after the restaurant had closed. By then it may have slipped her mind anyway. Coffs Harbour is a tourist town and there are plenty of restaurants. The odds against the travelling couple picking David's place are therefore high. Like so many coincidences, it can be analysed to the nth degree without either detracting from its qualities or finding any logic to it. Who would want to?

▶ 100-year-old Score Settled ▼

In 1977, Australia and England, the world's two oldest cricket rivals, played in a centenary test. Both the 1877 and 1977 matches were played in Melbourne in March on the Melbourne cricket ground. In the latter, England, going into their second innings, needed 463 runs to win in 590 minutes – not an impossible task, but no side in Test history had achieved it. At one stage it looked as though the Englishmen would actually manage it, as Derek Randall took the Australian bowling apart and scored 174. But Dennis Lillee pulled out all the stops and England finally went for 417, and Australia won by 45 runs – exactly the margin by which Australia had won 100 years earlier. As all followers of the game know, there are many permutations for an outcome of a cricket match – a win, a draw, a first innings' win, rain stopping play and so on. Yet the outcome for this historic game resulted in a coincidence.

▶ Bookmark ▼

Not all crimes in which coincidence plays a part are major ones. Early in January 1989, three women from a travel agency were discussing their favourite books during their lunch-break. *Riders*, the book by Jilly Cooper, came up and Gabrielle Thackray said she would lend it to Nikki O'Shea, when she got it back from a friend she had loaned it to more than a month before. Later that day, Nikki walked into a second-hand bookshop and saw a copy of *Riders*, reduced in price. The flyleaf bore the name: Gabrielle Thackray.

▶ Four Rules ▼

Angie Hartnell and Ricky Todd, who had lived for years four miles apart, were both born on 4 October 1954. They met on 4 October 1979, were engaged on 4 October 1980 and married on 4 October 1982. They had four bridesmaids and four ushers at the church in Silverton, Devon. They said the 4 October events in their lives were coincidence. They hoped to have four children.

▶ Cell-mates ▼

In 1965, Professor John McAleer of Massachusetts received a letter from prisoner Billy Dickson in response to a review the professor had written of a book by Theodore Dreiser. McAleer replied and a correspondence developed which eventually produced a total of 1,200 letters. For the first three months McAleer did not ask Dickson what he had done to deserve his jail sentence, or even how much time he had to serve. Dickson finally told him in a letter in which he said he appreciated that McAleer had not probed into these matters.

'On 12 June 1956, I held up the Centreville Trust and got away with $10,000. I took a bank officer hostage but let him go a little while later, unharmed.'

That night McAleer told his wife that he was corresponding with the man who had held up her sister. He wrote to Dickson and explained the circumstances, adding: 'A friend, a probability expert, told me that life was filled with million-to-one chances waiting their turn to happen . . .'

McAleer later helped turn a manuscript on Dickson's Korean war experiences into a saleable book. He says of the whole saga: 'Life sometimes serves up odd coincidences that writers are unwilling to credit.'

▶ Twin Lives ▼

Twins, of course, have most chance of being involved in co-incidences between themselves. But Chris and Christine Mikhael and their family have been more than surprised at the coincidences that have occurred so far in their young lives, especially by the sudden prediction made by their mother when their all-important Higher School Certificate examination reports arrived at their home on 11 January 1989. Before they had had a chance to open the envelopes, their mother said: 'I bet you'll score the same.' Moments later her prediction was proved correct.

Given the broad range of marks and the numbers of people involved in crediting them, the result can only be considered highly coincidental. Had they come within a few points of one another, it would have been remarkable.

Chris and Christine were born within half an hour of one another in 1970. Both attended the same school; Chris was captain and Christine vice-captain. In 1986 the two had been scalded by oil, in different locations but at the same time of day, Chris while on a camping holiday and Christine while filling in for Chris at his part-time job at a takeaway food bar. Chris says he and his sister often have the same thoughts: 'I'll say something and Christine will say, "I was just thinking of that."'

▶ Brysons at Brown ▼

Warren Weaver, the mathematician who was an expert on probability theory, told the story of a neighbour, one George D. Bryson, who was on his way to St Louis by train when he decided on a whim to stop *en route* at Louisville, Kentucky, since he had never been there. At the station he asked for the leading hotel and was sent to the Brown Hotel. After registering, and still in a whimsical mood, he stopped at the mail desk and asked if there was any mail for him. The clerk calmly handed him a letter addressed to 'Mr George D. Bryson, Room 307'. The name was correct, as was the room number. It turned out that the previous resident of the room had indeed been another George D. Bryson, who came originally from North Carolina.

Despite relating this anecdote, Weaver never believed there was anything special about coincidences.

▶ Love Seat ▼

The office chair at the Cardiff Arts marketing office looked innocent enough. But four salesgirls who sat in it during 1987 became pregnant. One of the chair's victims, Anya Tinsley, said, 'I thought nothing of the chair when I started work, then found myself pregnant almost straight away. Our male colleague will be allowed to keep the seat from now on – it can't do him any harm.'

▶ Mystery Run ▼

Author/journalist Malcolm Andrews was editing his book on great sporting heroes and had reluctantly decided to omit a passing mention of Alby Thomas, a former world three-mile record holder, for space purposes. Having done so, he took a break, turned on the TV news and on to the screen came Alby, whom Andrews had not seen for fifteen years. Later in the evening, he was continuing work on the book and had just reached his reference to Craig Johnstone, the Liverpool player, when from the radio came Johnstone's voice in an advertisement.

▶ **The Sun Also Rises** ▼

Shortly after reading a story from Koestler's case-book on coincidences, I found myself involved in an equally poignant situation which had relevance to the original story.

Koestler's case concerns a mother whose daughter was jilted for the second time. The mother could find no way of comforting her daughter or stopping her tears. She went into the kitchen to get a drink, praying desperately for guidance but realizing she was usually inarticulate in such situations.

Waiting for the kettle to boil, she distinctly heard the words 'As the sun sets, it also rises.' At the time she accepted this without astonishment and only afterwards did the full impact of that voice come over her. Returning to her distraught daughter, she gave her a drink and said the words, 'As the sun sets, it also rises.' They appeared to calm her daughter.

A year later her daughter was getting married. The mother booked the reception at a Jacobean country mansion recommended to her. Because there was insufficient sun to enable suitable pictures to be taken at the church entrance, the wedding party went to the garden entrance. Cut into the old stone of the door lintel under which the happy couple were posing was 'As the sun sets, it also rises.'

Like the mother, I too am inarticulate in such situations, though I feel deeply. What a gift it would be to be always able to come up with appropriate words of sympathy at the time they are needed.

About a week later, I received a call from a woman whom I had known through work for some years but had not heard from for some time. She was in the middle of a harrowing time. Her husband had left her, breaking up their twenty-year relationship, which she had come to consider secure. Not only that, he had left her less than a week before she was due to have a serious operation. I was appalled by the news but, try as I might, I could not think of the appropriate words of comfort which the woman so obviously needed.

In the middle of the night the words finally came to me with such force that I was immediately awake and alert and writing them down: *As the sun sets, it also rises.*

That day I went to a florist to order a bouquet of flowers to send her. The assistant showed me catalogues with so many arrangements and different types of flower that I was completely confused – I am a floral illiterate. For some reason, an arrangement of orchids attracted me, so I sent them with the quotation, hoping it would offer some comfort. I was rewarded with a joyful phone call from the woman, who said out of all the advice she had been given by friends and well-wishers, these words had had the most profound impact. But, she asked, why orchids? I said they simply seemed to stand out from the rest.

She laughed and explained her question: 'I'm working on a book about orchids and I have details about them all over my desk – they have been on my mind so much. In fact, having to think about them is the only thing that keeps me sane. Then your orchids arrive . . .'

▶ Known Criminal ▼

Ann Rule, an American police reporter, agreed to write a book about a mass-murderer who, police claimed, may have killed more than thirty young women. When the murderer was eventually caught and convicted, he turned out to be a close friend of Rule, Ted Bundy.

(Author's note: I am writing this case story a few days after the film of Bundy was shown on local TV.)

▶ Barrel of Torts ▼

Dr Ira Progoff, in his book *Jung, Synchronicity and Human Destiny* (1973), tells the following story:

One day a stranger came to Abraham Lincoln with a barrel full of odds and ends. He said that he was in need of money and that he would be much obliged if Lincoln would help him out by giving him a dollar for the barrel. The contents, he said, were not of much value; they were some old newspapers and things of that sort. But the stranger needed the dollar very badly . . .

Lincoln, with his characteristic kindness, gave the man a dollar, even though he could not imagine any use that he would have for its contents. Some time later, when he went to clear out the barrel, he found that it contained almost a complete edition of Blackstone's Commentaries. *It was the chance, or synchronistic, acquisition of these books that enabled Lincoln to become a lawyer and eventually to embark on a career in politics.*

▶ Healing Message ▼

In the late 1970s Canon Christopher Pilkingon, of Bristol, and his wife, Pat, set up a healing clinic with a volunteer staff. It had not been going long when one of its most successful volunteers, Penny Brohn, found she had breast cancer.

Because there was nowhere in Britain which offered the kind of alternative cancer treatment she wanted, Brohn, an acupuncturist, paid out a great deal of money to go to such a clinic in Germany.

After nine weeks, Pat Pilkington went to visit Brohn and found her in good shape both physically and mentally, if not financially. During the visit the two women discussed the possibility of setting up this sort of clinic in Britain, and before the visit was over they had decided to do so. Brohn insisted that it would have to be properly supervised by a medical doctor, one who was familiar with and sympathetic to alternative approaches to medicine. But, the women wondered, how would they go about finding such a doctor? The problem was uppermost in Pat Pilkington's mind as she flew home to Britain.

A large pile of letters was waiting for her at her Bristol home and, without taking her coat off, she opened one of them at random. It was from a clergyman friend asking if, by any chance, she could help a Plymouth hospital consultant, Dr Alex Forbes, who was looking for a small centre where he could try out his alternative ideas of medicine.

'I literally screamed at the ceiling,' Mrs Pilkington recalled. 'I was in the grip of something very strange at that moment.'

The new clinic opened in October 1980, with Dr Forbes as its head.

▶ The Theory of Relativity ▼

Nobel Prize winners Albert Einstein and Otto Hahn were both born on 14 March 1879. The Time Twins were great physicists.

The two great tenors Benjamino Gigli and Lauritz Melchior were born on 10 March 1890. Both were members of the New York Metropolitan Opera.

▶ Winning Dream ▼

José Silva is the creator of Mind Control, a widely acclaimed self-improvement programme which teaches people to use their minds at a deeper and more effective level – even while they are asleep – and which boasts more than 1 million users throughout the world. Silva tells of a coincidence which helped him to develop an important part of his course, the usefulness of dreams in problem-solving.

He relates that in 1949 he had been grappling for some time with the problem of whether or not dreams could serve a useful purpose when he was awoken by one: 'It was not a series of events like most dreams, but simply a light . . . very bright.' He opened and shut his eyes several times in the dark room and every time he closed them the light returned. About the third or fourth time, he saw three numbers: 3–4–3. Then another set of numbers: 3–7–3. The numbers returned several more times.

He lay awake for the rest of the night trying to figure out if the numbers had a meaning – a telephone number, an address, a licence number – but failed to make sense of them. The next day, just before he was to close his electronics shop, a friend dropped in and suggested they go for a coffee. His wife asked if, since he was going out, would he go over to the Mexican side of the border (Silva lives in the Texas border town of Laredo) and buy her some rubbing alcohol, as it was cheaper across the border.

On the way he was telling his friend about the dream when it occurred to him that, maybe, what he had seen was a lottery ticket number. They stopped at a store and bought the alcohol. As the salesman wrapped it, the friend called from another part of the store: 'What was that number you were looking for?'

'3–7–3, 3–4–3,' said Silva.

His friend told Silva to join him.

'There was half a ticket with 3–4–3 on it,' writes Silva. 'Throughout the Republic of Mexico, each of the hundreds of thousands of vendors, like this little store, receives tickets with the same first three numbers every month. This store was the only one in the entire nation which sold number 3–4–3. The number 3–7–3 was sold in Mexico City.'

A few weeks later Silva learned his half of the first lottery ticket he had bought had won $10,000, which he sorely needed.

'As elated as I was, I looked this gift horse carefully in the mouth and what I found was more valuable by far than the gift itself. It was foundation for a solidly based conviction that my studies were worthwhile. Somehow I had made contact with a Higher Intelligence. Maybe I had made contact with it many times before and not known; this time I *knew*.

'Consider the number of seemingly chance events that led to this. In a moment of despair, I dreamed of a number in so startling a way . . . that I *had* to recall it. Then a friend dropped in to invite me for coffee and, tired as I was, I accepted. My wife came by and asked me to bring rubbing alcohol, which led me to the only place in Mexico where that particular ticket was on sale.'

Silva adds: 'We have no objection to the word "coincidence" in Mind Control; in fact, we attach special meaning to it. When a series of events that is hard to explain leads to a constructive result, we call it coincidence. When they lead to a destructive result we call it accident. In Mind Control we learn to trigger coincidences. "Just a coincidence", is a phrase we do not use.'

▶ How the Stone Spoke ▼

A coincidence which has its origins in antiquity surfaced during the search to interpret the inscription of the famous Rosetta Stone in 1820. The translator, Dr Thomas Young, had received a parcel of manuscripts from a man named Casati in Paris, including one which bore in its preamble something resembling the text of the Rosetta Stone. Dr Young had made a certain amount of progress in attempting to decipher this material when he received some research material on ancient Egyptian art from Sir George Grey, who had just returned from Egypt, including several fine specimens of writing and drawing on papyrus which he had bought at Thebes. 'They were', said Dr Young, 'chiefly in hieroglyphics and of a mythological nature, but two contained some Greek characters written in an apparently pretty legible hand.'

Dr Young said Casati's material was the first in which any intelligible characters had been discovered among the many manuscripts and inscriptions which he had examined. Studying Sir George's manuscripts, he established that they were in fact – and astonishingly – of Casati's manuscripts.

Young wrote:

I could not therefore but conclude that a most extraordinary chance had brought into my possession a document which was not very likely in the first place ever to have existed, still less to have been preserved uninjured for my information through a period of near two thousand years, but that this very extraordinary translation should have been brought safely to Europe, to England and to me, at the very moment when it was most desirable to me to possess it, as the illustration of an original which I was then studying, but without any other reasonable hope of comprehending it; this combination would in other times have been considered as affording ample evidence of my having become an Egyptian sorcerer.

▶ Slaughter on the Mind ▼

On Sunday, 1 September 1991, Audrey Best borrowed from her local library a copy of a book called *Diary of a Country Parson*. She goes on: 'I did not start reading the book until the evening of 9 September, when I learned it was the edited diary of a Rev. Francis Witts, born in 1783, Rector of Upper Slaughter, a village in the Cotswolds, from 1808 until 1854.

'Although I knew of the Cotswolds, I had not heard of the village of Upper Slaughter.

'When I collected the office mail on the morning of 10 September, there was a letter from J. R. Brain, The Veterinary Surgery, Lower Slaughter, The Cotswolds.'

▶ Good for the Teeth ▼

A dentist is named Dr S. O. Chu.

▶ First Hole in One ▼

In 1992 Alan Leary, a video-shop owner, was convinced by his friend Stephen Hourigan that he should have a relaxing game of golf. Alan had never played the game, so it came as a surprise when at the par-three fourth he holed in one.

▶ Thanks, Dad ▼

In 1984 police booked Julia McArdie for failing a breath test – the machine had been invented by her father.

▶ Triple Texan Surprise ▼

Texan Ron Thompson found his family had grown by four in less than twenty-four hours when three of his daughters, Mary, Joan and Carol, gave birth to four boys in 1990.

Mary was driven to hospital by nineteen-year-old sister Joan, who was nine months pregnant. Five hours later Mary, twenty-eight, gave birth to Shane. Seven hours later Joan was driven by her sister Carol to hospital and gave birth to Jeremy a minute after midnight. Carol, twenty-four, then went into labour and gave birth to twin boys just before 3 a.m.

▶ Ill-met ▼

A news report on 27 December 1989 said that among the Christmas holiday death toll in Queensland were a father and son. The two had been driving separate vehicles when they collided head-on on a lonely dirt road.

▶ Nine Lives ▼

Jessica Lee Bromwell was born at nine minutes past nine on the ninth day of the ninth month in 1990, which means she turns nine on the ninth day of the ninth month in 1999.

▶ Lowdown on High Flying ▼

A baby born on a Royal Flying Doctor Service plane at 27,000 feet in 1991 had the surname Lowdown.

▶ Bondage Case ▼

In July 1992, a man admitted to a court that he whipped a teenage boy while the youth was strapped to a bondage rack. The man's name: Julian William Whippy.

▶ Pullar in Rowers' Town ▼

A dentist of Henley-on-Thames: Mr Pullar.

▶ Cop Copped ▼

In early 1991, some English police were viewing a video of a shoplifter in action. They recognized their own crime prevention officer. The officer was fined – and sacked.

▶ If the Shoe Fits . . . ▼

A chiropodist is named J. J. Trotter.

▶ Premature Drinks ▼

Lifeguards in New Orleans celebrated the fact they had gone a year without a fatality at any of the swimming pools they supervised with a party. While the hundred or so guards partied, a woman fell into one of the pools and drowned.

▶ Stitched up ▼

Solicitors – Weaver and Rugless.

▶ Have a Nice Day! ▼

Computer salesman Ian Murray was listening to a motivational tape as he drove to work one morning in March 1987. Just as it told him 'No matter what happens, never let it affect your selling day', his car was hit in the rear. 'I did what anybody would have done in that situation,' he told me. 'I turned off the tape.'

▶ Hot Seat ▼

Electrician C. W. Winterbotham advertises himself as an electrical heating specialist.

▶ Just Married ▼

While the wedding reception for Ian Smith and bride Cathy was in full swing, outside some of the guests were working on the groom's silver Commodore with shaving cream, tin cans on the bumper bar and straw stuck to the bodywork with honey.

Ian and Cathy eventually emerged and headed for their car. It was polished and immaculate. Those who had worked on the 'decorations' watched appalled as they drove away. They then had to explain to an irate man who had emerged from the pub opposite the reception hall to see what the fuss was about why *his* silver Commodore was not in the same state it had been when he'd parked it and gone in for a beer or two.

▶ Jury Duty ▼

Noelene Jury works at a courthouse.

▶ All Legal ▼

Roger Court, QC, is a Crown Advocate

▶ Not a Plant ▼

An agriculture scientist – Dale Weedman.

▶ Knows His Onions ▼

Owner of several gardening firms – Ernie Digweed.

▶ Family Firm ▼

A photographer named Father brought his son into the business and put up the sign Father & Son.

▶ Name Nags ▼

Horse Trail Riding Club president – Warren Gallop.

▶ Drinking on the Job ▼

Officials with the US National Soft Drink Association – Crawford Rainwater and Sidney P. Mudd.

▶ Last Drinks ▼

Melbourne's oldest pub, The Devonshire Arms, underwent a drastic conversion in the mid-1980s into a sobering-up clinic run by St Vincent's Hospital.

▶Hot Items ▼

On 28 January 1986, the worst space disaster in the US occurred when the shuttle *Challenger* exploded within a minute of take-off, killing all seven crew members. Later in the year a rocket ship-shaped child's bed canopy appeared in department stores bearing the name Challenger. It was made of 'washable FIRE RESISTANT nylon'.

▶ Despina's Despair ▼

Wendy Rozell attended a Christmas party at a Greek restaurant where waiters made a point of telling her friend, Diana, that her name was 'Despina' in Greek.

The following day, Wendy saw what she took to be a piece of crumpled paper on the pavement. What caught her attention was the name on it – Despina. It was a cheque from the income tax authorities for a woman for $571; she was reunited with it in time for a happy Christmas.

▶ Unsafe Safe ▼

A woman left her handbag behind in a supermarket and rang the store. A store employee told her not to worry, they would keep the bag in the safe for her to collect next day.

Overnight thieves broke in and the safe was burgled.

▶ Love Permit ▼

A planning permission notice for a brothel appeared in a local newspaper authorized by a Stephen Love.

▶ Security Slip ▼

One of a group of people sharing the one home told me they changed their front-door lock when one lost a key. Another of the tenants tried the old key on the new lock – and it worked.

▶ Astrologer's Reflection ▼

Astrologer Stella Recamier says that on the eve of the eighth birthday of her son, Roger, in 1976, she sent him on an errand to a shop. The circumstances triggered a memory of an incident on her eighth birthday.

On that day she had been travelling with her parents in France by bus. They had stopped in the city of Avignon in southern France, *en route* to Nice. In a shop her attention was caught by a small brass-framed mirror with a picture of Avignon on the back. Stella wanted to buy it but her parents hurried her away, saying they would miss the bus.

Her thoughts of that birthday disappointment were soon replaced by concern at the time Roger was taking. When he did appear he was completely unaware of the stunning impact the excuse he offered would have on Stella.

Roger said that on his way home he had seen a trash 'n' treasure stall and suddenly decided he wanted to buy her something. He produced his gift – the same brass-framed mirror she had seen in the shop in Avignon many years before, complete to the picture of the southern French city on the back. She had never mentioned the incident to Roger. In fact, it was only the fact of his eighth birthday that had reminded her of the incident on her own eighth birthday.

▶ Biting the Dust ▼

On 25 November 1991, after a radio news reported the death of Freddie Mercury, lead singer of the pop group Queen, the record that followed was the song 'Another One Bites the Dust', sung by Queen.

▶ Man to Man ▼

An expert in male infertility – Professor David Handlesman.

▶ Pope Pops Question ▼

On a children's TV quiz programme, Christ the Lord School competed against Our Lady of Mercy School. Quizmaster was Michael Pope.

▶ Betting Plunge ▼

Thirty passengers were killed when a New York commuter train left the rails while crossing the bridge over Newark Bay and plunged into the waters beneath.

The following day newspapers ran pictures of the carriages being winched back on to the bridge. One picture showed a carriage with its number clearly visible on a side panel – 932.

That day thousands of people took ticket 932 in the New York numbers game – and made a killing when the number came up.

▶ Lucky 13 ▼

Canadian journalist Dennis Passa told the following story – on Friday, 13 March 1992.

In 1985, on 13 April, he flew from Calgary to Toronto in seat 13a and became friendly with the occupant of 13b, Mary-Jo Stodola. On 13 February 1988 they were married.

They migrated to Australia, landing in Sydney on 13 February 1989. On 13 February 1992, he and Mary-Jo boarded a flight for a wedding anniversary holiday, their seats were 13a and 13b.

▶ Fighters for Peace ▼

At a Hiroshima Peace Rally in 1992, the star attraction was a rock band – the Urban Guerrillas.

► Met by Chance ▼

A car and a motor cycle collided in Stourbridge, England. The name of the driver, Frederick Chance, the name of the motor cyclist, Frederick Chance.

On a road near London two cars collided; both drivers were called Ian Purvis.

► June and October ▼

David Roberts was born 31 October 1957 and his sister, Lynn, on 31 October 1959.

David's daughter, Lisa, was born on 31 October 1985 and his son, Michael, on 31 October 1987.

► A Cotswold Country Garden ▼

Gwen Jurkowski was so impressed by a pretty cottage garden on a trip to the Cotswolds that she insisted her brother-in-law photograph her there.

Some months later, she was given a calendar called 'Country Gardens'. Glancing through it she found the garden which had so taken her fancy. 'Of all the thousands of gardens they could have had in the calendar . . .' muses Gwen.

► Curse of the Habsburgs ▼

In 1849, Emperor Franz Josef of Austria, then nineteen, was visited by an obscure Hungarian countess who accused him of having had her son murdered. Young Michael Karoli had been executed on the orders of Baron Julius von Haynau, general of Franz Josef's army, as he tried to put down the Hungarian revolt against the empire.

Countess Karoli followed her accusation with a five-part curse: 'May heaven and hell blast your happiness. May your family be exterminated. May you be smitten through the persons of those you love. May your life be wrecked. May your children be brought to ruin.'

The curse was to be appallingly fulfilled. More than a dozen of his close relatives met violent deaths. Others abdicated, were compromised in scandals or involved in bad marriages.

Franz Josef married sixteen-year-old Elisabeth, with whom he was smitten, but they remained faithful for only a few weeks before she found another lover and the emperor also sought consolation outside the marriage.

He soon had other problems. Austria fought a war against France, Sardinia and Prussia and lost every battle. His empire shrank and Austria was driven from the German Confederation. In 1867, his wife's brother-in-law Maximilian was rejected as Emperor of Mexico and shot by a firing squad.

From 1886, his wife's cousin, mad King Ludwig of Bavaria, committed suicide by drowning, his niece Sophie was burnt to death and his son Crown Prince Rudolph took his own life. His nephew John of Saxony abdicated and was then drowned at sea, while another nephew, Archduke William, died in a fall from a horse. Another niece was burnt to death and three more nephews committed suicide. In 1897, the Empress Elisabeth was murdered by an Italian in Geneva.

In 1914 his heir, Archduke Ferdinand, was assassinated in Sarajevo, his death triggering the First World War. Franz Josef died a lonely, exhausted figure as his army was being crushed by the Allies in 1916.

► The Law is My Shepherd, or Sheppard ▼

Retired stipendiary magistrate (SM) Frederick Sheppard of Armadale, in the state of New South Wales, tells this story of his own personal coincidence:

'In 1957 I was dealing with a case at Inverell and the police prosecutor read the antecedents of a defendant: Charleville Court of Petty Sessions (Queensland) before Mr Fred Shepherd SM – six months' hard labour. "That can't be right, sergeant," I said. "I have never been in Charleville and I would not have jurisdiction in Queensland." Inquiries showed that there was a Fred Shepherd, a magistrate in Queensland.'

Sheppard got in touch with Shepherd of Queensland.

Although their names were spelt differently, they found they had the same English great-grandfather and that their lives had followed similar patterns. Sheppard was born at Brewongle, NSW, in 1902. Shepherd at Brighton, England, in 1905. Both entered the Civil Service; both left it in 1924. In that year Mr Sheppard was appointed junior clerk in the petty sessions office in Albury, NSW, and Shepherd clerk in the petty sessions office in Maryborough, Queensland.

They passed examinations in the same year – 1929; were appointed clerks of petty sessions and coroner in the same year – 1948; and in 1954 were appointed as stipendiary magistrates, Sheppard at Glen Innes, NSW, Shepherd at Charleville, Queensland.

They met in 1957. Sheppard writes: 'It is said that everyone has his double and this makes me think it may be correct. Physically we are not the same but there is a family likeness and a remarkable coincidence of careers. He has a son who is a medical doctor and I have a son who is a doctor of philosophy.'

▶ Cop's Family Cop It ▼

Police Sergeant Ron King reports that on 10 June 1982 he had a serious accident at 1.30 a.m., driving a Toyota Corolla. He received many broken ribs and was left with a large scar under his chin.

On 10 June 1984 ('yep, at 1.30 a.m. exactly') his son, Peter, was also involved in an accident while driving a Toyota Corolla. He had no broken bones, but was left with a scar under his chin.

The coincidence did not end there. His daughter fell over late in 1986. Now she too bears a scar under her chin. They are all grateful they survived to tell the story.

▶ Media Match ▼

TV reporter Tory Hoarder and producer Chris Morris first met while working together on a current affairs programme. They discovered both were born on the same day. In July 1988, they each gave birth to their first child on the same day, both girls.

▶ I'm Putting You on Hold ▼

In October 1979, Anthony William O'Sullivan escaped from jail and managed to elude capture for many months.

One day in April the following year, he rang a house and was arrested shortly afterwards. He had made the call at the time police were searching it for drugs. Police answered the phone and asked some pertinent questions, such as where he was at that moment, without O'Sullivan being aware of whom he was speaking to.

▶ They Said It Wouldn't Work . . . ▼

US columnist Doug Robarcheck pointed out that General Motors spent a fortune promoting their new model, the Nova, in Latin America. Then someone told them '*no va*' is Spanish for 'no go', or 'it doesn't go'.

▶ Sound Friendship ▼

Qantas airlines security officer Bill Teunissen formed a 'phone friendship' with Tom Quincy, who was in military liaison at the US embassy in Canberra. The two organized flight bookings for service personnel.

After fifteen months, Quincy announced that he was being shifted. No, he did not know where. 'They tell you you're going, but not where,' the embassy man explained.

As he hung up, Bill thought wryly that he could hardly say he would not see his old friend again, as he had never seen him in the first place.

A week later, Bill flew into Auckland, New Zealand, on a job. By the time he reached the taxi rank, there was only one cab left. As he was about to step into it, a tall black man with a military bearing appeared and asked Bill if he was going down-town, and if so, could he share the cab as it was the only on the rank. Bill said of course he could. As they relaxed in the back seat, the man turned to Bill and said, 'You know, you have a familiar accent . . .' It was Tom Quincy, who had arrived to take up his new assignment at the embassy in Auckland.

CHAPTER NINE

Random Anecdotes: III

The startling, surprising, amusing and often amazing nature of coincidences becomes more apparent as you dip into the pages of these random chapters for items that catch your eye. Or, of course, alternatively you can simply begin with the first item and work your way through . . .

▶ The President's Been Shot ▼

President John Kennedy, who was elected 100 years after Abraham Lincoln, was deeply involved in civil rights for blacks, as Lincoln had been.

However, other coincidences linking the two assassinated presidents are much more significant: both were assassinated on a Friday in the presence of their wives; each had lost a son while living in the White House; Lincoln was killed in Ford's Theater, Kennedy in a Ford-made Lincoln convertible; Kennedy's assassin, Lee Harvey Oswald, fled from a warehouse into a theatre, Lincoln's assassin from a theatre into a warehouse; both men were succeeded by vice-presidents named Johnson who had been born 100 years apart – Andrew Johnson was born in 1808, Lyndon Johnson in 1908; John Wilkes Booth, Lincoln's killer, was born in 1839, Lee Harvey Oswald in 1939; both killers were assassinated before their trial; Lincoln's secretary, whose name was Kennedy, advised him not to go to the theatre, while Kennedy's secretary, Lincoln, advised him not to go to Dallas.

In 1980, Ronald Reagan broke a 140-year-old tradition when an attempted assassin's bullet was deflected by his rib. Beginning with the death of President William Harrison in 1840, a month after he was elected, every twenty years a president has died in office. Four were assassinated.

William Harrison, elected 1840, died of pneumonia
Abraham Lincoln, 1860, assassinated
James Garfield, 1880, assassinated
William McKinley, 1900, assassinated
Warren Harding, 1920, died of pneumonia
Franklin D. Roosevelt, 1940, died of cerebral haemorrhage
John F. Kennedy, 1960, assassinated

To complete this look at America and its coincidental chiefs, the second and third presidents, John Adams and Thomas Jefferson, died on the same day, 4 July 1826, the fiftieth anniversary of the US Declaration of Independence.

▶ Another for the Album ▼

Carl Jung told of a German mother who photographed her infant son in 1914. She left the one-shot film plate to be developed at Strasbourg, but the outbreak of the First World War prevented her from returning to Strasbourg.

Two years later she bought a film plate from Frankfurt, more than 160 kilometres away. She used it to take a picture of her daughter. When that plate was developed, superimposed on the picture was the earlier picture of her son. The plate had somehow been labelled unused and sent to Frankfurt, then sold to her. With cases like that being reported to him, no wonder Jung remained fascinated.

▶ Same Strikes ▼

Exact timekeeping, down to one-hundredth of a second, has just about rid the sporting world of dead heats. The only way they can occur now, it seems, is through coincidence. In the 1988 Olympic Games in Seoul, Australian Karen Lord and

Italian Manuella Carosi carved out their place in Games history when the two girls, swimming in different heats of the 100-metre backstroke, clocked identical times of 1 minute 4.69 seconds. Now, this in itself was not unusual, except it dead-heated them for sixteenth place and forced them into a swim-off for a lane in the consolation final.

But to the astonishment of the small crowd that stayed behind to watch at the end of the heats, the two girls again produced exactly the same time – to one-hundredth of a second – in the swim-off: 1 minute 5.05 seconds. It was all too much for the bewildered international swimming officials. *Never before had a swim-off produced a second dead heat.* 'Could the managers of the Australian and Italian teams please come to the office. I think we have a problem here,' said a message over the loudspeaker. Australian manager Evelyn Dill-Mackay did not think it was a problem. 'They can swim again,' she said.

So, in the early hours of Thursday, 23 September 1988, the two girls stood side by side. Through the first fifty metres the two matched each other stroke for stroke, and amazingly the electronic timing could not separate them at the turn. The time for both was 31.25 seconds. At the end of the last length they lunged at the wall together and finally the computer delivered its verdict: Carosi, 1 minute 4.62 seconds; Lord, 1 minute 4.75 seconds.

The coincidence of the whole affair in overcoming the highly accurate clocks has tied the girls together in time, as it has done with so many other people.

▶ Coupled ▼

Margaret Menzies was driving to the Melbourne suburb of Windsor in 1979 when she was involved in a crash with another car. Her car was wrecked and the other car badly damaged. Both drivers managed to escape unhurt and, to the amazement of the crowd that gathered, they threw themselves into one another's arms. Mrs Menzies had collided with her husband, Trevor. The accident happened near their home, so they walked the rest of the way and cracked a bottle of champagne when they arrived. 'We were both pretty emotional after the crash,' said Mrs

Menzies. 'But it must have seemed pretty crazy for passers-by to see two people who had just crashed into one another start hugging and kissing on the intersection.'

▶ Caught In-flight ▼

In early 1988, drugs squad detective Peter Miller arrested Stephen Rotaru, thirty-one, from Cleveland, Ohio, on charges of supplying and possessing cocaine and possessing cannabis leaf. Three weeks after the arrest, Miller went on holidays. At Sydney airport, Miller boarded Continental Flight 16, bound for Ohio via Miller's destination, Hawaii. As he made his way down the aisle, he saw Rotaru in a seat. Miller promptly rearrested the American. Rotaru had surrendered his passport after originally being arrested, but had then persuaded the US Consulate to issue him with a new one. Miller was not consciously searching in any manner for Rotaru. As far as he was concerned, the American, who hotly protested his innocence, fully intended to stand trial.

In addition to surrendering the passport, he had put up bail and was reporting to a police station twice a week. Miller had booked on the same flight for no other reason than he wanted to go to Hawaii for a holiday.

▶ Hot Feet ▼

In Lansing, Michigan, in 1986, a juror studying a defence witness spotted his stolen shoes on the feet of the witness. The witness was arrested on the spot: 'It was the darnedest thing that ever happened in my courtroom,' the judge is reported to have said.

▶ Father 0, Son 0 ▼

In 1955, famous cricketer Norm O'Neill began his first-class career badly. Playing for New South Wales, he was bowled off stump for 0 on the second ball he faced. In 1979, Norm's son

Mark made his first-class début – and he too was bowled off stump on the second ball, also for 0.

▶ Cross Reading ▼

The most common precognition coincidences concerning newspapers are 'seeing' the headlines or stories of an event that has not occurred yet, then does and is confirmed by the subsequent publishing of the story already seen. Herbert Greenhouse, in his *Premonition: A Leap into the Future* (1971), tells the story of Lady Rhys Williams. An economist, she would act on the information she 'saw' in newspapers, only to discover that the article was not there, although invariably the article would appear.

In 1957 she 'saw' a paragraph in *The Times* about a heavy drop in earnings of small farmers. She sat down and wrote a letter to the Prime Minister about this, but when she came to clip out the article she could not find it. She posted the letter anyway and the article appeared the following day.

A year later she 'saw' another paragraph about a three-bed-room house that could be built cheaply. She asked her secretary to clip out the article, but the secretary could not find it – until the following day, when it appeared just as she had described.

▶ Mental Picture ▼

A case similar to the one described above concerns a woman bank teller in Florida who congratulated a customer on his daughter's engagement and said, 'That was a beautiful picture of Barbara in last Sunday's newspaper.'

The man was puzzled. The announcement would not appear until 23 May and it was only the 13th. But the teller insisted she had seen the picture, along with the announcement, in the 9 May issue.

What was even more puzzling was that she had not even known that the man had a daughter. Yet she knew the girl's name and described her appearance, including the unusual hairstyle in the picture. She also said the picture had appeared in the second column of pictures, just off-centre. Barbara's picture finally appeared in the 23 May issue, in the second column, just as the teller had 'seen' it.

▶ Sisters Check-out ▼

In 1983, sisters Pat Speer and Madelaine Cook were reunited after eighteen years when they bumped into each other at a supermarket check-out in San Francisco. 'I saw her look at me,' Pat said. 'I did a double-take. I thought, "My god, those eyes are familiar!" Then I asked her if she was Mickey and she said, "Are you Patti?"'

They had not seen one another since Pat had run away from her adoptive parents at the age of sixteen. The sisters shortly afterwards found their natural mother – and a brother.

▶ Death Gun ▼

On 28 August 1988, Rogers, the young manager of the Rex Hotel in Sydney's red-light district, King's Cross, was held up as he was counting the night's takings. The twenty-three-year-old was pistol-whipped, then shot once, execution-style, in the back of the head. The killer fled with a total of $8,000.

On 4 October, the same year, William Rogers (note the same surname), a taxi driver, was killed behind the wheel of his cab, in the Sydney suburb of Ashfield. The killer, as in the earlier incident, fired only once, this time hitting the victim in the upper part of the body.

The first lead the police seemed to have was the fact that both victims had the same surname. Was it some kind of family feud? They soon established it was not, the two men were unrelated and had not known one another. But then another coincidence came into play: ballistics tests showed that the men were shot by the same gun, a .38 revolver. It would appear to follow, then, that the same killer took the lives of both men. However, police were able to establish that this was not the case. According to them, it is quite common for criminals, once a gun has been used in a crime, to then sell it in King's Cross.

In other words, two different killers were involved and the link between the deaths of the two men was their surname – and the gun. For them and their families, a bad coincidence. At the time of writing neither case had been solved.

▶ So Near, Yet So Farr ▼

Reporter Malcolm Farr telephoned Maureen Tangney of the Privacy Committee to discuss how people adopt other people's identities illegally. Tangney was reluctant to talk because she did not believe Farr was who he said he was. Her brother-in-law's name is – Malcolm Farr.

▶ Gone for a Tosca ▼

Commuter George Patas was waiting to catch a train when he suddenly felt like having a bar of chocolate. He put the coins into a vending machine and was about to make his selection when a heap of Tosca bars poured out. On each bar were the words: 'Where's George? Gone for a Tosca.'

▶ Lucky Hill ▼

In May 1989, British-born chairman of the Australian Broadcasting Corporation David Hill was asked to draw a prize for a selection of antiques from a top hat – and came up with his own number. Before doing so, he had warned that the last time he had been asked to draw a prize he had drawn his own number.

Jane Hall, star of the TV soap *A Country Practice*, was invited to draw the raffle at the Ultimate Sporting Club. Jane pulled out one entry and discovered the winner was – Jane Hall! She graciously drew a new winner.

▶ Yoke was on Mum ▼

In June 1989, Julianne Wright had just returned from hospital, where she had given birth to twins. She bought a dozen eggs at a supermarket – six of them were double-yokers.

▶ Lightning Strikes Twice ▼

Boston councillor Albert O'Neill, speaking in 1984 on radio, vowed he would look into the abortion controversy. 'May lightning strike me dead if I don't,' he declared. At that moment a lightning bolt knocked the station off the air. Nobody was hurt.

In 1988 lightning struck the Sydney Radio2KY transmitter and put the station off the air as racing commentator Chris Kearns was discussing the chances of a greyhound called Silence.

▶ Drilling for a Hole ▼

In 1980, an army chaplain and dentist found themselves involved in an amazing double coincidence at Australia's Royal Military College golf course when they shot holes in one with consecutive strokes. Major Peter Kentwell and Padre John Wessell had been drawn as partners in a club competition.

At the 167-metre par-three seventh hole, Kentwell's ball dropped just short of the hole and rolled in. The padre commented, 'That's a hard act to follow', then he sent his drive down the fairway to see it too drop short of the hole.

They walked to the green but could not find the ball. The Padre looked into the hole and there it was. The major went on to win the nine-hole competition with forty-four points. Padre Wessell came third. The balls were mounted and the event has been commemorated with a plaque at the club.

▶ Swings and Roundabouts ▼

In 1979, a woman punter picked up $584.77 in winnings at a racecourse. She arrived home that evening to find a letter from the tax office telling her that she owed them $584.77.

▶ November Débuts ▼

Jan Lynch says her mother, Olga, was born on 10 November 1909, her sister Coleen on 10 November 1938 and her son

Patrick on 10 November 1967. Her second son, David, was born on her father's birthday, 20 March.

▶ Taxing Relationship ▼

Two women in the US were brought together by the taxation office – the Internal Revenue Service – in a meeting full of co-incidence. In 1983, the IRS told Mrs Patricia Kern she owed $3,000 in tax for a job she held in Oregon. Mrs Kern wrote back and said she had never been to Oregon. The service finally traced a Patricia Dibiasi, who lives in Oregon and who did owe the taxes.

As a result the following facts emerged. The two women share the same maiden name, birthday and social security number. Both were born on 31 March 1942 and were named Patricia Ann Campbell. Their fathers were named Robert. They had both worked as book-keepers and studied cosmetics. The ages of the children of both of them were the same. Their husbands were servicemen. Both were married within eleven days of each other in 1959. Finally, they had never met.

▶ Shared Rooms ▼

Irving Kupcinet, Chicago *Sun-Times* columnist, tells the story of how he checked into the Savoy Hotel, London, in 1953 to cover the Coronation. In a drawer in his room he found some personal belongings of an old friend, Harry Hannin, a Harlem Globetrotter. Two days later, Hannin sent a letter to Kupcinet from the Hotel Maurice in Paris saying, 'You'll never believe this, but I've just opened a drawer here and found a tie with your name on it.' Kupcinet had stayed in that room a few months before.

▶ Firing Back ▼

Here is one of those stories that have stood the test of time. In 1893, Henry Ziegland, of Honey Grove, Texas, broke off his engagement. The brother of the girl, to avenge her honour, attempted to shoot Ziegland, but the bullet missed and buried itself in a tree. The brother, however, thought he had killed Ziegland, whose face had been grazed, and killed himself.

The story moves forward to 1913, when Ziegland was removing the tree which still had the bullet buried in it. He used dynamite and the resulting explosion 'fired' the bullet. This time it did not miss – Ziegland was hit in the head and died.

▶ POWs Reunited ▼

In August 1989, an American ex-serviceman in Santa Monica, California, asked the Australian army to help him trace a Dr Des Brennan, who had treated him in a prisoner-of-war camp in Mukden, Manchuria, in the Second World War. The army did so and Dr Brennan, then seventy-three and still practising in Sydney, wrote to the American with his name and address and arranged to meet him in Sydney in October.

However, by the time the letter arrived the ex-serviceman had found the address through another source. He had mentioned his search to a travel agent in Santa Monica and the agent responded by saying he had been at school twenty-three years before with Dr Brennan's son, Richard, also of Sydney, and he still had the family address.

▶ Earthquake to Order ▼

On Saturday, 14 October 1989, under the heading 'Series-ly, Let the Earthquake Begin', *USA Today* sporting columnist Tom Weir opened his story on the eve of the baseball World Series thus: 'OAKLAND. The only flavour still missing from this Bay Bridge World Series is an earthquake, and the Athletics and the Giants just might be capable of rattling one up without Mother Earth's help.'

A few days later the second worst earthquake recorded in the US hit the area, causing many deaths and injuries and leaving thousands homeless. Among the first victims was the World Series itself, which had to be postponed.

▶ Message from Beyond ▼

Comedian Michael Bentine tells of this supernatural coincidence in his book on the paranormal, *Doors of the Mind* (1984). Bentine has long been a student of the psychic and for some days a voice had disturbed him at night with the words: 'Blood sacrifice!'

One day, while relaxing in his home, his coffee table shook 'with a terrific bang *inside the wood*' (his italics) and the two words sounded again.

Just then the phone rang. His wife answered it and, looking shaken, told him it was a friend of his from Scotland Yard. 'He says there's been a bomb outrage and they think it's Airey Neave,' she said (the MP was killed in London by an IRA bomb). Bentine spoke to the officer, then returned to his sitting room to say a prayer for his wartime friend. As he did so, the coffee table cracked again, like a pistol shot – 'an unmistakable paranormal sound' – and immediately the same phantom voice spoke, this time loudly and triumphantly: 'And all the trumpets sounded for him on the other side' – a quotation from Bunyan's *Pilgrim's Progress*, which Bentine had not read for many years.

Shortly afterwards, he attended the memorial service for Neave at St Martin-in-the-Fields. Suddenly those words were being spoken again: 'And all the trumpets sounded for him on the other side.' The speaker was Margaret Thatcher.

▶ Living Portrait ▼

Scilla Rosenberg named one of her daughters Vashti, after a character in Sir Arthur Quiller-Couch's novel *Major Vigoreaux*, which she had read as a young woman. At the time of reading, the name itself, the character and, in particular, the haunting portrait of Vashti on the book's frontispiece had deeply impressed Scilla.

It was not until her daughter was grown up that Scilla learned that the young woman who had posed for the portrait of Vashti was one Dody Puckett, who is her grandmother and, of course, Vashti's great-grandmother! Vashti, like Dody, became a model!

▶ This is a Hold-up, Hold-up, Hold-up . . . ▼

Robyn Cooke was involved in four hold-ups between 1989 and 1990 at the bank where she worked as a teller. In one of them a bandit pushed a gun in her back and forced her to lie on the floor.

The Victims' Compensation Tribunal offered her $7,500 compensation for the shock and stress she experienced. However, Robyn contested the offer. As the subsequent hearing was under way, a fifth hold-up occurred at the bank and Robyn was once again a victim.

▶ More Money ▼

A bank teller is named Mr Cashmore.

▶ Born to Shop ▼

The manager of a shopping mall is a Mr Will Purchase.

▶ Backward Bra ▼

A brassière was produced in Britain in 1966 with its trade name 'EMBARGO' prominently displayed on each cup. Sales were brisk until it was pointed out what the word spelt in the reflection of a bedroom mirror.

▶ Spontaneous Combustion ▼

In one week in 1989, all the oven hobs in a block of Sydney units exploded without warning, no matter what their brand. When it was reported to the Department of Business and Consumer Affairs, the owners were told there had been a series of spontaneous explosions around Sydney, not only of the tops but also of oven doors. The cause of the sudden series of explosions was not traced.

▶ Copycat Gassing ▼

When Edward Zarnow died in his Milwaukee, Wisconsin, home in January 1989, his death was at first put down to natural causes. He was eighty-nine and had a bad heart. His son, also Edward, fifty-six, a retired school teacher of Orange, Australia, and his wife, Rebecca, matron of the local nursing home, flew to the US to organize the funeral. They stayed at the father's house with an American niece and her husband.

The next day, when other relatives called and there was no response, they broke in and found the four slumped in their beds. Edward II was dead, along with the niece and her husband. Rebecca was taken to hospital.

The medical examiner found all had been overcome by carbon monoxide leaking from a faulty gas furnace. When the body of Edward senior was re-examined it was found he too had been a victim of the faulty furnace.

The son of Edward II, Edward III, went to the States to arrange the funerals, with his wife – and their son, Edward IV.

▶ Seeing the Job Through ▼

A sales manager of a glass repair company – Mr Payne.

▶ Bright Names ▼

Among the university students who earned distinctions and high distinctions in 1991: Brilliante, Brain, Champion, Smart and Goodchild.

▶ Frate's Freight ▼

A salesmen with the Airborne Express Company – Nick Frate.

▶ Long Arm of the Law ▼

Michael Mitchell, forty, on the run from jail in Montana, was standing in a queue at a souvenir stand in Seattle, Washington State, when he felt a firm hand on his shoulder.

'You're under arrest,' Mitchell was told.

The man directly behind him was Jack McCormick, in Seattle on holiday from his job as a warden at Montana State Prison.

▶ No Worries ▼

In August 1991, Harold Hayward of Sydney, Australia, received a card from his daughter, Jennie, who lives in Ashford, Connecticut, for his fifty-eighth birthday. The card depicted an elephant and the words: 'Dad, don't worry about birthdays aging you . . . if being a father hasn't, nothing will.'

Amused, he put it down and opened the card given him by his other daughter, Meredith, who lives at home. On the cover was an elephant and with it the words: 'Dad, don't . . .' etc.

Both cards were made by Hallmark, the only difference was in the words 'aging' and 'ageing'.

In 1992, the same thing happened – two cards both the same!

▶ Pool on Ponds ▼

Liverpool University's courses for Further Education included one called 'A Pond in your Garden'. It was given by Dr Pool.

The same university's building course was run by a Mr Trowell.

▶ Stiff on Stiffs ▼

The Essex coroner is Mr Stiff.

▶ They Also Serve ▼

In the Australia Day 1992 Honours List, Oscar Elton Butcher received an award for services to the meat industry and John Charles Rivett for services to engineering.

▶ Home from Home ▼

'Spencer' told a radio programme phone-in on coincidences that he had migrated to Australia as a child in 1957 from Surrey, where he had been born and spent his early years.

In 1984 'Spencer' had an urge to return to Surrey for a holiday. He owned a motor bike at the time, a 650cc Triumph Thunderbird. Rather than leave it in his garage for the time he was going to be away, he decided to have it refurbished. He searched around for someone to do the work and settled on a motor-bike shop in the Sydney suburb of Narwee.

Once in Surrey, he went to the house where he was born and knocked on the door. An elderly woman answered and 'Spencer' told her of his connection with the house. She knew his name as she had purchased the house in 1955 from his father.

Spencer went on: 'She invited me in and there on the table was a slouch hat with corks on it.' I said, 'That's strange, I've just come from Australia. She said she had a sister in Australia. I asked her where.'

'New South Wales.'

'Where?'

'Sydney.'

'Oh yeah. What suburb?'

'Narwee.'

'Whereabouts in Narwee?.'

'Well, she's an old age pensioner and I send the letters to this gentleman who has a motor-bike shop . . .'

'Spencer' personally delivered a birthday card to the sister when he picked up his bike from the caring owner of the Narwee repair shop.

▶ Two out of Two ▼

Margaret, a caller to a radio programme on which I was appearing, told me her mother, a New Zealander, went to England and was introduced to an old woman in a wheelchair.

The woman said: 'I only know two other New Zealanders – one is Godfrey Bowen, the champion sheep shearer.'

Margaret's mother said, 'That's my cousin. Who's the other one?'

She said, 'It's a man called Stan Utting.'

'He's married to my cousin on my mother's side.'

▶ Star's Name ▼

Perceval Seymour is an astronomer.

▶ English Expert ▼

A Miami English teacher – Lilian Poms.

▶ Quantum Leap Year ▼

The Henriksen family of Ardenes, Norway, have three children, Heidi, born 1960, Olav, 1964, and Lief-Martin, 1968 – all their birth dates are 29 February.

▶ Home Brew ▼

The owner of a liquor store – John Brew.

▶ Expert at Work ▼

A notice from the local water board advising consumers of the measures it was taking to minimize 'nuisance odors' was signed by Rod Mould.

▶ Dim View ▼

An ophthalmologist – Dr Wong See.

► Car-pet Name ▼

The name of a carpet layer – Walter Wall.

► Registered Birth ▼

Pregnant Jeanette Ellis of Cobbs Creek, Virginia, realized early one morning in February 1992 that her second child was suddenly on its way. She climbed into the rear seat of their Ford Taurus station wagon while her husband, Tad, took the wheel. They did not make it to hospital before the birth. At 6.40 a.m. Jeanette gave birth to a boy in the back seat. The numberplate of the car: BOY 640.

► Blooming Unseen ▼

For years New Zealand botanists searched for proof the tiny *Corybas carseii* orchid had not become extinct. The *NZ Herald* reported that they found their evidence at the end of an expedition in 1992 which involved four days of wallowing in a peat bog.

Following a lunch-break, one of the botanists stood up, looked back and found he had been sitting on a specimen of the orchid, which blooms on just two days a year.

► Honest Crookes ▼

The successful tenderer for a detention centre at a jail: Richard Crookes Constructions. The company put up a sign at the site: THE ONLY HONEST CROOKES. Officials made them remove it.

► Apt Name ▼

A county pest exterminator – Len Roach.

▶ Defect Found ▼

A Sunday night movie, *Total Recall*, was sponsored by the Nissan car company

▶ The Near-dead Zone ▼

In October 1991, as a violent electrical storm raged, Jennifer Roberts, twenty-three, was tucked up snugly in a tent reading Stephen King's book *The Dead Zone* – then lightning struck her.

The bolt entered Jennifer's body through her watchband and burned a trail down to her toes. Doctors said the only thing that saved her was the fact she had been lying on a rubber mattress – and that she had removed her brassière.

It was an underwired bra and, because it had been jabbing into her, she had taken it off ten minutes before the strike. Had Jennifer still been wearing it, the lightning would have re-energized the wire and given her heart a double jolt.

The lightning burnt a hole through the 290 pages of the novel. The book's cover is illustrated with the head of a man from which lightning bolts are flashing!

▶ Caught in the Backwash ▼

Talking of storms ... Australia's worst shipping disaster occurred on 4 August 1845, when a hurricane drove the *Catarqui* on to a reef 500 metres off King Island in Bass Strait.

The 802-tonne migrant ship had sailed from Liverpool four months earlier with 415 men, women and children on board. Only nine made it to the shore, including the first mate, Thomas Guthrie, and the only migrant to survive, Sol Brown, whose wife and four children were among those drowned.

Guthrie took a job as skipper of a coastal vessel and was drowned a year later when his ship went aground off South Australia. Three years after the tragedy, Brown fell into a creek late one night when drunk and he too finally drowned, in a few inches of water.

▶ The Shipwreck Experts ▼

One of the most amazing coincidences at sea began innocently enough, with the departure from Sydney Harbour on 16 October 1829 of the schooner *Mermaid*, bound for distant Collier Bay on the north-west coast of Western Australia, thousands of kilometres distant. On board were eighteen crew and three passengers. The captain was Samuel Nolbrow.

The journey north along the east coat of the country went smoothly for four days. Then a sudden gale blew up as the *Mermaid* was entering the Torres Strait, between Australia's northern tip and Papua New Guinea. High winds and raging seas tossed the helpless schooner in every direction. Finally, a large wave dumped her on a reef and she began to break up. The only chance for those on board was to swim to a rocky peak that jutted from the boiling waters about 100 metres from where they had gone down.

When daylight came, a head count showed that all those on board had somehow made it through the raging sea. They were marooned there, cold and wet, for three days before another ship, the barque *Swiftsure*, appeared.

The *Swiftsure* took the survivors on board and continued on her way, heading west for five days along the southern coast of Papua New Guinea. Unexpectedly, she found herself under the influence of a strong current. Her crew unable to counter it, the ship was swept on to rocks and wrecked. The *Mermaid*'s crew found themselves abandoning ship for the second time.

This time the ordeal lasted only eight hours. The Schooner *Governor Ready* spotted their signals from the shore. The *Governor Ready* was already carrying thirty-two people and a full cargo of timber. However, she managed to squeeze the survivors from both the *Mermaid* and *Swiftsure* on board before continuing her voyage.

Only three hours later, the *Governor* mysteriously caught alight. The fire spread rapidly through the timber and the order to abandon ship yet again rang out. Everybody jammed into her long boats. Around them was nothing but a vast expanse of open sea and their prospects of yet another rescue looked slim. But a miracle occurred. The government cutter *Comet* unexpectedly appeared, and again all were rescued.

When the story so far spread among the crew of the *Comet*, there was some initial grumbling about the *Mermaid*'s crew being jinxed. But it was pointed out that rather than bad luck they were having a great deal of good luck. So far they had survived three shipwrecks in dangerous waters.

For a week the good luck argument prevailed – until another sudden squall sprang up. Soon the *Comet*'s mast was lost, her sails in tatters, her rudder gone. This time the only ones to abandon ship were the crew of the *Comet*. Their belief in the jinx theory by this time prevailed and they took to their boats, leaving their much shipwrecked fellow seafarers to fend for themselves.

For eighteen hours those left behind on the *Comet* clung to what was little more than a wreck. They had to fight off sharks as well as weariness throughout their ordeal. They were saved yet again when the packet *Jupiter* appeared and took all on board.

As they at last headed for port, the captains took the roll and realized that, although there had been four shipwrecks, not a single life had been lost.

An incredible story on its own! However, there was a final coincidence. On board the last vessel – *Jupiter* – was a passenger, Sarah Richey, an elderly Yorkshire woman. She was in Australia searching for her son, Peter, who had been missing for fifteen years. Peter was one of the crew from the first vessel, *Mermaid*.

▶ Mystery Ice ▼

In 1975, the Melkis family of Dunstable, Bedfordshire, were watching the film *Titanic* when a huge chunk of ice caved in their roof. The origin of the ice is unknown.

▶ It's an Ill Wind . . . ▼

Camille Flammarion, the late nineteenth-century astronomer and writer, was working one day in his study when a sudden gust of wind forced open a window. The wind, blowing in from the south-west side of the study, picked up the papers from his desk and carried them through the open window on the east side, scattering them over the avenue. Almost immediately a rainy squall hit. Flammarion, obviously a man with a pessimistic disposition, decided it would be useless to retrieve the material as the rain would have ruined it.

Three days later he received page proofs of the 'lost' chapter from Lahure's printing house. The printer's was about half a kilometre from the observatory. Had the wind carried the complete chapter to it? The answer was more mundane, but still intriguing. A porter who worked for the printer's had earlier on the day of the storm picked up some other chapters of Flammarion's for typesetting. He happened to be passing the observatory later that day, following the shower. He saw the pages lying about and figured he must have dropped them from the earlier pick-up. He carefully gathered the pages, delivered them to Lahure's and ensured they were typeset correctly, even though the ink had, as Flammarion had surmised, been smeared across the pages. The chapter in question had to do with the force of wind.

► Judgement Day ▼

San Francisco judge Samuel King, annoyed that jurors were unable to make it to court because of continual heavy rain, issued a decree: 'I hereby order that it cease raining by Tuesday.'

That was in 1986 and drought hit California for the next five years. In 1991, he was reminded of his decree by colleagues and proclaimed: 'I hereby rescind my order of 18 February 1986 and order that rain shall fall in California beginning 27 February.'

On that day a fierce storm swept over the Pacific, drenching the state with more than 100 millimetres of rain. In the next few days two smaller storms added more rain. Squalls continued for the next fortnight.

► Quake Date ▼

Severe earthquakes struck Japanese cities in 827, 859, 867, 1185, 1649 and 1923, in each case on 1 September of the year concerned. The 1 September 1923 quake was the worst in Japan's history, levelling Tokyo and Yokohama and killing 143,000 people.

▶ Youth Who Missed the Train ▼

In the early hours of 20 May 1988, a nineteen-year-old youth was hit by a train while walking on the tracks. Police searched the man's shredded clothing for some identity and found the address of a young woman. Assuming it to be that of the man's girlfriend, they went to the address, which was near the scene of the accident, and asked her to describe her boyfriend. She did so, including details of his height, colour of hair and tattoos and other body markings. 'She described him to a T,' said an officer. She also gave them the address of the boy. When police went there, the boyfriend's parents said their son was asleep in his bed. Through an amazing coincidence, the son had identical tattoos and body-markings to the train victim, a case of the wind of coincidence blowing both good and ill omens.

▶ Well Named ▼

Vera Cragg's marriage certificate is a personal record of a family coincidence. It shows both marriage partner's parents sharing the same first name, the same middle name and the same occupation.

Vera married Thomas in October 1938, at St Matthew's Church. The marriage certificate shows both fathers' first names recorded as Alfred Ernest and the mothers', Rose Hannah. The fathers were both wool scourers and the occupations of both mothers were given as 'domestic duties'.

There's more. Vera's matron of honour was Lillian Hunt and so was the bridesmaid – they were mother and daughter.

Commenting on all this some years ago, Mrs Cragg said: 'The minister thought we were having him on. He told us he had never come across anything like it in the twenty-three years he had been marrying couples.'

▶ The Law's a Dog ▼

Senior constable Neal Cremen, who admits to the nickname 'The Dog', was assigned to investigate a complaint about a savage dog. When he called at the owner's house, the animal provided all the evidence he needed by biting him.

In hospital 'The Dog' was treated by a Dr Bassett. The owner was taken to court and the prosecutor was Constable Barker.

CHAPTER TEN

Random Anecdotes: IV

A final chapter of coincidences selected at random.

▶ Timely Mailman ▼

Mrs Willard Lovel, of Berkeley, California, found herself locked out of her house when the front door accidentally shut. She stood there for ten minutes, pondering her next move, when the postman arrived with a letter from her brother, Watson Wyman of Seattle, Washington State, who had stayed with her recently. The letter contained the spare key to her front door that he had borrowed during the visit.

▶ Off the Rails ▼

On 24 August 1983, the Amtrak Silver Meteor train set out on its regular run from Miami to New York. At 7.40 p.m. in Savannah, Georgia, the train struck and killed a woman who was fishing from a bridge. At 9.30 p.m., just twenty-seven kilometres further on, it hit and destroyed a truck parked too close to the lines in Ridgeland, South Carolina. The crew were so shaken by the two events that rail officials decided to replace them.

At 1.10 a.m. the following morning, the train hit a tractor-trailer on a crossing at Rowland, North Carolina, and two passengers cars were derailed, sending twenty-one people to hospital – including the engine driver. Once again, Amtrak officials brought in a new crew and the train continued its journey. At 2.37 a.m. in Kenly, North Carolina, it ran head-long into a car that ignored the warning lights at yet another crossing.

The National Transport Safety Board then stepped in. They had no reason to doubt the quality of the machinery or to question the competence of the crews, but they declared Amtrak 117 to be a 'rogue train' and cancelled the rest of the journey.

▶ Prime Ministers Foretold ▼

The coincidence of numbers has dogged Tony Taylor. In the early 1950s, he bought a house in Liverpool, England, Lot No. 201, which eventually became No. 47. His local Labour Member of Parliament was Harold Wilson, who became Prime Minister for a period in the 1960s and 1970s.

Mr Taylor moved to Australia early in the 1960s and bought a house at Liverpool, a city near Sydney. The suburban sprawl swept out from the city centre, finally engulfing Liverpool, so that it now is a western suburb of Sydney, although still retaining its city status. When Mr Taylor bought his new house its address was Lot 201. It also became house No. 47.

His local MP was Gough Whitlam, Labor, and Mr Taylor could not resist writing to him to tell him on the basis of his coincidental experience he would become Prime Minister – he did in 1972.

▶ Characters ▼

Shelley Boa received as a Christmas present from a married couple a book of short stories. In one of the stories the names of the two characters were Miss Bristow and Philippa. The wife of the givers' was Philippa Bristow. Another one of the characters also had the uncommon name of Shelley. 'The gift was without the knowledge of the contents of the book. Amazing!' she commented.

▶ Last Act ▼

Mr M. N. Hervey ran his own repertory company in the UK. One day, half-way through a rehearsal of *All My Sons*, he put the script down and told the cast they would have to manage without him for a while because he was going home. 'On entering my home my mother told me that my father had died of a heart attack – seemingly at the exact moment I left the theatre.'

▶ Random Search ▼

Dame Rebecca West went to the Royal Institute of International Affairs to check on one of the accused in the so-called minor Nuremberg (war crime) trials. She was horrified to find the trials were published in a form almost useless to the researcher.

After hours of searching, she came across an assistant librarian at one of the shelves and complained to him about her inability to find the reference. As she was doing so, 'I put my hand on one volume and took it out and carelessly looked at it, and it was not only the right volume, but I had opened it at the right page.'

▶ The Genes Trap ▼

Clive Tippits, a young British detective, had a major problem on his mind when he sat down to relax in front of the TV. He was investigating the rape of a victim who had been paralysed from childhood with polio. He and his colleagues had narrowed the field down to four suspects, but there they seemed to be stuck.

He turned on the TV and found himself watching a science programme. This, he thought as he sat back, would take his mind right away from the case. The programme described a technique developed in 1984 by Dr Alec Jeffries of Leicester University. Known as genetic fingerprinting, it is the surest way of identifying an individual from a minuscule amount of tissue.

It reveals an individual's genetic pattern. Everyone who is not an identical twin has a unique genetic pattern, repeated in every body cell. Tippits was suddenly far from relaxed. Here, staring him in the face, was a possible way forward in the rape case. His enthusiasm for what he had heard persuaded his superiors to contact Dr Jeffries. As a result, one of the suspects was positively identified and prosecuted.

Blood, semen, hair, even skin scrapings found under a victim's fingernails, can lead to the attacker's identity being revealed. Since it was first tried, genetic fingerprinting has been used around the world to solve crimes and successfully prosecute rapists and murderers. Had the 'coincidence sense' not led Tippets to turn on that TV programme, a rapist could still be walking around today.

Of course, it is quite possible that Tippets would have heard about genetic fingerprinting from some other source. However, he was acutely conscious that he needed to find an answer to the problem and such awareness can make us coincidence-prone.

▶ Significant 7 ▼

The number 7 has played an important part in the life of Dianne Randall's family. They lived in a house with a street number 7. The family – five children, two parents – totalled seven. Her eldest brother was born on 7 July 1943, her second eldest brother on 7 May 1945, the third brother on 7 August 1948, and she herself was born on 7 March 1950. Her youngest brother was born on her third eldest brother's birthday, 7 August 1952.

▶ Just Missed ▼

Alf Apperley just missed being part of the significant birth date of his family. His mother and her sister each had two children born on the same date, his two sisters on 17 April 1934 and 17 April 1936; his cousins on 17 April 1942 and 17 April 1944. Alf was born a few minutes after midnight on 18 April 1932.

▶ Turn for the Worst ▼

In 1987, Mexican-American Francisco Sandoval, forty-six, was killed when his car overturned on a bend on Highway 94, between San Diego, California, and the Mexican border. Thirty-six hours later, a hearse carrying his body was involved in an accident on the same bend.

▶ Feeling the Pinch ▼

On the Great Western Highway, west of Sydney, a semi-trailer carrying two soldiers overturned, trapping the occupants. The accident happened on a bend known as Soldiers Pinch. Neither man was seriously hurt.

▶ The Park-bench Job ▼

Pratt Whitfield, a fifty-five-year-old disabled merchant seaman, was sitting on a park bench in the tough Bronx district, minding his own business, when he heard a fellow bench-sitter talking to a friend about a robbery they were planning for that night. When they mentioned that they planned to use a shotgun that one of them was carrying, Whitfield pricked up his ears. He rose from the bench as casually as possible and walked to a police station near by.

Whitfield did more than report a planned robbery. Five years previously, two men had broken into his home. One had held a knife to his throat, the other aimed a shotgun at his wife. They had robbed the couple and had never been caught. But Whitfield had never forgotten the menacing voice of the robber ... Returning to the scene with two cops in tow, he confronted the men.

'Do you remember me?' Whitfield asked thirty-three-year-old James King. 'You robbed me and my wife five years ago with that gun!'

There was no menace in King's voice as he faced Whitfield this time. In fact, King was speechless. He gave up without a struggle and was sent to stand trial for a number of robberies, including the Whitfield job. King had a long list of convictions.

The story does not end there. The statute of limitations for robbery runs for five years and this fateful reunion at the park bench happened *the day before* the five-year limitation on the Whitfield robbery was up.

▶ Noisy Line ▼

Wellington (NZ) resident Gael Woods called the city's central police station one weekend in May 1989 to complain about a noisy party. The police gave her the number of the city council's noise control officer. When she dialled the number, she heard a recorded message asking her to leave her name and address. She did not hear back from the office, but on Monday the Association of the Deaf rang her asking about the strange message she had left on their machine. The association's welfare officer said they had received a number of calls in recent months, there had always been noise in the background and the people had sounded weary and irate. The cause of the confusion was uncovered by a quick check in the phone book. NZ Association of the Deaf . . . 849682; noise control officer . . . 849628.

▶ Red-marked 'Girl' ▼

In London in 1971, author George Feifer lent a friend an advance copy of his novel *The Girl from Petrovka*. He had been reluctant to do so because it was a unique version, full of corrections for the forthcoming American edition – 'labor' for 'labour', and so on. There were four or five red marks to a page, the result of considerable work, which gave the copy, since he is American, almost as much sentimental as practical value. Within a week, Feifer's friend had lost it from his car. Frantic searches and the offer of a reward failed to locate it.

In November 1973, Feifer went to Vienna, where the book was being filmed, and met Anthony Hopkins, who plays one of the film's major characters. Hopkins told Feifer that, having signed to do the part, he went to central London to buy a copy of the book. On his way home at the end of a fruitless trip, he noticed an abandoned book on a bench in Leicester Square underground station. He at first suspected it might be a bomb but eventually picked it up. (Author's note: At this stage the IRA were particularly active in London and Hopkins's initial reaction is not surprising. Bombs were being left at underground stations. What is surprising is that he picked it up at all.)

Turning it over, Hopkins read the title, *The Girl from Petrovka*. He told Feifer he was still confounded by the marks scattered on most pages. 'Might that copy have some personal meaning for you?' he asked the author.

▶ Gift from a Prince ▼

British actor Edward Sothern, in his book *The Melancholy Tale of Me*, tells how the Prince of Wales gave his father an engraved gold matchbox. His father lost it while hunting, but had a duplicate made, which he eventually gave to Edward's brother, Sam, who in turn gave it to an Australian named Labertouche.

Many years later, when Sam was himself hunting, he was approached by an elderly farmer who had heard that Sam's name was Sothern. That morning one of the farmhands had found the original matchbox while ploughing. Sam was amazed by the coincidence and wrote about it to his brother, Edward, who was then touring the United States. Edward read the letter on a train on which, by chance, he was sharing a compartment with another actor, Arthur Lawrence. When Edward told Lawrence about his brother's find, it was Lawrence's turn to be amazed. He produced the duplicate matchbox, which had been given to him several years before by Labertouche.

▶ Mid-air Meeting ▼

Golfer Kevin O'Brien saw his ball hit mid-flight by another belonging to a player further down the fairway who was playing a recovery shot in the opposing direction (having strayed from the adjacent fairway).

O'Brien and the other golfer met at the collision point and

introduced themselves. This revealed the second coincidence – the other player was also named Kevin O'Brien.

As they chatted, the second O'Brien mentioned he lived on McArthur Avenue. That revealed the third coincidence. The first O'Brien also lived on McArthur Avenue, but in a different suburb.

▶ Ad with Bite ▼

Just before the commercial break, a TV news service ran an item about a ship going down in the Caribbean with sharks attacking and killing many of the passengers and crew. More than 100 people lost their lives.

The commercial then came on with a jingle which began: 'Does a tiger shark bite?'

▶ The Queen of Soaps ▼

A woman who was born on the day of Edward VIII's coronation in 1936 was named Coronation. She married a Mr Street, so, like Britain's longest-running soap, she is also called Coronation Street.

▶ PIN Prediction ▼

Film researcher Peta Newbold found herself in need of cash and decided to use an Automatic Teller Machine. The trouble was, she seldom used her card and was uncertain of the Personal Identification Number (PIN) the bank had given her, although something told her it was 1234 (not, of course, the real number).

Peta pushed the card into the slot and punched out the numbers. Wrong, gloated the machine. She tried again, still convinced the numbers were 1234. Wrong again! A third time and the machine told her she could not have the card back.

The next day she explained to the bank what had happened and arranged to be issued a new card. Some weeks later she received the new PIN number the bank had selected for her – 1234!

As PIN numbers are selected by a machine on a random basis, there can be no question of Peta having asked for 1234, or in any other way having influenced the process by which she received the numbers that had lodged so persistently in her mind.

▶ PIN Prediction II ▼

When Paul Hudley from Bedlington, Northumberland, arrived in Australia to be reunited with his girlfriend, Christine Franklin, he found they had something extra in common – the same four-figure PIN number. He banks with the NatWest in England, she with the National Australia.

▶ Specialist Writer ▼

A story in a medical journal in June 1992, dealing with possible links between lung cancer and contraceptives, was written by reporter Samantha Overy.

The previous month the magazine had run a story about chronic fatigue, quoting a Professor Denis Wakefield.

▶ Top Tapp ▼

The head of a Norfolk (UK) typing school – Ms Tapp.

▶ Literate Company

A Dublin firm of printers and stationers – Reid and Wright.

▶ Leak in Hull ▼

A man fined for urinating in a public place in Hull (UK) – Mr A. Leak.

▶ String Vests ▼

The manager of a clothing factory – Mr Holes.

▶ Role Model ▼

John Glover, dubbed the 'granny killer' for the murder of five elderly women in Sydney, changed his name to John Wayne Glover after the American movie star – as did John Wayne Gacy, the American serial killer of teenage boys.

▶ Three to Won on ▼

A triple dead-heat occurred in a race in 1903 and the three horses involved, High Flyer, Loch Lochie and Bardini, ran again – and once again dead-heated.

▶ Tee-Terred ▼

In 1929, a golfer on the Belmont, Massachusetts, course hit off from the second tee and saw his ball reach the edge of the hole. The golfer, a James Cash, peeved he had missed out on a hole in one on the par-three course, had just started down the fairway when an earth tremor rocked the course – and dropped his ball into the hole.

▶ Plot Involving PC J419 ▼

Mrs J. T. Farr's father served thirty years in the London Metropolitan police force, stationed in the north-east suburbs, in what was known as J division. His number was J419. He died in the early days of the Second World War. Years later, when Mrs Farr's mother died, aged eighty-six, the grave number of her cemetery plot was J419.

▶ Final Round ▼

On the night her husband died, Rhonda Kellie watched with him a film on TV about the boxer Jack Dempsey – he had been very interested in boxing. When they placed his memorial plaque in a rose garden, she noticed the adjoining plaque was one for a Mr Dempsey.

▶ Putting Her Back into the Job ▼

TV reporter Sheryl Taylor, assigned to produce a two-part special on bad backs, set to work with a will. She read books on the subject, interviewed specialists and sufferers, and offered her own insights as a qualified nurse. Shortly before her story went on air, she was pushing the corners of a new liner on her rubbish bin into place when there was 'an incredible explosion of pain in my back'. Sheryl had to lie on the floor until the pain subsided. Instead of putting the finishing touches to her story, she was in the hands of a physiotherapist.

▶ Hit for a Six ▼

In *The Road Less Travelled* (1978), American Dr M. Scott Peck tells of an eerie coincidence which happened shortly after he and his wife arrived at night for a holiday in Singapore. It was their first visit and, after settling in, they went for a stroll. Peck goes on:

> We soon came to a large open space at the far end of which, two or three blocks away, we could just about make out in the darkness the vague shape of a sizeable building.
> 'I wonder what that building is,' my wife said.
> I immediately answered with casual and total certainty, 'Oh, that's the Singapore Cricket Club.'

The words had popped out of Peck's mouth spontaneously. He'd had no reason for uttering them. Not only had he not been in Singapore before, he had never seen a cricket club before – in daylight, much less in darkness. To his amazement, when they reached the other side of the building, they saw at its entrance a brass plaque reading 'Singapore Cricket Club'.

▶ Poetic Justice ▼

French poet Émile Deschamps dined out on his coincidence, which began with a meal. The story is told in Camille Flammarion's book *The Unknown* (1900).

As a schoolboy Deschamps happened to dine once with a M. de Fortgibu, who had recently returned from living in England. Fortgibu asked the student to try a plum pudding, a dish then unknown in France. Deschamps enjoyed it and its taste stayed with him.

Ten years later he spotted a plum pudding on display in a restaurant window and went in to buy it. But he found that pudding had already been ordered, by M. de Fortgibu.

The story moves forward many years, to a dinner party he was invited to at which a 'real English plum pudding' was to be served. As they sat down to eat, Deschamps joked with the hostess that M. de Fortgibu would surely join them. The words were hardly out of his mouth, when the door opened and a servant announced that M. de Fortgibu *had* joined them.

Deschamps remembered later that his hair stood up on his head. The now ageing Fortgibu had indeed been invited to dinner, but by a friend who lived in a different apartment in the same building. The old gentleman had mixed up the apartment numbers.

▶ Pop Pope Day ▼

On 18 October 1405, Pope Pius II was born; on the same day in 1417, Pope Gregory XII died, as did Pope Pius III in 1503.

▶ Doing It by Dates ▼

The following coincidences come from two people who phoned a radio programme on which I was appearing.

First: 'I was born on Friday the 13th. I celebrated my thirteenth birthday on Friday the 13th and today I'm celebrating my eighteenth birthday' (it was Friday, 13 March 1992).

Then: 'I married on 24 February 1979. I was divorced on 24 February 1984 and my ex-husband was found dead on 24 February 1990.'

▶ Job for an Expert ▼

The general manager of the New Zealand Beef and Lamb Marketing Bureau – Ian Lamb.

▶ Planes down, Number up ▼

In March 1977, two 747s collided in the Canary Islands. The death toll was close to 600. It was one of the worst aviation accidents on record. A few days later the number 7470 came up in the Massachusetts state lottery. There were three times as many winners as usual.

▶ Haunting Memories ▼

New Yorkers Joyce Walp and Michael Bachman were awarded damages because of the trauma they went through when the body of their pet dog was thrown into a mass grave and not buried in its own plot. Bachman is a pseudonym of Stephen King, the best-selling horror fiction author, who wrote *Pet Sematary*.

▶ Ho-hum ▼

A yoga student, 'Bruce', told me that when he was doing a meditation exercise with about 120 people in a large hall, the teacher suggested that, for a variation on the usual start, each member of the class should hum for as long as he/she felt like it, then go into the exercise.

'We began and after a few moments I decided I would stop when I ran out of breath,' Bruce said. 'At the precise moment I stopped every other person in the class also stopped. There was instant silence.'

▶ He's Watching ▼

TV producer Simon Townsend was working on a list of 1,000 controversial topics in 1992. One he wrote was: 'The devil exists and, like God, is aware of everything we do.'

It was only after he'd written a few more topics that he glanced back and noticed the statement was Controversial Topic No. 666.

▶ Removal Van ▼

In *The Blackbird – The Unauthorized Biography of Paul McCartney* (1991), author Geoffrey Giuliano says that on the day of Lennon's death, McCartney was standing with his close friend Denny Laine at the window of a recording studio in London overlooking Oxford Circus. He happened to notice a green removal van going by with 'Lennon Furnishings' written on it.

Until then Paul had been numb from shock. At the sight of the van he broke down.

▶Governing the Governers ▼

The same governess taught two British prime ministers, who ended up on opposite sides of the political spectrum: the Conservative's Winston Churchill and Labour's Clement Atlee.

▶ Seeing is Believing ▼

In 1971, long-distance truck driver Edwin Robinson was left blind and almost deaf as a result of a bad road accident. Doctors gave him little hope of recovery and over the years he learned to adapt to his afflictions.

One day, with a storm brewing, he went into the back yard of his home in Maine to check on his pet chickens. As he passed a poplar tree, a bolt of lightning struck, knocking him unconscious.

Twenty minutes later he returned to consciousness to discover he could see again – in fact, better than he had nine years earlier – and also his hearing was fully restored.

A month after the accident, there was an additional bonus. He told *The New York Times* how hair had begun to grow on his bald scalp. He had been bald for thirty-five years, believing it to be an hereditary condition, something he had to accept, like his blindness and deafness . . .

▶ Say It with Roses ▼

Francis King, in his book *Ritual Magic in England* (1970), tells the story of a magician, A. O. Spare, who announced he was going to cause fresh-cut roses to fall from the air. He waved various magic symbols around and chanted the word 'roses'. In the middle of this ritual, the overhead plumbing suddenly burst, drenching Spare and his witnesses with raw sewage.

▶ Mmmm! ▼

The first word most children in the world speak begins with an 'm' sound. In nearly every language the word for mother begins with this sound.

▶ Short Term ▼

George Barnham became mayor of Wembley, in Greater London, on 8 July 1937 and died the same day.

▶ Right Name, Wrong Street ▼

In his *Mathematician's Miscellany* (1953), John Littlewood tells the story of a woman who set out to visit her sister, Florence Rose Dalton, a servant who resided at 42 Walton Street, London.

The woman was not familiar with the area and ended up at 42 Ovington Square, without realizing it. When she knocked on the door, she was told that Florence Rose Dalton did work there as a servant but had gone away for a two-week holiday and her sister was standing in for her.

There were indeed two women by that name working as servants and residing a few streets apart at houses whose numbers were 42, unknown to one another.

Littlewood, who did not give much credence to coincidences, admitted that this story struck him as 'genuinely remarkable'.

▶ Tough Music ▼

Rick Lovel was lying in bed, listening to the radio and waiting for a late-night programme which is heralded by a distinctive musical theme to start. As it played this night, he thought to himself how aggressive it sounded. When it concluded, the presenter came on and muttered, 'My God . . . that's an awfully aggressive theme.'

▶ Golfer Scored a Duck ▼

In October 1988, a golfer scored a birdie and a duck on the same hole, during a round at the Bayview Club.

The duck came first. The ball hit it and it went down with feathers flying. Then came the birdie. The ball, after hitting the duck, dropped on the fairway close enough to the green to give her a four on the par-five hole.

▶ Conception Day ▼

Mum Jennifer Crozier, thirty-nine, and her daughters, Emma, seventeen, and Gina, twenty, all became pregnant at the same time in 1989.

▶ Lucky Friday the 13th ▼

On Friday, 13 September 1991, at the annual meeting of the Greenoaks Private Hospital, the wife of the managing director drew the lucky seat prize, No. 13 – the winner, the managing director Dr Warwick Roscoe.

Roscoe insisted on another draw and the wife drew again – No. 13 once more. It was a case of third time unlucky for No. 13, on the 13th, as somebody else walked away with the prize – a bottle of champagne.

▶ Watts in a Name? ▼

A real estate agent was having trouble selling a property despite its attractions, a 'year-round resort, complete with five bedrooms, four bathrooms, landscaped gardens and solar-heated pool'. The problem was it was too close to high-tension wires. Its name: Watts Place.

▶ Death Cakes ▼

Jane Stearn tells this story about her mother and father.

'My mother was an excellent cook and a very generous person. Visiting a sick elderly friend, she took some cakes in the hope they would tempt her waning appetite. They did . . . when she arrived the following week with the cakes, it was to find the friend had died earlier that day. My mother left the cakes and they were used at the funeral tea.'

Some years later, an uncle had a heart attack but was supposedly progressing well. Jane's mother made and took him some cakes, only to find when she arrived he had died suddenly.

Once again the cakes became part of the funeral tea. She goes on:

'In September 1961, the daughter of the uncle developed cancer and in mid-1962 my mother realized that my cousin would not be able to make her own Christmas cake, which would have been a tragedy of enormous proportions in our family. I was sent to visit with the message that my mother would make the cake if my cousin so wished.

'The offer was gratefully accepted and the cake duly made. We always made our cakes and puddings in August, in time for them to mature by Christmas. I took the cake to my cousin and at her request put it on the top shelf of the pantry, out of the way of the small children in the family.

'By Christmas my cousin was desperately ill and cake was the last thing on anyone's mind. My cousin died at the beginning of February 1963 and again cake made by my mother was used at the funeral tea.

'It was not until some months later that the dreadful coincidence of the three events dawned on my mother. One evening, on returning from work, I found my mother in tears. For some reason that afternoon the three incidents had coalesced in her mind. She begged me not to tell father, who was a sceptic, as she feared he would ridicule her. However, as she was so upset and my father was a very practical man, I said we should.

'My father finally convinced my mother that it was just a dreadful coincidence and she should not worry about it. He said if the people had *eaten* the cakes before they had died, then we would all have cause to worry. This light-hearted note cheered my mother, but she never offered to make cakes for anyone ever again.'

▶ Peter Principle ▼

Debby Howe says she finds the name Peter everywhere she looks. Her brother and stepfather are named Peter; her dog's show name is Demrose Little Peter; her husband's brother and a cousin are named Peter. When her best friend married, it was to a Peter and a next-door neighbour is Peter – and his wife is called Debby.

▶ Dr Apts ▼

GPs – Dr Savage and Dr Gore.

▶ Cop Shot ▼

Chief Inspector George Henry Taylforth of the New South Wales police force and his wife, Leslie, entered a competition at the Mollymook Golf Club in 1991. Leslie hit the first hole in one in her golfing career on the eighth and George his first on the eighteenth in the same game.

▶ Coloured Post ▼

In her teens Mrs S. Ryan went on holiday with three friends, Misses Black, Brown and Brindle. Her name at the time was Gray. When they asked at the local post office if there was any mail for Black, Brown, Brindle or Gray, the red-faced postmaster told them to clear off or he would call the police.

▶ Birds of a Featherstone ▼

Frank and Pat Featherstone, on their way to Britain from Australia, started chatting to the couple who joined their flight in Bangkok and sat next to them. After some polite questions, the couple asked where the Featherstones were going. Beckenham in Kent, they said. So are we, said the couple. What address? Foxgrove Road. Us too! What number? 28A. We're staying at 30A.

▶ Clean Sweep ▼

Shortly before a major convention in his city, San Francisco mayor Frank Jordan decided to sweep prostitutes and beggars from the streets. The man he picked to do it was Police Commander Michael Brush.

▶ Reminder Calls ▼

Esther Gordon was doing the shopping when she remembered she had left a pot on the stove. She saw a phone and headed for it to warn her daughter. She was just beaten by another woman, also making a hasty dash for the phone.

The other woman was apologetic. 'I won't be long. I just have to call home and tell my son I've left a pot on the stove.'

▶ Phantom Pays ▼

Phantom ('the ghost who walks') fan Michael Tetley bought an overcoat to wear as a Phantom costume to a fancy-dress party in a second-hand shop in 1991. The overcoat, along with a hat and dark glasses, is the Phantom's civilian disguise as Mr Walker.

In one of the pockets Tetley found a receipt from Tansey & Co., general drapers of Bray, Ireland, dated 7 January 1947, for £6 10s., made out to Mr Walker, Putland Road, Bray.

▶ Future Mourning ▼

Years ago reporter David Evans had coffee with another young journalist who was extremely upset – almost suicidal. The other man, Harold, said his girlfriend had just died in a plane crash in Africa. He told Evans the plane had taken off, failed to gain height and crashed. Most of those on board had been killed. Evans says Harold named the airline, the type of plane and the airport involved.

'Since there had been nothing in the papers or on the radio about the crash, I took his story with a pinch of salt and forgot about it,' he wrote. 'Until three days later, there was an air crash in Africa – exactly as Harold had described it. Unfortunately, I never got a chance to ask him about it because I never saw him again.'

▶ Cheesed off ▼

When a National Smile week was held in Britain in the late 1970s, the person involved who found it most difficult to smile was Miss Moya Church, Miss National Smile herself.

Within minutes of winning, Miss Church's crown was misplaced. It was found in a pile of rubbish. Its recovery did allow her a grin, about the only one for the week.

Someone in the crowd at a 'Smile' reception spilled coffee over her sash and her £100 dress. Both were ruined. The following day she locked herself out of her house. The next day her car broke down and when she left it to call the garage she got a parking ticket.

After her final photographic session she missed her last train home.

▶ Thought Painters ▼

Samela Harris attended a party at which all the guests were required to have their faces painted in a design meant to show their inner personality.

Because she does not like 'gunge' on her face, Harris asked the two artists to paint a simple design on her cheeks. When she looked in the mirror, she found they had painted a pair of dolphins, which both stunned and impressed her.

On her office desk is a dolphin 'shrine', a photo of two dolphins swimming, given to her by a photographer friend who felt it would help ease the tension of her demanding job as a daily newspaper columnist. The photographer later added a small statuette of two dolphins to make up the shrine.

'These are the objects I spend so much of my spare time looking at,' she said. 'They mean so much to me – of all the objects the artist could have chosen . . . it shows some pretty amazing mental agility.'

▶ Food for Thought ▼

Gourmet caterer Victoria Bright was having lunch with an old friend from her home town and the friend's new lover. Several times during the conversation, the couple stressed to Victoria not to mention she had seen them or that they were holidaying together, should she be speaking to anyone from their home town. They explained that the boyfriend, John Flavel (not his real name), was going through a difficult divorce from his wife, Brenda, and it would be most embarrassing should she know they were together.

Victoria assured them she would not mention anything – she did not know Brenda and certainly did not intend to become involved in a domestic dispute.

After lunch she returned home, from where she runs her business, and checked her answering machine. The first message was from – Brenda Flavel, asking Victoria to call her as soon as possible!

She was shocked. How did Brenda find her number? What was she going to say to her? What could she say to a scorned woman? A further thought struck her: the number Brenda had left was local. Was she in town and had she been spying on them?

With trembling hand she picked up the phone and dialled the number. 'Oh, yes, Miss Bright, thank you for calling back. I would like you to cater a luncheon for me . . .'

Same name, completely different woman!

▶ Chuffed Muffy ▼

New in town and accommodation-hunting, Myfanwy Marshall arrived outside a house in February 1994 to find a trailer in the street by the gate. On it was a launch, its name clearly visible across the back: MUFFY. Myfanwy then and there knew the place was going to suit her. No one in town knew her family pet name was Muffy. Also she knew there are strict rules about naming boats – they are not allowed to have the same name.

'I felt the coincidence was not only rare but meaningful, and, as it turned out, it was,' said Myfanwy, happily settled into her new home and planning to buy the only boat in the country with her name on it.

▶ Shared Rooms ▼

In May 1992, John Hoskins, producer of the popular *Beyond 2000* TV series, was covering a story in Winterthur, Switzerland, when he lost his passport. In March 1994, reporter Iain Findlay from the same programme was in Winterthur to do an update on the story Hoskins had covered (about a super motor bike) when he found under the back seat of his rental car Hoskins's missing passport.

▶ Young Doctor ▼

The director of obstetrics at Sydney's King George V Hospital is a Dr Child.

▶ All in the Mind ▼

A US sociologist specializing in mental illness – A. T. Scull.

▶ Schoolgirls' Reunion ▼

Anita Cronshaw and her husband became acquainted with a couple living a few streets away while they were building their house at Gosford in New South Wales. 'One evening they invited us to dinner,' she relates. 'When we arrived, they said some friends of theirs had unexpectedly turned up from Sydney. On meeting this other couple, my husband said to the girl: "I recognize your accent."

'Not only was she from the same area as myself, Greenford, Middlesex, in the United Kingdom, but she turned out to be an old schoolfriend of mine with whom I had walked to school and sat with at school almost all through primary and high school. Her family had emigrated to South Australia when she was sixteen or seventeen. We emigrated when I was just twenty. We had not seen or heard from one another for almost twenty years.'

▶ Cost a Packet Trips? ▼

Headline from *Travel Trade Weekly* on the merger between the French cruise line Paquet and the Italian line Costa Cruises: 'Costa-Paquet cruise merger may set up Europe's top line.'

▶ Rollover Funds ▼

Under the heading 'Revolving Funds', a Fiji government brief outlining defence expenditure lists $263,000, for its army helicopter unit.

▶ What Came First? ▼

The Big Bird Kindergarten in Slacks Creek, Queensland, is on Sesame Street.

▶ Dogged Him ▼

Police combing the Buttonville, California, area for a murder suspect called in Alf, the police dog. Alf sniffed out the man very quickly – he was hiding in a dog kennel.

▶ You Wouldn't Read about it ▼

Dr Tim Flannery lost everything when his home went up in flames during the worst bushfires for many years on the outskirts of Sydney in 1994. Only two books survived. One was entitled *Burning Bush: A Fire History of Australia*.

CHAPTER ELEVEN

Time Twins

▶ Wondering Wandas ▼

The Washington Post reported this story of Time Twins under the headline: 'The Case of the Two Wandas'.

Wanda Marie Johnson lives in Adelphi, in Prince Georges County, and works as a baggage clerk at Union Station, Washington, DC.

Wanda Marie Johnson lives in Suitland, Maryland, also in Prince Georges County, and works as a nurse at the District of Columbia General Hospital in Washington.

Both Wanda Marie Johnsons were born on the same day – 15 June 1953. Both are former District of Columbia residents who moved to Prince Georges. Both are mothers of two children. Both are owners of 1977 two-door Ford Granadas. The eleven-digit serial number on their cars are the same except for the last three digits. Their Maryland driver's licences were identical because a computer determines each licence number by name and birth date. As a result, Wanda Marie Johnson of Adelphi found herself the victim of medical records mix-ups, harassment for payment of debts she didn't owe, telephone calls from strangers and a misunderstanding with Maryland Department of Motor Vehicle officials, who insisted that she wear glasses while driving. The other Wanda wears glasses.

It all became so troublesome for Wanda Marie Johnson of Adelphi that she sought frantically to find the other Wanda. 'People I talked to thought I was crazy,' she said, and she began wondering about that herself.

Her problem began while both women still lived in the District of Columbia – one on Girard Street and the other on New Jersey Avenue. They both had babies at Howard University Hospital and attended the Howard clinic. It was there that the Wanda on Girard Street discovered something was wrong, when doctors at the clinic began consulting with her while using the other Wanda's medical information.

A Howard University official confirmed the existence of the two sets of Wanda Marie Johnson patient records and said they were identified by address and social security numbers, which 'are very close' (the first four numbers of their nine-digit social security numbers are identical; the next two digits are the same, but transposed). A credit company threatened to sue the Adelphi Wanda for non-payment of a bill for furniture that Wanda and Michael Johnson of Suitland had bought. The Adelphi Wanda didn't even have an account at the store, but that did not satisfy the collector, who had heard stories like that before.

'Are you trying to say your name isn't Wanda Johnson?'

'No,' she said.

'Are you trying to say your birth date isn't 15 June 1953?'

'No. I'm just saying that's not me.'

The Adelphi Wanda learned to drive in 1977 and bought her Granada. But each time she tried to apply for a Maryland driver's permit, she was told she already had a licence with a restriction requiring her to wear glasses.

Presumably they worked something out.

As the above story indicates, this chapter deals with what may well be another aspect of the Clustering Effect: people born at the same time of different mothers whose circumstances of birth and ensuing lives are full of coincidences – Time Twins.

Such cases are by no means rare, judging by the records. In some the children are related, but in others there is a more subtle effect.

▶ Common Lives ▼

One of the most famous Time Twin cases involved Samuel Hemming. He was born on the same day and at the same time as George III (4 June 1738).

The commoner and the king were very much the same in appearance and their lives ran along similar lines – though, of course, at different levels. Hemming set up as an ironmonger on the day George succeeded to the throne.

Both were married on 8 September 1761. They had the same number of children of the same sex, became ill and had accidents at the same time, and both died on 19 January 1820 of similar causes.

George IV also had a mirror-image Time Twin, born within the same hour. The twin was only a lowly chimney sweep, but was equally renowned for gambling, philandering and spending, and both were addicted to racing. The prince raced thoroughbreds and the sweep donkeys. On the day the prince was kicked by a horse, his 'twin' was kicked by a donkey. Both took the same amount of time to recover and when the prince went bankrupt, so did the sweep.

▶ Sisters and Aunts ▼

Two sisters gave birth to boys within three hours in 1984. To add to the coincidence, in January 1951, the two aunts of the sisters had had babies on the same day. Experts at the time said the odds against two sisters giving birth on the same day were thousands to one against, and as high as several millions to one against it happening twice in the same family.

The coincidences did not end with the births. In the later dual-births case, the sisters had been due to give birth on the same day but were admitted to hospital a week early. Thirty-three years earlier, their aunts' children had both arrived twenty-five days early. Given the two events, the odds become meaningless.

In some cases, mothers have said they felt their babies delayed their entry into the world so they could be born with the other child. This may sound like wishful thinking on the mothers' part, but in the animal world controlled coincidental births are not considered extraordinary.

The male ostrich has a number of hens and each of the hens in strict order, starting with the dominant female, lays five or six eggs. The last clutch of eggs could be laid as long as three weeks after the first. But all hatch within a few hours of each other. Some eggs synchronize their births by listening to each other within their shells. They do this because of the need to cluster for survival purposes. Dual births with humans could warrant further study.

▶ Shared Interests ▼

Diane Ireland and Margaret Gorrie met while they were studying at a teachers' training college. They quickly became close friends and after graduation were placed at the same school.

There they met and married men who were also best friends and who, like them, shared a flat in the same area. Sixteen months after their marriage they found out on the same day that they had both become pregnant.

Margaret and Diane booked into hospital – and found they had been placed in the same room. Margaret gave birth to a boy, Benjamin, two weeks early and a day before Diane's girl, Jesslyn, was born – a day late.

Diane said in an interview that they don't really like telling people about the coincidences in case it is thought that the two of them are making things up. She said: 'Neither of us is superstitious, but there must be something in all this.'

Other people also are reluctant to speak about the phenomenon. A regard for medical ethics rightly or wrongly inhibits many doctors involved from going public, while in other cases the mothers themselves, or their husbands, relatives or friends discourage talk for any number of reasons: fear of branding the children, modesty, superstition. Or it may be that those concerned do not see anything remarkable in the event. In any case, doctors, medical staff or relatives of a more prosaic bent simply shrug it off, the way many people do with other coincidences, considering them unremarkable, a part of the natural order of things.

Those who strongly favour the psychic elements of coincidence see in these births a further reinforcement of their belief that our lives are ruled by some great cosmic force that controls not only our coming into the world but also our going out of it.

▶ Late, Early ▼

In November 1986, sisters Kathleen Donachie and Maria Trushiem gave birth to boys on the same day at the same hospital. The intriguing thing about this is the ostrich-egg effect: Maria was twelve days late giving birth, while Kathleen had been admitted on the day of the joint births, eleven days early.

▶ Two Births ▼

On 7 November 1984, Gail McClure and her sister, Carol Killian, gave birth to daughters within an hour of each other at Mesa's Lutheran Hospital in Arizona. Three years later they did it again at the same hospital. On 11 February 1987, Gail had a son, Benjamin. Forty-five minutes later, Carol had another girl, Christi, when the same doctor who had delivered the first children carried out a Caesarean section.

'After we did it the first time, we talked about doing it again,' said Gail. 'We tried to plan the due date in March but both got pregnant sooner. Then we didn't talk about it, because we both thought we had ruined the plan.' It wasn't until they were both three months pregnant that they found out both were due at the same time again. Gail was due on 1 February and Carol a week later. 'She waited for me,' said Carol. 'Is that amazing or what?'

▶ Look, Think, Dress Alike ▼

The following case once again takes us to the labour ward and to a case of Time Twins where the coincidences that piled up will almost certainly ensure that the children involved are headed for similar destinies, as happened to their mothers because of their birth dates. Between 2 a.m. and 2.30 a.m. on 8 November 1982, Jenni Miller and Rhonda Shorter each gave birth to babies at Sydney's Crown Street Hospital.

One of the nursing sisters noticed that the new mothers had both been born on 29 October 1956. This got the two women chatting in the four-bed ward they were sharing. They found both were first-time mothers who had been through ten-hour labours before giving birth twenty minutes apart. The children themselves were a 'pigeon pair' – fair skin, blue eyes and blond hair – although Jenni's was a boy, Jay, and Rhonda's a girl, Rosemary.

Each had trained as infant and primary school teachers and lived within a few kilometres of each other in Sydney. They were both the same height, 160 centimetres, took the same shoe size and wore size 12 clothes. The final round of coincidences came when their husbands visited. Both were dark-haired computer programmers who were each 200 centimetres tall.

▶ Kerrie, Kerry ▼

And yet another variation, also full of coincidences. Two women with almost the same name gave birth on the same day, both two weeks early, on 31 March 1988, prompting people who first heard the story to talk of an April Fool's Day joke. The two women, Kerry Mason and Kerrie Mason, live within five kilometres of one another. Both babies were boys. The women had the same doctor.

The details were confirmed by both women, their gynaecologist and the hospitals in which they gave birth. Neither knew the other before the births but were put in touch by their doctors, who said the women were expected to give birth within two days of each other, but both went into labour two weeks early.

▶ Twin Packages ▼

When Dawn and Shaune Shannon gave birth within four hours of each other in Dallas, Texas, on 25 June 1987, it was just another coincidence in a long line. Twins Ronnie and Donnie Shaw had proposed to them on the same day in 1979, the couples married on the same day, honeymooned in the same city and now lived on the same street.

The sisters were due to give birth on the same day, but were both admitted to hospital early, without the other knowing.

Shaune, already the mother of two daughters aged four and one, had a boy, Aaron Michael, and Dawn a girl, Lacey Alexis. She had had a son the previous year.

▶ Dead on Time ▼

Yet another Time Twin story. In New York a furniture manufacturer named Richardson met by chance a man named Negrelli who looked exactly like him. Negrelli was born in Italy on Richardson's birthday. Four days after the chance meeting, Richardson was run over by a car and died two days later. In a different part of the city, Negrelli had been run over by a car and, though this had been two weeks earlier, both Negrelli and Richardson died on the same day as a result of their injuries.

▶ Unrelated but Twins ▼

Another well-known case. On 28 July 1900, at Monza in northern Italy, King Umberto I was introduced to a restaurant owner and commented on how much alike the two of them looked. In further conversation they discovered they had been born on the same day at the same time, had married wives with the same name and both had a son called Victor.

The restaurateur had gone into business on the day the king had ascended the throne of Italy. He told the king he was due to take part in a shooting match the following day in which the king was to present the prizes. The king said he was looking forward to meeting his double again.

However, before the event the king's Time Twin accidentally killed himself while cleaning his gun. The king asked to be taken to the scene of the accident and on the way was himself shot and killed by anarchist assassin Gaetano Bresci.

West and Toonder, in their *The Case for Astrology* (1970), say:

Astrologers . . . insist the documentation is now sufficiently strong to provoke the interest of the scientifically minded. Astrologers are confident that large-scale research would prove beyond a doubt that cases of Time Twins are not ascribable to

*coincidence, and that physical and psychological similarities
could be excepted to recur.*

Like many researchers who believe they are on the point of
validating a new scientific truth, the two writers try to avoid
the role coincidence plays. They might do better to accept the
role of coincidence and look more closely at it, rather than
rejecting it in the hope that this will somehow validate their
findings.

▶ Alikeness ▼

Two unrelated women, both named Edna, met for the first time
in a hospital in Hackensack, New Jersey. Both had been born
on the same day and were now in hospital for their first
confinements. Their babies were born within an hour of each
other and both had been named Patricia Edna in advance.

Both women were married to men named Harold, who had
both been born on the same day. Both men were in the same
business and owned the same make, model and colour car. Both
couples had been married on the same day. Both women had
the same number of brothers and sisters and belonged to the
same religion. Both families had a mongrel named Spot.

That story is from *Case for Astrology*. The book goes on to tell
the following, similar, story with a bit more detail. Joyce Ritter
and Jean Henderson were born within five minutes of each
other in the same nursing home on 20 February 1947. At the
age of six they came to live next to each other in White Plains,
New York. From this time on, not only their teachers but also
their parents had trouble distinguishing between them. They
were remarkably alike physically and also shared the same likes
and dislikes. Both came from families of five children. Both had
fathers who held similar jobs at the same airport.

▶ Generation Gap ▼

For a variation on the sister-birth theme, here is the case of
Cheryl Bushby. Her baby was nine days past its expected birth

date. Then, on 18 January 1985, the baby came with a rush, thus linking three generations of the family – all girls – to the same birth date. Baby Amanda had arrived on Cheryl's twenty-third birthday. Her grandmother, Mrs Shirley Nicholls, had been born on the same day in 1939 and had given birth to Cheryl on her twenty-third birthday. 'It's almost as if she knew,' said Cheryl.

▶ Unknown Mates ▼

Here is a case of two mothers who had never met, yet they gave birth to children on the same dates, twice. On 5 May 1981, Denise Weldon and Cheryl Tynan gave birth at the Baptist Medical Center in Birmingham, Alabama. Weldon had a boy and Tynan a girl.

Twenty-three months later they were back at the same hospital and gave birth again almost at the same time. This time Weldon had a girl and Tynan a boy. All four children were delivered by a Dr Ronald Goldberg. Both had visited him, usually on Mondays, during their pregnancies and both had visited him on the Monday before the birth. Neither of them had ever met.

▶ More Sisters ▼

Three Kelley sisters of New York all became pregnant at the same time in 1981 and, in February 1982, all gave birth within thirty-four hours of each other.

In 1982, Margaret Wright, twenty-seven, and her *older* sister, Dianne, twenty-nine, gave birth together. In October 1984, Margaret was back in hospital about to give birth again, as was her *younger* sister, Wendy, twenty-three. The two went into labour together but Margaret gave birth six hours earlier than Wendy – a boy, Samuel, weighing 4 kilos. Wendy had a girl, Heidi, weighing 3.35 kilos. The two sisters were put in a labour ward side by side, with the doctor running between the two. The women said the double births were entirely coincidental. 'It was a real surprise to me when I found out Wendy was pregnant,' said Margaret. 'We were actually due two weeks apart but we were both praying we'd have the babies together. When it came to the time, our prayers were answered – Wendy was a week late and I was a week early. We both went into labour together. It was a tremendous help to know Margaret was going through labour just as I was. I kept reassuring myself that I would get through it because Margaret was.'

► Double Act ▼

On 30 May 1982, Denise Falster gave birth to twin boys in the Sydney Adventist Hospital, after previously having had two children. Falster's two older sisters, Julie and Jane, each had two children before each gave birth to twins. Falster said: 'The really odd thing is that there is no history of twins in either of our families.'

► Twin Share ▼

On 11 September 1964, Jean Watts was born at 6.25 p.m. and her twin sister Angela, at 6.50 p.m.

On 11 September 1991, Jean gave birth to identical twin boys at 6.14 p.m. and 6.23 p.m.

► Related Coincidences ▼

Similar circumstances to those already discussed appear to be at work in cases involving relatives who have been separated for years and yet find when they meet that their lives are full of coincidences.

One example: Mervyn Conway, forty-four, and Glenn Plath, forty-three, lived in the same Queensland town, Bundaberg, for most of their lives without knowing they were brothers.

Their mother had been forced to have them both adopted at birth. Mervyn and Glenn met as a result of the easing of disclosure restrictions in Queensland's adoption laws in 1991. Among the strange coincidences they found when they compared notes: each brother had a daughter named Amanda Lee and each had lost a brother from their adoptive family in road accidents in the same year, 1967.

Mervyn's first wife had married Glenn's best mate and Glenn had helped Mervyn, a truck driver, unload steel from his vehicle and sign his delivery dockets.

Another case: Judith Robertson was reunited with her brother, Michael Roe, after more than forty years. They too had been given up for adoption. They were struck from the first at the similarities between them: same tastes in music, food and sport. They had each named their eldest son Anthony.

In Robert Ripley's *Book of Chances* there is the story of the 'Jim' twins, who were brought up apart. A 1979 study at the University of Minnesota showed significant coincidences in their lifestyles, including the facts that both had married women named Linda and both had divorced them and married women named Betty. One had called his first son James Alan and the other called his James Allen. Both named their dogs Toy.

▶ Brothers-in-Arms ▼

Two youths walked into the Newport army recruiting office in Wales one morning in 1979. They had never met. However, an NCO noticed they had the same surname and, when he looked up the family details, found they were brothers.

Graham Far, twenty-seven, lived with his father and grand-parents in Newport. His younger brother, Stephen, was brought up in a children's home and was living with foster parents in Gwent, South Wales.

Stephen said he had been told he had a brother somewhere, but did not expect to find him by joining the army on the same day as him!

CHAPTER TWELVE

Famous People

As noted earlier, the philosopher Schopenhauer said the real significance of coincidences exists only in relation to the persons who experience them. However, coincidences affecting the famous, and the infamous, do have a compelling fascination for the rest of us.

▶ Hot Tips ▼

On the day Prince Charles and Lady Di married, 9 July 1981, a quarter of the horse-races in Britain were won by starters with names such as Tender King, Favoured Lady and Wedded Bliss.

Of the 200 horses that ran that day, eleven had 'royal' or other suitable names and, of those, six won or came second in seventeen races at combined odds of 54,000 to one against such an occurrence, and not one was a favourite.

▶ Coincidence Joins PMs' Destinies ▼

On the same day on opposite sides of the world, two women became prime ministers of their country. A woman national leader is rare enough, but the compelling forces behind psychic patterns take no note of percentages – except to defy them, in this case in countries as different as east is to west, with women who were in both cases comparative newcomers to politics.

It began in the Turkish capital, Ankara, on Tuesday, 14 June 1993, when members of the ruling True Path Party voted in Ms Tansu Ciller. Ms Ciller, forty-seven, was adviser to the man she replaced, Mr Suleyman Demirel, who became president.

Only hours later in Ottawa, more than 3,400 delegates to the ruling Conservative Party convention elected the then Defence Minister, Ms Kim Campbell, to the top post. The forty-six-year-old Vancouver lawyer replaced Mr Brian Mulroney.

In both cases, although the polls were held to choose a party leader, each automatically became prime minister.

In her acceptance speech, Ms Campbell told delegates that their task was to win the trust and confidence of their fellow Canadians and to renew in them a new sense of hope for the country. In her speech, Ms Ciller said that the Turkish people wanted and expected change, something new.

▶ Presidents' Tape Talks ▼

In the second week of March 1974, the US House of Representatives judiciary committee instructed its lawyers to subpoena President Nixon's Watergate tapes and documents. Twenty years on, to the week, a special federal counsel under force of a subpoena called for documents and other material such as electronic messages on computers relating to the Whitewater affair, involving President Clinton and his wife, Hillary.

In 1974, the House committee's senior counsel was Bernard Nussbaum. Hillary Clinton had been a member of his staff.

In 1994, Mr Nassbaum was the White House counsel – until forced to quit over his handling of the affair. The White House admitted he removed files from the office of his deputy, Vincent Foster, within hours of Foster's suicide and only very reluctantly surrendered the files. Hillary and her Little Rock law firm were also accused of shredding Whitewater-related documents; Nixon and his staff had been accused of wiping tapes.

▶ Sheep Baaa to Book Vet's Shoo ▼

James Herriot, the veterinary who wrote *All Creatures Great and Small*, which led to the popular TV series, was sent flying by a herd of black-faced ewes in his seventy-seventh year, when he attempted to shoo them from his garden in Thirsk, North Yorkshire, and ended up in hospital with a broken leg.

▶ Coincidence Cost Millions of Lives ▼

In his book *The Occult* (1971), Colin Wilson gives details of some deft detective work he did which shows that, but for a coincidence, the First World War may not have happened! It is an incredible claim. But the components build up in their usual mysterious fashion.

Wilson begins with the point that one of the two main characters in this story is Rasputin, the monk who had so much influence over the last Tsar and Tsarina of Russia. On two occasions Rasputin successfully persuaded the Tsar not to go to war over the Balkans, which were claimed by Austria.

The other character is Archduke Franz Ferdinand of Austria, who was assassinated at Sarajevo by a young Bosnian patriot, Gabriel Princip, in June 1914. As a consequence, Austria declared war on Serbia. This meant the world's destiny was in the hands of the Tsar, for he had to make up his mind whether to stand by Serbia and declare war on Austria or let the Balkans solve their own problems.

This was the point where Rasputin's further advice would have made all the difference between war and peace. Unfortunately, Rasputin was not around to give advice. He had been stabbed by a would-be assassin in his home village of Pokrovskoe and hovered between life and death for weeks.

When Wilson was writing his book on Rasputin, he noted the coincidence - that Rasputin and Archduke Franz Ferdinand had been struck down about the same time. Intrigued, he set about pinning down the timing more accurately. Accounts differed on the date when Rasputin was stabbed. Historian Sir Bernard Pares seemed to think it was Saturday, 26 June 1914. But Maria Rasputin's book on her father states quite definitely that the stabbing took place on the following day. This was made even more likely by the fact that he was stabbed after he had returned from church. This meant that Rasputin was stabbed *on the same day* the Archduke was shot. Maria Rasputin gives the time as shortly after 2 p.m.

As for the Archduke, he had felt certain he was going to die even before visiting Sarajevo, telling his children's tutor: 'The bullet that will kill me is already on its way.'

Shortly after 10 a.m. that Sunday, a home-made bomb was thrown at his motor car but the Archduke and his wife were uninjured. They attended a ceremony in the town hall, leaving half an hour later. It was on the drive back through Sarajevo, at about 11 a.m., that Princip, a consumptive young student involved in the earlier attempt (see next anecdote), leant forward and fired two shots, killing the Archduke and his wife.

There are 50 degrees of longitude between Sarajevo and Pokrovskoe, so the time in the two places differs. Wilson worked out the difference. It is a simple sum: the earth passes through 360 degrees when it does a complete turn in twenty-four hours – that is, 180 degrees in twelve hours, 90 degrees in six hours, 45 degrees in three hours.

So, to turn through 50 degrees it takes exactly three hours and twenty minutes. The Archduke Ferdinand was murdered shortly before 11 a.m. Rasputin was stabbed at 2.15 p.m., and 10.55 a.m. in Sarajevo was exactly 2.15 p.m. in Pokrovskoe.

Wilson concludes: '*The man whose death caused the First World War, and the man who could have averted the war, were struck down at the same moment.* The coincidence is as extraordinary as any I have come across.'

▶ Wrong Turn ▼

While we are on the subject, we should note another extra-ordinary coincidence relating to the assassination of the archduke and his wife (above).

Princip and the other would-be assassins were walking along a street in Sarajevo, bemoaning the fact that their first attempt had left the Archduke and his wife uninjured (shortly after

10 a.m. that morning they had thrown a home-made bomb at the Archduke's car) when, to their amazement, the car appeared again, travelling slowly. Its driver had become lost and had taken a wrong turn – into the very street where the assassins had wandered.

Princip did not let this second opportunity slip by. He leant into the slow-moving car and shot the Archduke dead.

Before the last shot of the First World War had been fired, a further 18 million had died.

▶ The Way of the Dragon ▼

In his short life Bruce Lee rose to international stardom with a series of martial arts films which grossed millions. His sudden death on 20 July 1973, at the age of just thirty-two, sent the media into a frenzy of speculation about conspiracy theories: a mysterious martial arts sect had been hostile to Lee for divulging kung-fu secrets to the West; Triads, the Chinese Mafia, had killed him for refusing to pay protection money . . .

Officially Lee died from an acute reaction to aspirin. On the last day of his life he had been at the film studio, working through the script of his latest movie with his leading lady, Betty Ting-pei, when he complained of a headache and took a break. Several hours later attempts to wake him failed and he was rushed to hospital.

The coincidence in this anecdote came about when almost twenty years later (31 March 1993) Lee's son Brandon, also an actor, also became ill on the set of a movie and died suddenly, reviving once again the bizarre stories about Lee's surprise death.

▶ Touching Time ▼

Hugo Weaving plays a blind photographer in the film *Proof*. In one scene Weaving runs his fingers over his mother's tombstone to feel the date, 15 August 1965. The première of the film was 15 August 1991.

▶ Class Monsters ▼

School class photographs of the young Hitler and the young Stalin bear striking resemblances. The photos were taken when each was about ten, Stalin's in 1889 and Hitler's in 1899. They appear in the centre of the back row of their classes. Each is wearing a distinctive look of defiant superiority that somehow demands attention.

The coincidences do not end there, according to Lord Bullock, author of *Hitler and Stalin Parallel Lives* (1991). Bullock points out both men had bullying fathers and doting mothers. Both were short men, the German dictator 167.6 centimetres and the Russian dictator 162.5 centimetres. Both were women-haters who had female lovers who shot themselves. Neither had much interest in sex. Both were seriously underestimated by their political rivals, who dismissed them as boorish little men. Psychologically they were narcissistic. Neither could handle the slightest criticism. They were revenge-obsessed, nocturnal, anti-Semitic and unpredictable.

Bullock goes into detail of how both men mastered the arts of revolutionary politics; how they were genuises, their timing superb. They were congenitally deceitful and had an instinctive understanding of where power lay. They claimed ultimate power over their separate nations in the same year, 1934.

▶ Why Did Hitler Adopt Chaplin's Mo? ▼

Another astute observer has traced significant coincidences between Hitler and Charlie Chaplin! Professor Harry Geduld of Indiana University points out the coincidences between the dictator and the comic began with the proximity of their births. Chaplin was born on 16 April 1889, in London, Hitler four days later in Braunau-am-Inn, Austria.

Geduld, a prolific author and professor of comparative literature, notes that both were born into working-class families and both (as we saw above with Hitler) had bullying fathers whom they detested and sickly, indulgent mothers whom they adored.

As young men they had artistic aspirations. Chaplin wanted to be England's greatest dramatic actor, Hitler a great painter. Each grew into temperamental adults given to unpredictable, sometimes terrifying, tantrums.

But, says Geduld, the most striking coincidence was their celebrated moustaches. Hitler imitated Chaplin in this, whether he was aware of it or not. Chaplin adopted the moustache in his second film, *Kid's Auto Race* (1914), while Hitler did not trim his moustache into its famous shape until after the First World War, by which time Chaplin had appeared in dozens of movies with his distinctive tache. Geduld says Hitler's motivation for adopting the most famous 'trademark' of a man who exemplified all that he most abhorred is a mystery.

The most intriguing parallel of all, says Geduld, writing in the January/February 1989 edition of the US magazine *The Humanist*, is that both men endure as an image on film.

► London Pride ▼

Charlie Chaplin was born in Kennington, next to the local music hall, in a poor area of south London. Kennington was where fellow actor Michael Caine was brought up. Once, having a nostalgic look around his old neighbourhood, Caine came across Chaplin doing the same thing.

Three years later, says Caine in his book *And Not Many People Know This Either* (1985), he was making a second trip down Kennington's memory lane, when he again found the famous comic doing the same thing.

► The Micklewhite Mutiny ▼

Actor Maurice Micklewhite tells how he came to get his now-famous stage name. In 1954 he had been offered a walk-on part as a prison warder in Jean Anouilh's play *The Lark* – he had to take Joan of Arc to her trial. His agent told the young actor that if he wanted the role, he would have to change his name as there was already a Maurice Micklewhite on his books (incredible as that sounds).

He had until 6 p.m. to come up with another name. He had already decided on Michael, but a suitable surname eluded him. In a coffee bar across from the Odeon Theatre, Leicester Square, the cockney spied the neon title of the film playing there, *The Caine Mutiny*. 'Caine hit me – and it has stuck ever since,' Michael Caine relates in his best-selling book *Not Many People Know That*.

▶ Oppy's Odyssey ▼

In 1931 legendary cyclist Hubert 'Oppy' Opperman was cheered by hundreds of thousands of French people as he rode to victory in the famous Paris–Brest–Paris road race.

The following year he returned to Australia to lead the procession of cyclists at the opening of the Sydney Harbour Bridge – one of Australia's engineering marvels.

Exactly sixty years later, 'Oppy' was back in Paris, where he was presented with one of France's highest honours, the Gold Medal of the City of Paris, to mark the centenary of the race he had won so many years before. As happened in 1931, hundreds of thousands of French people turned out to cheer him.

(In the 1930s, his popularity was so great that more than 1 million readers of the French sporting journal *L'Auto* voted him Sportsman of the Year, ahead of their tennis greats Henri Cochet and Jean Borotra.)

In 1992, at the age of eighty-eight, Oppy led the parade of the first cyclists to open another great Australian engineering marvel, the Sydney Harbour tunnel, built to take pressure off the Harbour bridge he had helped open in 1932.

▶ Blackhead's Return ▼

US General Norman Schwarzkopf, of Gulf War fame, has the same name as the people who created the world's first civilization in that region more than 5,000 years ago.

George Michanowsky, a New York-based specialist in the Sumerian language, says they called themselves Sag-Gig, which translates as 'black heads' and black head in German is *Schwarzkopf*.

► Tony out, Tony in ▼

When international cricket commentator Tony Greig left the Lion Insurance Company, he was replaced by a Tony Gregg.

► Saintly Sinner ▼

The head of the Catholic church in the Philippines is Cardinal Jaime Sin.

► Farewell Festival ▼

For many weeks leading up to the Cannes Film Festival of 1992, France had been bombarded with black-and-white photographs of that epitome of screen glamour, Marlene Dietrich.

Her posters had been chosen as an advertisement for the festival. Just as the festival got under-way, the screen star died in Paris, aged ninety.

► On the Beach ▼

TV star Peter Phelps played an Australian lifeguard in the Hollywood TV surf saga *Bay Watch*. His acting career had begun when a local TV producer spotted him – on a Sydney beach.

► The Return of the Donor ▼

British actor Alfred Molina has long loved and admired the talents of Tony Hancock, whose tragi-comic life came to an end with his suicide in 1968.

Some years ago Molina was having lunch with writer William Hubble and they were swapping anecdotes about the comedian. Molina found himself saying that one day he would like to play the role of Hancock, although there was at the time no plan to make such a film.

Eighteen months later a recently completed script for the film *Hancock* was offered Molina – he was to play the lead role.

Molina's performance in the 1992 film is a *tour de force*. The *Sunday Telegraph* said: 'At moments the impersonation is so true that he seems to have been taken over by the ghost of the man who saw his success as failure.'

Molina denies there was anything supernatural about his performance, but then confesses the incident he most remembers about the film was the re-creation of *The Blood Donor*, one of the most famous comedy sketches written.

They had started filming when somebody pointed out that of all the studios in the BBC, they were working in the one Hancock had used to do the original sketch.

▶ The Ides of Marsh ▼

In February 1992, the day vice-captain Geoff Marsh was dropped from the Australian cricket team, a horse at Werribee in Melbourne called Marsh was scratched along with another named Hits 'n' Memories.

▶ Fixxing It ▼

Jim Fixx, the man who set the world jogging, dropped dead while out on a run.

▶ O Café Man ▼

Actor Malcolm McDowell began his working life as a coffee salesman. In one of his first major films *O Lucky Man!*, he was a coffee salesman.

▶ How People Change ▼

In his best-selling *The Road Less Travelled* (1978), Dr M. Scott Peck tells a story (pp. 258–60) that made him aware small miracles of coincidence can happen at any time anywhere.

Having a couple of hours to spare between appointments in another town, he asked a colleague who lived in that town if he could use his study to work on a book about spiritual growth. At the house the colleague's wife met him. She was 'a distant and reserved woman who had never seemed to care for me very much and had been actually hostile to me on several occasions in an almost arrogant way'.

In a stilted conversation, Peck told her what he was doing there, then retreated to the study. Within half an hour he had run into a snag, a section on the subject of responsibility suddenly seemed to him completely unsatisfactory and would obviously have to be extensively enlarged – yet he felt this would detract from the flow of the book. On the other hand, he did not want to delete the section.

He battled with the dilemma for a frustrating, unfulfilling hour. At this point the wife came quietly into the room. She was timid and hesitant. Respectful yet 'somehow warm and soft, quite unlike in any encounter I had had with her previously', she asked if she was intruding. Peck said she wasn't, that in fact he had hit a problem and was not going to make any progress for the time being.

The woman was carrying a little book in her hands, which she now proffered, saying that she had happened to find it and thought it might interest him, although she was not certain why. Peck was, of course, up to his ears in reference books and he did not see how he would be able to get around to reading it. Instead of rejecting her offer, her 'strange humility' evoked a different response. He told her he appreciated her kindness and took the book with him. That same evening he felt compelled to look at the slim volume, entitled *How People Change*, and to his surprise found much of it concerned issues of responsibility. One chapter in particular eloquently expressed what he would have tried to say had he enlarged the difficult section in his book. The following day he condensed the section of his book to a small paragraph and referred the reader to the other book. His dilemma had been solved.

'The event was both extraordinary and ordinary,' writes Peck. 'Such highly unlikely beneficial events happen to us all the time, quietly knocking on the door of our awareness.'

▶ Stranger than Science Fiction ▼

In the August 1991 edition of *Locus* magazine, Arthur C. Clarke wrote of a coincidence that must have helped cheer him up during his recovery from an operation he underwent at University College Hospital, London, for the removal of a massive diverticulum (bladder extension) and prostate. The operation lasted two and a half hours, was difficult and he lost five pints of blood. When he woke up, he found himself with three tubes inserted at strategic spots.

A few weeks after returning home to Colombo, Sri Lanka, he came across a passage in Ronald Clark's *JBS: The Life of J. B. S. Haldane* (1968):

> Haldane returned to London during the first days of November [1963]. Rather reluctantly, he entered University College Hospital . . . an operation was necessary . . . when he recovered consciousness from the anaesthetic, Haldane wrote to Arthur Clarke, the noted writer of science fiction, he became aware of three tubes which had been inserted into him.
>
> 'I was fed through one into a vein, another went via my nose to my stomach . . . the third was a urethral catheter, which I considered a great luxury. To judge from some S.F. [science fiction] this is a foretaste of the future. What little is left of our natural bodies is to be attached to a variety of gadgets . . .'

Clarke says he had completely forgotten this letter. Reading the passage twenty-seven years later gave him 'a most peculiar feeling'. As he said: 'To have woken up in the same place, with the same number of tubes in me as JBS, certainly does seem to strain the bounds of probability. And there's no way the choice of location could have been an unconscious self-fulfilling prophecy. UCH was chosen by my surgeon . . . and, in fact, as a Fellow of King's College, I feel guilty at defecting to a rival establishment.'

▶ Dark Cloud ▼

British Prime Minister Edward Heath owned three yachts, each called *Morning Cloud*. All were wrecked. In one, two crew members lost their lives. Heath posed for publicity pictures with one of the yachts for a book called *The Prime Minister's Boat is Missing*. Five days later it too was wrecked.

▶ Kennedy Capers ▼

Joe Kennedy, patriarch of the American Kennedy clan, claimed that it cost him $US2 million to seduce Gloria Swanson in 1929. Kennedy Sr chased the 1920s screen idol for months, before inviting her to stay as a guest at the mansion he had bought on North Ocean Boulevard, just outside Palm Beach, in Florida.

Swanson said later that Kennedy Sr had bolted the door of her upstairs bedroom and grabbed her – while she was still holding the suitcases she had arrived with. The price? Swanson wanted her own film company and Kennedy paid for it.

Seventy-two years later, the grandson, William Kennedy Smith, son of Joe's daughter, Jean, found himself in deep trouble when he became involved in just such a brief encounter at the same compound – just beneath the window of the bedroom in the huge mansion where the Kennedy–Swanson coupling encounter had occurred.

Charged with rape, the junior Kennedy was eventually acquitted, but not before he had learned, like his grandfather, the high price of passion.

▶ Rebellious Soul ▼

Errol Flynn's first film was the low-budget movie *In the Wake of the Bounty*, in which he played Fletcher Christian, the leader of the crew members who mutinied against the *Bounty*'s captain, Bligh.

The swashbuckling star was suited for the role. He was descended on his mother's side from Midshipman Young, who was another one of the mutineers. The connection did not end there. One of Flynn's uncles married one of Christian's descendants.

▶ Hollywood Legend ▼

James Dean (1931–55) became a symbol of restless youth, starring in films such as *Rebel Without a Cause*. His early death in a car accident turned him into a figure around whom legends have grown. One of the first concerned the car in which he died. A mechanic who was working on the wrecked vehicle had both his legs broken when the engine slipped and fell on him. It meant he was not there when a fire damaged the workshop.

A doctor eventually bought the engine and had it installed in his racing car. He died in a race shortly afterwards. Another driver had the drive shaft of Dean's car installed in his car; he also died in the race.

Eventually the car was repaired and then sold for display purposes. In Sacramento, California, it fell from its stand and broke the hip of a teenage fan. In Oregon, the truck on which it was being carried smashed through the front of a shop. In 1959, it once again slipped from its steel supports and broke into eleven pieces.

▶ Double Dip ▼

Kelly Hall won an *Achille Lauro* cruise as part of her 1990 Penthouse of the Year prize. While on the cruise in March 1991, she filled in one of those questionnaires about the on-board service, etc., and it was placed in a barrel for a prize draw. Kelly won – the prize, a cruise on the *Achille Lauro*!

The following year, she was back on board, making the most of her recurring prize. She and a friend once again filled in the questionnaire. Came the draw – and the prize was won by the friend.

▶ On Guard ▼

Australia's chief censor, who regulates the amount of sex allowed in cinemas, videos and literature, is John Dickie.

▶ Minister, Minister ▼

A priest serving as education minister in the Nicaraguan government in the 1980s: Father Hernando Cardinal.

▶ Viewed from Afar ▼

In an idle moment theatre critic Andrew Urban flicked on the TV in his hotel room in the French city of Rheims to find the credits of the steamy old Australian soap *Number 96* running. As he settled back, the next thing he saw was his wife, Margaret Louise Keller, who had played a few cameo roles in the long-running series.

Urban picked up the phone and rang Margaret at their home in Sydney and told her that at that moment he had his eyes on her.

▶ Sleeping out ▼

Consider a case involving Jean Harlow, the Hollywood heart-throb who died tragically at the age of twenty-six. Only two weeks after she had been married her husband shot himself. A boyfriend of the woman who later bought Harlow's house was shocked to learn his bedroom was the scene of the shooting and went to stay the night at the house of a friend, Sharon Tate. Coincidence could not have dealt him a worse hand. Charles Manson's band murdered him and four others that night at the friend's house.

▶ *Rescue* Fails to Rescue Rescue Squad ▼

On the night the second series of the international TV hit *Police Rescue* opened in Sydney, the New South Wales government announced it was axing most of its real-life police rescue squads. The series is based on the adventures of a fictitious NSW police rescue squad.

'*Rescue* fails to rescue Rescue,' quipped Steve Bastoni, one of its stars.

▶ Long Shots ▼

Harold Nicolson, in *Small Talk* (1937), tells of an uncanny event involving Bismarck, the nineteenth-century German statesman, which began dramatically in May 1866 with his attempted assassination. Bismarck, then fifty-two, was riding along Berlin's Unter den Linden when student Cohen Blind produced a revolver and fired four times at point-blank range. Despite the closeness, two bullets failed to hit; the third entered Bismarck's shoulder and the fourth his lungs. Eventually the gun used in the attempt was presented to Bismarck as a souvenir.

Nicolson goes on:

> *In 1886, the father of my friend Leopold was staying with Bismarck to whom he was related by marriage. There were several ladies staying in the house, and after luncheon the Princess Bismarck took the ladies around the rooms, showing them the historical objects which they contained. Bismarck himself and the men guests remained in the smoking-room . . .*
>
> *The voices of the ladies could be heard. 'This is the pistol which Blind used in 1866 . . .' There was a murmur of interest, followed by a loud report. Bismarck leapt from his chair and dashed into the adjoining room; the ladies were standing looking at each other in astonishment; a smell of powder hung in the air. The pistol, still smoking, lay upon the ground. The Chancellor gave way to one of his rare outbursts of fury. He thundered, how could anyone have been so foolish as to touch the revolver? It was a miracle that no one had been killed. Never must anyone be allowed to touch that weapon again.*

The story moves on to 1906, some eight years after Bismarck's death. On a wet afternoon, Nicolson's friend Leopold was staying with some other young people at the Chancellor's house. Leopold showed them the study, where the pistol was now kept on the Chancellor's writing desk. He took it up and announced, much as the woman had done in 1886, that this was the pistol Herr Blind had used in his attempted assassination. Leopold then went on to describe what had happened when the women had been inspecting the pistol. He demonstrated how they had 'foolishly' pulled the trigger. With that there was a flash and a report. White-faced, the young people found themselves staring at one another. One of the girls had been slightly hurt in the hand. Leopold was bleeding from a finger and his hand was burnt with gunpowder. The bullet, the sixth and last in the revolver, had embedded itself in Leopold's biceps.

▶ Related Allies ▼

This is one of the most intriguing cases of distant relatives having matters in common. Three of the major figures in the Second World War were related – Winston Churchill, General Douglas MacArthur and President Franklin D. Roosevelt.

William Manchester, in *American Caesar* (1978), says MacArthur was eighth cousin to Churchill and sixth cousin, once removed, to Roosevelt. All were descended from one Sarah Barney Belcher of Taunton, Massachusetts.

▶ Trollope-Inspired ▼

American author Dominick Dunne is one of those creative people who enjoy making life imitate art and art imitate art through coincidence. He wrote three blockbusters in the 1980s, stories that concentrate on powerful people, their money, old and new, interlocking, against backdrops of hushed-up scandals.

Dunne started with *The Two Mrs Grenvilles* (1986), followed by *People Like Us* (1988) and *An Inconvenient Woman* (1990). The first two quickly became TV mini-series.

As an example of the way he mixes his characters, in *An Inconvenient Woman* the Vicki Morgan character, an actor-waiter, at one point does a screen test for a role in the mini-series of *The Two Mrs Grenvilles* that eventually goes to Ann-Margret – as it did in reality.

In *People Like Us*, a financier who goes to jail for insider trading buys a country estate that is the former home of the Grenvilles.

'Life's like that,' Dunne told Phillip McCarthy, the *Sydney Morning Herald*'s New York correspondent in 1990.

> *I am always fascinated by the links between people, particularly in these small rarefied circles we are concerned with here.*
>
> *Actually I stole the idea from Anthony Trollope, whose people come and go through his books, and it makes a point about how interconnected we are. You can be sitting next to a woman at dinner and it turns out her mother has a beach house next to someone you know, or someone infamous. Or your elevator man's sister is the pedicurist of the man you are writing about.*

Dunne makes coincidences happen to his characters the way he has found they happen to him in real life.

CHAPTER THIRTEEN

War

As in peace so in conflict . . . coincidences abound.

▶ Last Toast ▼

Former British intelligence officer Arthur Seaborn was dining one evening in June 1944 at the Tehran Club in Iran with his friend Captain John Holder of the Dorsetshire regiment. At the time, John was aide-de-camp to Major General Lochner while he was on the General Staff HQ for the Persian area.

The purpose of the dinner was to celebrate Holder's engagement to a corporal in the South African Women's Auxiliary Army Service unit, stationed near Cairo.

It was a warm summer's evening and dinner was being served in the garden, where tables were set among the trees and shrubs. On each table stood a small electric lamp in the shape of a candle, providing just sufficient light for the diners to see by.

Seaborn called a waiter and ordered a bottle of champagne. When the waiter had filled their glasses, he raised his and said: 'Well, John, here's happiness and good health to both of you.' But before they could drink the toast, an extraordinary thing happened. The candle-shaped globe of the electric light suddenly popped out of its socket and struck Seaborn's right hand, so that the wine glass was knocked almost from his grasp and its contents were spilled over the tablecloth.

They sat there dumbfounded as the waiter hurried to the rescue, removed the soiled tablecloth and relaid the table, carefully replacing the offending lamp globe in its socket. Seaborn was given a clean glass, which the waiter immediately refilled. Again he raised his glass and began to repeat the toast. Half-way through the second toast everything happened as before. The globe popped out of its socket, only this time it hit and shattered Seaborn's glass.

Holder was considerably shaken, insisting that he was superstitious enough to believe that this startling occurrence was a bad omen for his forthcoming marriage. Seaborn remembers that he was not feeling too happy about it either. He tried to allay the other man's fears, but was not surprised when Holder forbade him from attempting the toast a third time.

Next morning at HQ, an ashen-faced Holder walked into Seaborn's office. He was holding a signal form. The gist of its message was that a military transport plane carrying service personnel from Alexandria to Haifa had crashed the previous day near Cairo at 2015 hours (8.15 p.m.). There were no survivors. Holder's fiancée had been one of the passengers.

They had ordered dinner at the Tehran Club for 8 p.m. hours but had sat down five minutes late. By the time the waiter had brought the bottle of champagne and filled the glasses, it had been right on 8.15 – the exact moment the plane had crashed!

▶ Old Soldiers Never Fade away ▼

In his syndicated column, Canadian writer Allen Spraggett mentions how a chance remark about a wartime comrade led to a curious story. Spraggett said a US government official told him this story.

'I was in Washington for a day on official business and somehow in the course of the conversation the Korean War came up. I said that I had served as a medic in an infantry unit. That led me to mention, for no particular reason, the commanding officer of the unit. I recalled that the last time I saw him he was very badly wounded and was being put aboard a plane to fly him to hospital. He probably died, I said.

'Well, this conversation got me thinking about my commander – for the first time in years. I couldn't get him off my mind. I wondered if he had died after all.

'Anyway, later in the afternoon, on my way to the train, there, sitting in the station, was an army officer who looked strangely familiar. Curious, I couldn't resist going up to him and starting a conversation.

'You guessed it! He was, so help me, the man I'd been talking about earlier. He was alive and well and still in the army.'

▶ That's *Life* ▼

Dick Paget-Cooke was at Eton in November 1937 as a member of the Wall Game XI. Arms linked with his team-mates, he marched on to the field of play as the breeze blew the long purple and white team scarves around their boots. Unknown to the team, a *Life* magazine photographer took a picture.

Just before VE Day, 1945, when Paget-Cooke was a staff officer with 5 Corps HQ, he had permission to pass through Venice, which the last of the German forces had left only a few days before. There he entered a paper shop and saw a *Life* magazine. It hung on a rack near the ceiling. The proprietor dislodged it with a long pole. Paget-Cooke says it fell on to the counter open at a page with the picture of himself walking on to the field at Eton in 1937.

▶ Old Comrades ▼

Retired Lieutenant-Colonel Jim Ellis was interrupted in his home office by the ringing of the phone one evening in June 1989. He left his desk to answer it, but his wife, who had been watching TV, beat him to it. Ellis, now a self-employed farrier, takes business calls on most evenings, so he lingered at the hall phone to see if it was for him. As he did so, he glanced into the sitting room, where the TV was still playing – his night calls seldom give him a chance to watch TV. On the screen was a man he had never expected to see alive again.

'It's him, it's him,' he yelled at his wife, trying to divert her attention to the TV set. By the time she realized what he wanted her to look at, the face had vanished. The man who had appeared so briefly was Nguyen Van Te, who had worked for the Australian army in Vietnam and become close friends with Ellis.

The coincidence had begun in Hong Kong with a story by Australian Broadcasting Corporation reporter Geoffrey Sims about Vietnamese refugees in the Crown Colony. Out of the thousands of people there, he had chosen Te because he spoke good English. Te had revealed his association with the Australian army during the war and had written in the sand on the beach where the interview had taken place the initials of his former commanding officer, whom he wanted to contact. Sims had edited out that segment because he thought it may have been a ploy on Te's part and 'also because we didn't want to look as if we were milking every emotion we could'.

The initials he had written were JE (Jim Ellis), who, moments after seeing Te, was on the phone to the *Report* programme, asking for more information about the man who had worked for him on his two tours of duty in Vietnam. The producer rang Sims at home and Sims admitted he broke down when he heard the news. Te had battled for fourteen years to escape to freedom. Ellis said the Vietnamese would have been a marked man in his own country as a result of his service with the Australians and was surprised he had survived, let alone made a successful escape. By the following year, Ellis had managed to have Te sponsored to live in Australia. Ellis calls that brief glimpse at the TV set one of his most amazing coincidences in an amazing career.

▶ Clarion Call ▼

The following is an extract from *The War at Sea*, edited by John Winton (1967):

Captain Harold Hopkins, RN, relates an incident that occurred when he was officer-of-the watch on the bridge of HMS Cleopatra on 16 July 1943. With one other cruiser and two destroyers, they had spent a tense, sleepless night, patrolling off Sicily to give protection from the sea to the northern flank of the Allied invasion forces.

The captain finally retired 'dead beat' as dawn approached, saying to call him if needed.

Hopkins goes on: 'The melodious swish of the bow wave as we zigzagged at twenty-six knots provided the right background music for the emergence of Mount Etna from the clouds, and, with the exception of Sicily and a few seagulls, there wasn't anything in sight. But I knew some calamity was about to occur. I cannot explain why, but I was positive that I ought to call the captain. I pressed the buzzer, hard. 'What is it, commander?' the captain asked me, speaking through the voice-pipe.

'I don't know,' I replied weakly. 'Everything's quiet and there's nothing in sight, but I think you ought to come up on the bridge.'

As the captain reached the bridge the explosion occurred; a sickening, shuddering explosion which stopped the ship, dead, from twenty-six knots. HMS Cleopatra *listed over to starboard, while the screech of escaping steam drowned the noise of the men tumbling up on deck.*

▶ Leg-endary Flyer ▼

The traditional narrow columns of most newspapers mean a good deal of hyphenation, leading in some cases to some unfortunate howlers. For example, the *Guardian* obituary of the Second World War air ace Sir Douglas Bader referred to him as a 'leg-end in his own lifetime'. Sir Douglas had had both legs amputated.

The same newspaper reported that President Jimmy Carter was being treated for aggravated haemorrhoids by his personal physician, a Rear-Admiral William Lukash.

▶ Fooling the Nazis ▼

Hiltgunt Zassenhaus's brave story of her quiet resistance to the Third Reich, along with a handful of her fellow Germans, is told in her book *Walls* (1974). It is a story replete with timely coincidences. She worked as an official Nazi censor for Scandinavian prisoners. Her job included going to the prisons where they were held. She risked her life by smuggling in food, tobacco, papers and other banned items, and, more importantly, offering them hope that some Germans cared.

On top of this, she had to fit in her medical studies in her home town, Hamburg, which was being bombed almost nightly. As the examinations loomed, realizing how much she had neglected her studies and feeling helpless, Hiltgunt opened a textbook at random and read: "LIGHT. Only the rays with wavelength visible to the eye can be seen. There are other rays, X-rays, ultraviolet and infra-red rays, which the eye cannot see. Still they are there . . .'

The night before the examination, Hamburg was hit by its worst raid to that date and she spent the night in a shelter, unable to sleep. Next day, exhausted, she made her way through rubble, destroyed buildings and still-burning fires on roads crowded with refugees fleeing the city, to the examination room. A professor examined the students in groups. When it came to her turn, the professor asked his question: 'Can you tell me about visible and invisible rays?' She says:

Something happened inside me. It could not be accidental that I was asked this particular question. I heard my voice answering, strong again and without hesitation, 'Only the rays with wavelength visible to the eye can be seen . . .' My doubts and despair were gone, the ruins were only expressions of fear, hate and doubt, of human minds gone astray.

She tells of a later coincidence, when some of the prisoners secretly gave her slippers they had made from heavy felt with a note, 'for the last leg of your journey', meaning the time until the war's end. On her way back to Hamburg that night, the train stopped kilometres from the city; bombs had ripped apart the lines. With a loaded suitcase, she set out to walk the rest of the way. Eventually her exhaustion was overcome by her anxiety to find out whether her mother had survived yet another air raid in their house that had so far miraculously escaped damage. Her feet had given out.

*My shoes felt like a vise, tightly clamped around my swollen feet
. . . then I remembered the green felt slippers in my suitcase,
designated for 'the last leg of your journey'. Strength came
from them and I walked on with renewed vigor.*

▶ Cavalry's Calvary ▼

In British history two famous battles were fought on 25
October, the first in 1415 – Henry V's victory at Agincourt, in
which 1,500 French cavalrymen were killed. Then in 1854
came the Charge of the Light Brigade at Balaclava, during the
Crimean War, in which nearly 250 British cavalarymen were
killed, in less than twenty minutes.

▶ Fighting the Deadline ▼

Correspondents from *The New York Times*, Japan's *Asahi
Shimbun* and the *Sydney Morning Herald* chartered a ten-metre
sloop to sail from Djibouti to Marxist South Yemen, then in
the throes of a bloody coup. After three days' hard sailing
– gale-force winds shredded the mainsail and rough seas
slowed progress – they made it.

Aden, the capital of Yemen, was effectively closed to the
outside world. The three intrepid journalists had the story
to themselves. Survivors told gruesome tales of massacre and
counter-massacre. They were able to verify much of this
and put together what they expected to be acclaimed and potent
firsthand and front-page stories.

On the very day they filed their stories – 28 January 1986
– from the few surviving telex machines, the *Challenger* space-
craft blew up a minute after it was launched, killing all on
board . . .

▶ Driven to Drive ▼

A man who served as a driver in the Royal Marines was named
Maurice Driver – Driver Driver.

▶ Extradition Block(ed) ▼

The defence counsel involved in the extradition proceedings of suspected IRA terrorists from the US was Ira H. Block. (H-block is the notorious wing in the Ulster prison where terrorists are held.)

▶ Battle Days ▼

In the First World War the US forces went into their first major battle on 6 June 1918 – the date now best remembered as D-day, when the American, British and Canadian forces invaded Europe in 1944.

▶ They Call Him Tiger! ▼

Air-force helicopter pilot – Tim Moth.

▶ Love at First Flight ▼

An ex-air-force man, Charlie Clark, told me pilot Dean Swift married transport driver Judy Speedie at his air-force base.

▶ Troubling Note ▼

The man who wrote the lines of the wartime song 'Pack up your troubles in your old kit bag and smile, smile, smile' committed suicide.

▶ Backwater of History ▼

A leading British naval authority between the world wars became known as 'the man who invented the Pacific war', because he devised the basic strategy used by Japan, commencing with the attack on Pearl Harbor. His name: Hector Bywater.

▶ Apt Name ▼

Group-Captain Graeme Killer, a Royal Australian Air Force doctor.

▶ Birch-like ▼

T. E. Lawrence (Lawrence of Arabia) developed a liking for pain after being beaten by Turkish soldiers in 1917. He paid a man to whip him. His name was John Birch.

▶ Escape Notice ▼

The story is told in *Escape and Liberation 1940–45*, by A. J. Evans (1946) of the feat of Wing-Commander Basil Embry in 1940 which is ranked as one of the great escapes in either of the world wars. It was a coincidence that precipitated him into the attempt.

Embry baled out from his Blenheim bomber over France, landing in an orchard near St Omer, and was soon in German hands. Some days later, he was part of a long column of prisoners of war being moved eastwards along a poplar-lined road. Embry had resolved he would make an attempt at the first opportunity.

Suddenly he saw on the side of the road a signpost for a village they were approaching: 'Embry'. He was initially surprised that there was a village carrying the family name. His second reaction was that this was a clear sign he should make his attempt at that moment.

Without hesitation, he dived out of the column and into the ditch beside the road. His problem at this point was that the ditch provided little cover. Yet, incredibly, as though the signpost was in fact a message that providence was watching over him, he lay there for some time as German convoys passed without detecting him.

Finally he made it into some woods. For the next few months, his life was a series of adventures, with good fortune still smiling on him as he made it across occupied France to Spain, then back to England.

If it had not been for that telling moment, he may well have spent the bulk of the war in a prison camp.

▶ Red Beach ▼

In *The Pacific War* (1981), author John Costello tells of an ill-fated attempt by an officer to stimulate his men to storm ashore on the first day of the invasion of Tarawa, in November 1943.

'Come on men,' Lieutenant-Colonel Herbert R. Amey Jr was heard to yell as he waded ashore on Red 2 beach. 'We're going to take the beach. Those bastards can't stop us.' With that, he was cut down by a bullet and fell into the litter of bodies and dead fish staining the shallows crimson.

▶ Just Imagine ▼

In April 1982, author and journalist Max Hastings was sitting at his desk in Northamptonshire, trying to conjure up what it would be like to crouch in a landing craft approaching a hostile shore. He was straining his imagination as he worked on his masterful *Overlord D-Day and The Battle for Normandy* (1984), which began with the dawn landings by Allied forces on French beaches on 6 June 1944.

Less than two months later, 'by an extraordinary fluke of history', he no longer had need of his imagination to provide the picture he sought. As a war correspondent, he found himself crouched in a British landing craft as it approached the Falklands in the South Atlantic.

Hastings writes: 'I had an opportunity to witness an amphibious campaign whose flavour any veteran of June 1944 would immediately have recognized, even to the bren guns, oerlikons and bofors hammering into the sky.'

▶ The Spy Who Came out of the Plot ▼

In June 1957, as Norman Mailer worked on his novel *Barbary Shore* in his New York apartment, a Soviet spy began to emerge in the plot. At first the spy was a minor character, but as Mailer proceeded he became a major one, eventually becoming *the* dominant character.

When the novel was finished, the FBI arrested Soviet master spy Rudolph Abel – who lived in the same apartment building as Mailer.

Mailer, like other writers, had somehow snatched both facts and the future from time and space.

▶ Fighting Family ▼

Over the years three generations of the Jackson family have sailed under the colours of the Royal Australian Navy. In 1942, young sailor John Jackson was in the battle of the Coral Sea, when the combined US–Australian forces took on the might of the Japanese fleet and stopped its southward thrust.

Exactly fifty years later, his grandson, Todd, was involved in joint US–Australian commemorative exercises off the Australian coast, codenamed *Operation Coral Sea*.

Todd is a Gulf War veteran and the third-generation Jackson to have been at war. His father, Peter, did five tours of Vietnam during the 1960s aboard *HMAS Sydney*.

However, it is the links between Todd and his grandfather that are most remarkable. When young Todd joined the navy on 10 January 1989, it was fifty years to the day since John Jackson had signed on. Just eighteen months after Todd joined up he found himself getting his first taste of combat in the Gulf War. The day his ship left Fremantle, the last Australian port of call before setting out to cross the Indian Ocean for the Gulf, it was fifty years to the day since his grandfather's ship had sailed from Fremantle for Britain and his first taste of hostilities.

▶ Single Thought ▼

Fred Howell writes: 'During the First World War "comforts" were sent by members of the public in the UK to troops in the trenches in France. In 1916, William Howell received a packet of 10 Gold Flake cigarettes and had just lit the last one and thrown the empty packet on to the ground when he heard the whistle of an enemy shell. He threw himself on to the ground and right under his eyes was the empty packet and a previously unseen note on its back which read: 'If single drop a line – if married never mind.'

Howell was single and did drop a line to the writer, a Jessie Anne. Some weeks later Howell was gassed and suffered a shrapnel wound to his leg. He was returned to the UK as a stretcher case and ended up in a hospital in Scotland.

A reply from Jessie Anne caught up with him in hospital. She was a nurse at the hospital and delivered her letter personally. Fred Howell concludes: 'William and Jessie became my mother and father, as well as parents of two other brothers and two sisters.'

▶ Co-pilot ▼

Martin Caidin, in his book *Ghosts of the Air* (1991), tells of a letter he received in which Captain Robert Tyler relates this story:

> *I was flying F-100s in the United Kingdom right out of pilot training and, like all good fighter pilots, liked to make the rounds of the English pubs. One night shortly before closing I had an uncontrollable urge to go outside and into a local cemetery. To this day I don't know why, because I don't like cemeteries, and especially wouldn't normally go to one at night.*
>
> *In any event, I was drawn outside and found myself looking at headstones in the moonlight. In fact, I was unerringly drawn to one particular headstone which read: Flt Lt. Robert Tyler, RAF, downed flying Spitfires during the Battle of Britain, 15 September 1940.*

Captain Tyler had been born on 15 September 1940.

▶ Doppelgänger ▼

Private Bill Spencer found himself wandering aimlessly through the streets of Adelaide. Instead of enjoying his twenty-four-hour leave, he was feeling, for reasons he could not fathom, strangely uneasy.

He had an early evening meal and was killing time until he could attend a film or a dance and then return to his anti-aircraft battery at Outer Harbour, on the outskirts of the South Australian capital.

In Rundle Street, which was even in 1945 the main shopping centre, he paused and something made him glance back towards the intersection with King William Street. He noticed a military policeman there with another soldier.

As the two men spoke, they were looking at him and obviously the conversation was about him. He expected the MP to approach and ask for his leave pass. As it was in order, he was not concerned and made no attempt to move away. However, it was the soldier who approached.

Standing directly in front of Bill, he said: 'Good day.'

Bill responded uncertainly: 'Good day.'

The soldier was surprised at Bill's lack of enthusiasm. 'Don't you remember me?'

Bill said he had never seen him before in his life. At this, the other soldier became agitated. 'You *must* remember me. We were in the same tent for six weeks in Rottnest.' Rottnest is a tiny island off Western Australia.

Bill took a step back and told the other soldier: 'I've never seen you before and I've never been out of South Australia in my life.'

Then, to Bill's amazement, the man said: 'You're Bill Spencer, aren't you?'

Bill agreed he was.

At this the soldier became insistent. The same tent. Six weeks. Same name. Why didn't he want to admit knowing him? What was wrong?

As the soldier grew more upset, Bill was at a loss. All he could do was stand by what he had said originally.

Eventually the other man calmed down and went on his way, still obviously thinking he had run into the Bill Spencer he had known on Rottnest.

In 1948, Bill happened to move to Western Australia, where he still lives. He made several attempts to find the man who was both his namesake and lookalike, but without success. At first he assumed the other Bill Spencer had been killed in the last few months of hostilities or had moved elsewhere. But then people started telling him they had seen him in places he knew he had not been. 'Saw you in Perth today', or Victoria Park, or the beach. This has gone on for years. He has made a number of appeals through the WA media, but without success.

'I would like to have found this other Bill Spencer who looks so much like me,' Bill remarked. 'But I'm going on for seventy-six, so there's not much hope now.'

▶ Picking a Picture ▼

In 1978, a Canadian newspaper, the *Moncton Transcript*, in New Brunswick published a feature article based on a long and poignant letter written fifty years before by a Canadian soldier, Private Ronald Blakeney. At the time, he was serving in the trenches at Vimy Ridge. Before the story was published, the newspaper contacted the Canadian Press wire service and asked for photographs depicting a First World War scene, preferably one showing a Canadian soldier. A photograph was selected at random and sent to the *Transcript*. After the story and photograph appeared, a number of people telephoned the newspaper to say they recognized one of the soldiers in the photograph. Of the hundreds of thousands of war photographs, the Canadian Press wire service had chosen to send one clearly showing the author of the letter, Private Blakeney.

▶ The Tsarina is Dead ▼

The tendency to seek signs and portents outside reality became frantic among the Nazi leaders as the end of the war came closer.

Hugh Trevor-Roper, in *The Last Days of Hitler* (1971), recounts that by coincidence in this period Goebbels told Count Lutz Schwerin von Krosigk, the Nazi minister for finance, that he had read to Hitler from Carlyle's *History of Frederick the Great* (Hitler's favourite book).

The extract detailed the desperate situation faced by the

German king (on whom Hitler modelled himself) in the winter of 1761–2, the darkest period of the Seven Years War against Russia. All Frederick's generals and ministers were convinced that he was finished; the enemy already looked upon Prussia as destroyed.

In a letter to one minister, Count d'Aregenson, Frederick gave himself a time limit: if there was no sign of a change in the situation by 15 February, he would give up and take poison. Then, on 5 February, the sign! The Tsarina died. Peter III, who succeeded her to the throne, immediately sued for peace.

Goebbels said the words had brought tears to Hitler's war-weary eyes. All they now needed, he told von Krosigk, was a sign.

Late at night on 12 April came news of the death of the American President. Was this another portent? When he heard the news, Goebbels called for champagne, then made another late-night call to Hitler. 'My Führer, I congratulate you!' he shouted into the telephone. 'Roosevelt is dead. It is written in the stars that the second half of April will be the turning point for us. Today is Friday, 13 April. It is the turning point.'

Some writers say Hitler did take the coincidence of the Tsarina's and President's deaths as corroboration that providence had made a final miraculous intervention. But any exhilaration generated as a result soon evaporated.

Roosevelt's death did not affect the outcome of the war and within days Hitler had done what Frederick had been saved from doing 200 years before – he committed suicide by taking poison, as did Goebbels.

▶ Ghostly Presence ▼

In the march that was finally held to 'welcome home' Australian Vietnam veterans, volunteers carried flags bearing the names of their comrades who had been killed in that bitter war.

One of the volunteers – who gave his name only as Pat when he told his story on a radio programme – said that at the end of the march, while they were still in their ranks waiting to hand in the flags, he had a sudden urge to look around. His attention was caught by a man about a dozen or so rows away whose back was to him and whom he thought he recognized.

Pat moved over to the man and said, 'You're Graeme Belleville, aren't you?' At this the man turned and Pat realized he did not recognize the other man, who said, 'No, but I'm carrying his flag.'

Acting Captain Belleville, thirty-two, from Ballarat in Victoria, was killed at Ai Van Pass on the 'Freedom Road' High-way just north of Da Nang in February 1966. He was awarded the Republic of Vietnam Medal of Honour (First Class).

▶ Coincidence of the Transitory ▼

Arthur Koestler relates in his book *The Invisible Writing* (1954) that during the Spanish Civil War he was imprisoned for three months by the Franco regime as a suspected spy and threatened with execution. The International Red Cross eventually negotiated his exchange for a hostage held by the Republican forces.

As Koestler writes:

In such a situation one tends to look for metaphysical comforts, and one day I suddenly remembered a certain episode in Thomas Mann's novel Buddenbrooks. *One of the characters, consul Thomas Buddenbrook, though only in his forties, knows that he is about to die. He was never given to religious speculation, but now he falls under the spell of a 'little book' – which for years had stood unread in his library – in which it is explained that death is not final, merely a transition to another, impersonal kind of existence, a reunion with cosmic one-ness. Mann continues: 'There clung to his senses a profound intoxication, a strange, sweet, vague allurement . . . he was no longer prevented from grasping eternity . . .'*

Remembering that passage gave Koestler the comfort he needed. The day after he was released, he wrote to Mann and thanked him. The two had never met and, as Koestler adds, it was the first 'fan' letter he had written.

The letter was written from the Rock Hotel, Gibraltar, on 16 or 17 May 1937. The title of Schopenhauer's essay was expressly mentioned in the letter. Mann's answer reached him a few days later in London. Its contents were not easy to forget.

Mann explained that he had read the Schopenhauer essay in 1897 or 1898, while he was writing *Buddenbrooks*, and had never wanted to read it again because he did not want to weaken its original strong impact. The day before, however, sitting in his garden, he felt a sudden impulse to read the essay once more, after nearly forty years. He went indoors to fetch the volume from the library; at that moment there was a ring at the door and the postman handed him Koestler's letter.

▶ Unforgettable Number ▼

Donald Baird has never forgotten this bizarre coincidence, even though it happened to him more than fifty years ago. He had enlisted with the RAAF as aircrew and was posted to Winnipeg, Canada, for training. Shortly after he arrived, he visited the airmen's club, a social meeting place for the enlisted men and local people. A young woman with whom he was dancing invited him to her parents' house for dinner on his next leave. She gave him her telephone number: 403706.

Baird wondered for a moment if she was trying to pull his leg. His air-force number was 403706. But she wasn't and for the next three months he found himself dialling his own number.

The coincidences continue. The woman's name was Jan Crawford, and she had a sister called Eleanor. The name of the girlfriend Baird had left behind was June Crawford, whose sister was also Eleanor. Finally, the airman's club in Winnipeg was in Donald Street.

▶ The Fourth Man ▼

The following is taken from *Escape*, edited by H. C. Armstrong (1935).

Commander H. G. Stoker was a First World War Royal Navy officer imprisoned by the Turks. He made two attempts at escape but was recaptured each time and remained a prisoner until the end of the war.

Stoker first escaped with two other naval officers on 23 March 1916 from the Afion-Kara-Hissard camp in the middle of Turkey, with the aim of reaching the coast, just under 200 kilometres distant. Steering by the stars, they headed due south, walking sometimes above the snow line and struggling to stay warm. After some nights, Stoker poisoned himself when a purifying tablet reacted with the colouring material used in his water bottle and he became delirious. It took some days for the effects to wear off.

On the eleventh night, in an effort to avoid guards, they had to make a forced night march through a pass in the Taurus Mountains, which lay between them and the sea. They were exhausted and dispirited, yet their nerves were taut. They saw the guards' fires and stealthily crept past them. Signals lamps flashed in the dark and gale-force winds whistled through the peaks. Stoker says the effect was one of unreality, like a weird sort of dream bordering on a nightmare.

Then, in the middle of the night, he felt they were not three men struggling along in line but four. A Fourth Man was following at the end of the line. Stoker goes on:

When we stopped for a few minutes' rest he did not join us, but remained in the darkness out of sight; yet as soon as we rose and resumed our march he dropped into his place forthwith. He never spoke, nor did he go ahead and lead us; his attitude seemed just that of the true and loyal friend who says, 'I cannot help, but when danger is at hand remember always that I am here to stand – or fall – with you.'

Stoker had at first thought he was again delirious and did not mention the 'presence' to the other two. Some hours later, they had made it safely through the pass and were resting in a safe hiding place. Then one of his companions mentioned that he had seen the Fourth Man and the other officer also admitted seeing him. All three had seen the man during the moments of greatest danger that night.

We were agreed as to the effect his presence had on each of us individually – the sense of friendliness and comfort; we were agreed that the moment he left us was when we felt we had put the danger behind.

In fact, their 'lucky' Fourth Man had left them too early. From that point on their progress slowed, they were captured by brigands, threatened with death, robbed, then released and finally, within sight of the sea, were recaptured by the Turks.

After the war, seeking an explanation for the eerie presence, Stoker came across Sir Ernest Shackleton's book *South* (1919), which describes how the Antarctic explorer and two companions crossed South Georgia in a desperate attempt to find help for his marooned party. Stoker found this passage:

I know that during that long and racking march over the unnamed mountains and glaciers of South Georgia it seemed to me often that we were four, not three. I said nothing to my companions on the point, but afterwards Worsley said to me, 'Boss, I had a curious feeling on the march that there was another person with us.' Crea confessed to the same idea.

Stoker found the coincidence striking: that in two cases, three men battling against hardships and in fear of their lives, one in Asia Minor in April 1916, the other thousands of kilometres distant in South Georgia in May 1916, should feel the reassuring presence of a Fourth Man.

▶ Peeled off ▼

In *The Anzacs* (1978), author Patsy Adam-Smith tells an eerie tale concerning a relative in the Gallipoli campaign.

In the disastrous attack by the Australian troops on the Nek on 7 August 1915, hundreds of men died, among them her cousin Mick Byrne. On hearing of Mick's death, her Aunt Anastasia cried out a seemingly irrelevant remark, 'He must have taken his jacket off.'

There was a legend he had been born with a caul covering his face – the skin some babies do not slough naturally which is removed by the midwife. The caul has been revered through the ages as a protection against sudden death.

Adam-Smith says that Aunt Anastasia had told her that when Mick went to war, she had stitched his caul in the left breast pocket of his jacket.

'In August 1975, when I was on the Nek it was humid and heavily hot. I removed my jacket and suddenly remembered the photographs I'd seen of the troops waiting for the hop-over on 7 August 1915 – they were all without jackets under the hot sun.'

► The Shot Not Heard around the World ▼

In an essay he wrote in 1931, Winston Churchill illustrates with a compelling personal story the way chance can change the course of history.

In 1899 Churchill, then twenty-five and a war correspondent in South Africa, went on a reconnaissance mission with a force led by Captain Haldane (who as Lieutenant-General Sir Aylmer Haldane led the British Sixth Corps in the First World War). This particular mission took the form of an armoured train of five wagons carrying 120 men. The engine propelling the wagons was placed in the middle to prevent it being derailed while running over any sabotaged track.

In the event, the Boers ambushed the train by placing a rock on the line, thus blocking it. In the ensuing fight Churchill climbed in and out of the engine cab a number of times as he helped clear the line while under heavy fire. His Mauser pistol kept getting in his way, so he removed it. The essay goes on:

> But for this I should, forty minutes later, have fired two or three shots at twenty yards at a mounted burgher named Botha who summoned me to surrender. If I had killed him on that day, 15 November 1899, the history of South Africa would certainly have been different, and almost certainly would have been less fortunate.
>
> This was the Botha who afterwards became commander-in-chief of the Boers and later Prime Minister of the South African Union. But for his authority and vigour, the South African rebellion which broke out at the beginning of the Great War

might never have been nipped in the bud. In this case, the Australian and New Zealand Army Corps, then sailing in convoy across the Indian Ocean, would have been deflected from Cairo to the Cape. All preparation to divert the convoy at Colombo had actually been made. Instead of guarding the Suez Canal, it would have fought with the Boer insurgents. By such events both the Australian and South African points of view would have profoundly altered. Moreover, unless the Anzacs had been available in Egypt by the end of 1914, there would have been no nucleus of an army to attack the Gallipoli Peninsula in the spring and all that tremendous story would have worked out quite differently. Perhaps it would have been better, perhaps it would have been worse. Imagination bifurcates and loses itself along the ever-multiplying paths of the labyrinth.

But at the moment when I was climbing in and out of the cab of that railway engine in Natal, it was a thoughtless and unwise act on my part to lay aside the pistol upon which my chance of escape from a situation in which I was deeply compromised might, in fact, in a very short time depend. No use to say, 'But if you had known with your foreknowledge that he was not going to shoot you and that the Boers would treat you kindly, and that Botha would become a great man who would unite South Africa more strongly with the British Crown, you need not have fired at him.' That is not conclusive.

. . . If I had kept my pistol I should have been slower getting in and out of the engine, and I might have been hit by some bullet, which as it was missed me by an inch or two, and Botha galloping forward in hot pursuit of the fugitives from the wreck of the train might have met – not me with my foreknowledge but some private soldier with a rifle who would have shot him dead, while I myself, sent with the wounded into the unhealthy Intombi Spruit Hospital at Ladysmith, should probably have died of enteric fever.

No need to point out that the world today would be a very different place had the young Churchill himself succumbed in that skirmish, or as a prisoner. Some would argue, as he himself says, 'Perhaps it would have been better, perhaps it would have been worse'. As it was, he was captured on that day, although he escaped and made his way back to British lines.

In his essay, Churchill reflects on the question of whether he would like to live his life over again, retaining his memory of his present life so as to profit by his own experience. He concludes that life is made up of such incalculable chances that it would be impossible to profit permanently by any single piece of knowledge.

You might win a fortune by betting on one Derby whose outcome was known to you, but your action would so influence bookmakers and owners that next year's winner would be different from what it was in your first life . . .

▶ Ghostly Gordon ▼

Judith Oliver of Rochester, Kent, told me the following story concerning her and the legendary nineteenth-century soldier General Gordon.

She was born in her grandparents' home in Sheffield in 1947, when there was a shortage of maternity hospital beds in the post-war baby boom.

'The house was in Khartoum Road, so you can guess when it was built,' she commented.

(For those whose British history may be a little weak, Charles Gordon was killed in 1885, while defending Khartoum against Arab rebels.)

Oliver goes on: 'When I was nine months old my father was one of two soldiers sent on some mission or other to Khartoum, returning when I was eighteen months old.

'When I was about five, he was transferred to Yeovil, an army camp in the south-west of England, and we were allocated a privately rented house about ten miles away from – lo and behold – General Gordon's old home, a Georgian pile called The Chimes.

'In the entrance hall there was a bust of the General which was so strong a likeness of my father that most visitors thought it was him and asked who the sculptor was.

'That seemed to be it until 1972, when I moved to Kent and found this town is riddled with relics of Gordon's life.

'The small hotel about 100 yards down the High Street is

named after him and there are hundreds of other references. It seems he did his Royal Engineers training here before going off on his travels.'

▶ Name, Rank and Numbers ▼

A letter to the *Sunday Times* from former soldier D. J. Page of Surrey tells of the coincidences that ensued when in July 1940 another soldier opened an envelope containing his wedding photographs.

The soldier was in another troop and the mistake was not surprising seeing that both their names and numbers were so similar. The other soldier was Pape, No. 1509322; Page's number was 1509321.

After the war, Page went to work for London Transport as a bus driver. The letter goes on:

> *One particular pay day I noticed that the tax deduction was very heavy and complained. Imagine my amazement when I discovered that my wages had been mixed up with a driver who had been transferred to the garage . . . the very same chap from my army days. The weirdest thing of all, our licence numbers were: Page 29222 and Pape 29223.*

▶ Muddy Meetings ▼

George Best was a private with the Sherwood Foresters in the First World War. He and another soldier from the regiment were fleeing the Germans, when the other man slipped and ended up face-down in the mud.

Best helped his colleague to sit up. He had hurt his ankle and told Best to leave him. With the Germans closing in, it was the obvious thing to do. In the end, however, both were captured, although sent to different POW camps.

Best, in fact, escaped three times, and bore a small scar on his face for the rest of his life, a reminder of the rifle butt a German guard had smashed into it.

In 1929, Best and his wife were visiting relatives in Leicester for Christmas. The ex-soldier and one of the male relatives went to a football match. As the one-sided match drew to a close, they joined the growing exodus. Suddenly there was a commotion behind him and Best turned to see a man had slipped and was lying face-down in the mud. Best bent to assist the man and found himself looking at the soldier who he had last seen in that position shortly before the two of them were captured in 1917.

CHAPTER FOURTEEN

Premonitions

I don't go out of my way to collect premonitions as such. However, within the space of two days, I heard from people with tales of personal premonitions which they considered were coincidences. In each case, the experience had profoundly affected them. Their stories are too intriguing for anyone to argue against their inclusion in this book on grounds of terminology. The coincidence of timing, with the stories being related consecutively, even although those involved were unknown to each other, is enough of an example of the Clustering Effect to justify inclusion.

In the first case a film producer – I will call her Wanda – attended a weekend seminar at which a personable man with a good sense of humour and an easy-going manner impressed others – especially the women present.

After the first day Wanda had a dream which disturbed her. In it the likeable man appeared and started pushing her violently across the room. She was upset by the dream; no one had treated her in such a manner in real life.

On the final day of the seminar, she found herself instinctively steering clear of the man – and feeling guilty about it, which annoyed her, because he was as pleasant as he had been the previous day and she could not reconcile him with the angry man of her dream. Nevertheless, whenever he showed any interest in her, she became distant, while telling herself she was being foolish.

Some weeks later she rang a friend, who happened to be about to take a distressed and injured friend to the doctor's.

This friend's husband had beaten her, and not for the first time. Wanda found herself asking for the name of the culprit. The friend told her. It was an unusual name – that of the man she had dreamed of, a true Jekyll and Hyde character.

The following day I was given the next two premonition-coincidences within the space of a few hours.

▶ Face of the Future ▼

Canadian social counsellor Dorothy Herron had a dream which had a very strange outcome. She found herself in a bathroom with her mother. They were both staring into the bathtub. In the water was the head of a child with black hair looking up at them, a stream of blood laced around its neck. The dream was so chilling it left her disturbed for some time. In fact, some months later, her daughter visited and Dorothy warned her to be extra careful with her children in the water, so convinced was she that what she had seen was some kind of premonition. It was, but not the way Dorothy thought.

About a year later, when Dorothy had virtually forgotten the dream, she had a call from a friend in an advanced stage of pregnancy at the birthing centre of a local hospital. The friend asked her to bring some clothes to her.

When Dorothy arrived the baby was on the point of being born and the centre's staff and the father invited her to stay and witness the event. Dorothy was both surprised and pleased. Before she knew it, she was shown into a room where the mother lay in a bath filled with water.

As she watched, the scene she had first seen well before the mother had become pregnant repeated itself: the baby emerging under water from her mother's womb had black hair and a ring of blood around its neck and it looked up into her eyes.

▶ Dream of Terror ▼

The second intriguing account on the same day as the above came in a letter from solicitor Otto Stichter. The letter was waiting for me when I arrived home from my meeting with Dorothy at which she gave me the previous item.

Otto, admitting he is somewhat of a sceptic, wrote that he and his wife live about a couple of kilometres or so from the Strathfield Plaza in Sydney. She has two children from a previous marriage – a daughter, aged sixteen, and a son, aged twelve, Matthew. The family often went to the plaza and usually stopped for coffee and something to eat at the coffee shop.

In the early hours of one winter's morning, Matthew knocked at his parents' bedroom door and said he had had a bad dream and was frightened. 'We took him into bed with us and comforted him,' Otto wrote. 'He seemed quite distressed.'

Matthew went on to describe the dream with these words: 'We were sitting in the coffee shop and a man with a rifle started shooting people.'

On Saturday, 17 August 1991, Wade Frankum, thirty-three, murdered one young girl with a knife and killed six with a semi-automatic rifle. He injured seven other people before turning the gun on himself. His rampage began in the Strathfield coffee shop.

Otto clearly remembers Matthew saying *the* coffee shop. They had all known which one he meant. When Matthew heard news of the massacre, his words were, 'It's just like my dream.'

Would-be sceptic Otto sums up: 'Whenever I have heard of these stories, I have always dismissed them with the thought, it's easy to say *after* the event that someone had a dream about it beforehand. However, this dream by Matthew was told to me before the event and I am therefore not able to dismiss it in the same way.'

▶ What Are the Differences? ▼

Some researchers invoke the word 'premonition' to discredit coincidences, and indeed the psychic world in general. Apart from these deliberate attempts to blur the definitions, there is some general confusion about what counts as premonition and what as coincidence, and this cannot be easily sorted out.

Certainly, similar emotions can be aroused by both premonitions and coincidences – illogical feelings that may lead to,
or reinforce, a belief in a sixth sense. However, anyone
who experiences a *significant* premonition will be in no doubt
about it. Unlike coincidences, which are so often wry and
amusing, premonitions are mostly full of foreboding and
portent. Those experiencing them find they cannot dismiss
them as nightmares or a sudden, involuntary surfacing of
hidden fears or fantasies, and I speak personally here. Like
coincidences, premonitions can relate to something happening acausally in a different space at the same time. However,
unlike coincidences, premonitions can be visions seen as
though they were occurring in clear view when, in fact, they
occur at some later moment. Coincidences generally lack the
element of foreboding.

Let's now consider some further examples. As we do, you may
want to make your own judgement as to which category these
anecdotes fall into – remembering that coincidences can be
found in that mysterious borderland described by Arthur
Koestler as shrouded in fog which blurs the front between
chance and design . . . which may be the place that we also find
premonitions.

► Relative Read ▼

Flora O'Dea seldom reads a newspaper on Sundays. But one
Sunday in December 1990, on the way to a Christmas party,
she felt an urge to buy one. In it she found an advertisement
placed by Martin Cochrane, asking readers to contact him if
they had information on Sir James Martin. Cochrane is an
ancestor of Sir James; so is O'Dea.

► Fired Her Imagination ▼

Penny Evershed was driving home on 31 March 1990, when
she happened to look back towards the city. Just to the south of
it, she saw a huge red glow in the sky. 'It was from a large fire,'
she said. 'I have been in a couple of them so I know what a big

one looks like.' Once home, she told her mother and they turned on the TV, but saw no mention of it in the news programmes. Penny thought no more about it until the next night, when she was again watching TV and saw scenes of a big fire on the south side of the city, exactly like she had seen the previous night.

A gas container had exploded and hundreds of homes around it had to be hurriedly evacuated in a major operation.

Over the years there have been attempts to harness premonitions as forewarnings of catastrophic events, but unfortunately with little success. Too often the details have been vague, or understandable only in hindsight, as was Penny's fire vision.

▶ The Final Deliverance ▼

One day in 1984, television news producer Judith Rogers awoke with a start. She had just 'seen' the final scene from the movie *Deliverance*, directed by Sam Peckinpah, in which the hand of a drowning body clutches at the air while the river swirls around it. At work that day she glanced at the teleprinter as bells rang to denote a newsflash item – the story was announcing the death at the age of fifty-eight of Peckinpah.

▶ My Firsthand Account ▼

My personal premonition story begins on the night of 1 June 1983.

I was asleep. What I experienced was a typical traumatic premonition that forced me awake with a feeling of being greatly disturbed. The time was 1.45 a.m. I had an urgent need to write down as fully as possible the details of the experience and searched around for paper and pen. As I wrote, I found I could not shake off the feelings of fear and remorse – remorse because I felt there was something I could have done but failed to do.

The premonition in the early hours of that morning related to an event that happened within the next few days. Here are extracts of what I frantically scribbled a few minutes after awakening – I still have the original papers.

> *Nightmare garbled but I was waiting in some kind of office, hotel or boarding house, near a port, harbour or beach on an assignment to do with murder inquiry – six women. Phone rings. I'm called to it. Voice that fills me with chill speaks. Gives his name, but can't hear it properly . . . attempt to write . . . Man on phone becomes exasperated as I can't get name right.*
>
> > *'Oh, look, you're . . .'*
> >
> > *'No, no, sorry, too much noise here.'*
>
> *Says he knows about murders . . .*
>
> *I have written down Fredirickstein [later I remembered that I first got Frei. . .Stein. It was something in between I could not get, before settling on Fredirickstein]. His voice not quite foreign, I say: 'You're him, you're the killer.' He grows anxious, then I hear sirens, black police car . . . vehicles coming as I look out window. Voice grows anxious, then hangs up.*
>
> *Wake up feeling frightened, still chilled by voice of man.*
>
> *Remember initially Fredirickstein . . . killed six. Also remember in hubbub that someone in room says that could [or must be] him [man on phone].*

A few days later, on 4 June, I read a brief item in the stop press of a newspaper under the heading 'Six Shot Dead in School Rampage':

> *Six people, including three children, were killed yesterday when a man with a gun opened fire in a school at Eppstein outside Frankfurt, West Germany. The others killed were a teacher, a policeman and the gunman. Thirteen children were wounded, two of them critically. The gunman apparently was trying to take hostages. He shot himself dead as police closed in.*

I turned to another newspaper and on page 8, under the headline 'Children Shot', was this story:

> *Five people, including three children, were shot to death and 11 injured today by a gunman who burst into a school classroom and then took his own life, police said.*

One teacher, three children and a traffic policeman were killed by the man in the Freiherr von Stein *[my emphasis] school in Eppstein-Vockenhausen, a suburb on the north-west of Frankfurt.*

The following day, 5 June, this story appeared with a picture:

This was the heart-rending scene yesterday as a father was reunited with his daughter. She was one of the survivors of a school attack by a Czechoslovak psychology graduate who killed three children and two adults in the small town of Eppstein, West Germany.

Police said the killer, Kared Charvas, fired about 40 bullets into crowded classrooms of the Freiherr von Stein school yesterday before shooting himself.

A police spokesman said a search of the Prague-born gunman's Frankfurt home produced no clue to his motive.

When I look at what I 'received', two things are instantly confirmed:

1. The number of dead: I had written 'murder inquiry – six women' originally, but changed this at the end of that scribbling to just 'six dead', without being aware of it at the time.
2. The name: Fredirickstein is a close approximation of the school's name and in any case, having no other clues to associate it with Germany, it was to me a nonsense name.

► More June Doom ▼

A young New York businesswoman had a dream with which I can relate, not only because of the date but also because there are some similarities about the details I find personally eerie (see previous story).

On the night of 4–5 June 1968 (my premonition referred to an event that took place on 4–5 June 1984) she dreamed that she too was on the phone. On the other end of the line was her business partner, who said: 'We think you should know this

– Mr Keller was shot last night.' Keller was the firm's accountant. She, like me, woke greatly disturbed and it was some time before she managed to get back to sleep.

In the morning the phone woke her once more. It was her partner, who told her that Robert Kennedy had been shot; Keller was not harmed. She felt then that her dream had been a confused message about Kennedy's death, as I had felt my dream telephone call was a premonition of violent death. The names Keller and Kennedy being similar, she had simply substituted them. Robert Kennedy was killed on 5 June 1968 in California.

▶ Premonitions Bureau ▼

An article in *Family Weekly* on 4 May 1968 tells the story of a London piano teacher who reported 'seeing' Senator Robert Kennedy being shot (see previous story). She said at the time that she felt it would happen while he was on a tour of the western US. She had received one earlier premonition of the shooting and had had two since, on 5 and 11 April.

▶ Rue Regicide ▼

On 18 January 1935, the London *Evening News* ran a story about an expatriate Englishman identified only as H. Richards of Dieppe, France.

The report said he had warned French authorities about the assassination in Marseilles of King Alexander of Yugoslavia and the French Foreign Minister Louis Barthou. On 9 October 1934, a revolutionary associated with a Croat terrorist group had gunned down the two men in a Marseilles street. The king and the politician had been on a tour of Europe in quest of an alliance against Nazi Germany.

The *News* reported that the night before the assassination, Richards had gone to Paris for a visit. In his hotel room, between 2 a.m. and 3 a.m., he had had a vivid dream in which two men were shot in a street he could not recognize in a town that was also unknown to him.

Richards did recognize one of the victims, Barthou, from pictures he had seen often in the newspapers. The other he identified as the king from pictures in the following morning's newspapers.

The Briton told his friend, one of the chiefs of the Sûreté Nationale, of his dream. The official was not a sceptic and recognized Richards's description of the street he had seen as being in Marseilles. The official phoned his colleagues in that city but was laughed at. That afternoon brought the tragedy exactly as Richards had foreseen.

This could all be considered pure premonition, except that, unbeknownst to Richards, his hotel had given him the room that had been occupied the night before by one of the conspirators in the plot.

▶ King's Premonition ▼

While many people have predictions and premonitions about the deaths of the leaders of countries, one leader had one about the death of his dog. The feeling of foreboding for long-serving Canadian Prime Minister Mackenzie King began when his watch fell to the floor, the hands stopping at 4.20 a.m.

King, who denied he was psychic, nevertheless said: 'I knew, as if a voice were speaking to me, that Pat [the dog] would die before another twenty-four hours went by.' During the night, Pat crawled into his master's bed, and died there at 4.20 a.m.

Talking of animals, it is often argued that they possess abilities of prediction and/or premonition as great as those of humans. The next few cases back the claim . . .

▶ No Walkies ▼

In 1965, the San Francisco *Call-Bulletin* ran an item with strong tones of premonition. It involved a woman named Welcome Lewis and her boxer dog.

Lewis, from Los Angeles, brought her dog with her on a visit to San Francisco. She took him to the city's Lafayette Park for exercise. However, the boxer refused to leave the car. He barked and became quite agitated. So Lewis took him back to her hotel, where the dog leapt quite happily from the car. The following day she was driving past the park and saw that a huge tree had fallen on a car in the exact spot where she had parked with the reluctant dog. Lewis also discovered the tree had fallen just minutes after she had driven away.

▶ Deserting Rats ▼

Actor Raymond Massey and his wife told Broadway columnist Danton Walker a tale of apparent animal premonition during the 1940s. They bought a town house in Manhattan's East 80s. Across the street was a large brownstone mansion unoccupied when they moved in, but later bought by a socially prominent woman.

She told the Masseys she could not get rid of the hordes of mice in the building. A few days later, the Masseys were astonished to see a mass exodus of mice from the house, as though they were panicky and confused. Several days afterwards the woman committed suicide.

The building stood empty for a time, but was finally sold to a 'wealthy playboy'. His death made front-page news, but before it did the Masseys once again saw a frantic exodus of mice from the building.

The next owner was a prominent businessman. One morning while tending to plants in a windowbox, Mrs Massey again saw an exodus of mice. A few days later the businessman, flying his own plane, crashed into the Hudson River and drowned.

▶ When the Ivory Crumbles . . . ▼

At the end of a visit to New Zealand, Sir Michael Young was about to fly out of Auckland on his way to Canada when a premonition convinced him to change his travel plans. A miniature ivory elephant his mother had given him as a good-luck charm had inexplicably crumbled to dust in his pocket and he took this as an omen.

He arranged to travel by sea. When the ship arrived in Sydney, he learned that the plane he had been due to catch had crashed into the Pacific. All on board had perished.

▶ Death Vision ▼

Comedian Michael Bentine writes, in his book *Doors of the Minds* (1984), of the stark visions he began having while with Bomber Command in England in 1943–4. This was the height of the winter bombing operations against Germany, when losses among air crews were high.

Bentine says that he would know immediately he saw the crews at their meal before an operation which ones would die that night – their faces would change into a skull. His 'dreadful' experience was 100 per cent accurate and, although he tried desperately to shut it out, he had too close a rapport with the air-crew members to avoid them.

▶ Visions of Mirages ▼

Tom Hamilton, a long-serving member of the Royal Australian Air Force, was not aware of Bentine's premonitions (see above) when he gave me the following account of his own frightening premonitions.

'As early as 1966 I was walking past the Wagga base canteen when I had the distinct picture in my mind of a Rolls-Royce Dart engine attached to a burning wing. That afternoon a commercial airline Vickers Viscount crashed near Winton, Queensland (nearly 1,600 kilometres north of Wagga) with the loss of all on board. The Viscount is fitted with Rolls-Royce Dart engines.

'From Wagga I was posted to Williamstown. One night I was walking back to my quarters when I pictured a Bristol Britannia crash while landing. The Britannia had an enviable safety record to that time, but had been overtaken by pure jet-engined planes. Within months of my vision, no fewer than three

Britannias were involved in major accidents. This incident disturbed me and I mentioned it to a priest who was a very close friend. He told me such phenomena were not unknown when someone was as close as I was to the subject matter.

'Some months later, as I was driving down the Mirage flight line at Wiliamstown, I visualized a Mirage crashing into the sea. The odd thing was that the plane was camouflaged. All Mirages were silver. However, unknown to me the air force had begun painting its ground-attack Mirages and at the time had two in service.

'That afternoon Wing-Commander Vance Drummond, a Korean War POW and veteran of several hundred missions in South Vietnam, had broken formation and dived into the seas, flying one of the camouflaged craft.

'Two months later I had a "vision" of a Mirage crashing behind the married quarters. The next morning one crashed and the pilot, a flight-lieutenant, was killed. The crash took place in the spot I had seen in my vision.

'In 1977 I had a premonition of an aircraft aborting its landing and the two crew successfully ejecting at low level. The next day a crash took the life of a pilot. Later that day I was discussing it with the base printer and pointed out it had been nothing like my premonition.

'But two months later a twin-seat Mirage crashed and its crew escaped in the same circumstances I had envisioned. Since then I have been spared further incidents.'

▶ Knowing the Way in Bombay ▼

The Reader's Digest book *Into the Unknown* (1982) quotes the American writer William Chapman White as the source for this story of what I would call instant premonition (come to think of it, 'instant premonition' is a handy – and English – way of describing *déjà vu*). It concerns an American couple, Mr and Mrs Bralorne, who were on a cruise in Indian waters. They went ashore at Bombay, a city they had not visited before.

The husband found himself saying as they walked along a street, 'When we round the corner we'll come across the Afghan church.' They did. Shortly afterwards he said they would be coming to De Lisle Road. They did. He continued to identify every street and every building as though he had lived there all his life.

They asked a policeman if there was a big house at the foot of Malabar Hill with a large banyan tree in front. The officer told them there had been such a house and tree but both had been torn down years before – his father had worked as a servant in the house, which had belonged to a family called Bhan. Bhan? The couple had named their son Bhan Bralorne for no other reason than it seemed most fitting.

▶ **Warning Signs** ▼

Pamela Biron is a happily married mother of five adult children and has six grandchildren. She is also one of those people whose senses are extra alert.

She recalled that when her children were young she decided to take them to visit the grave of her mother. It had been quite an effort to organize the five children – the youngest was then only a baby – but finally they made it to the cemetery. At first she had not been able to find the plaque and they began searching randomly. Then, on impulse, Mrs Biron looked down and found she was standing directly over it.

She goes on: 'As I lay the flowers, all other thoughts left my mind except one, which seemed to suddenly appear: "Go home right now, you left the saucepan boiling on the stove." Somehow I knew it was Mum who made me remember this. We left immediately and arrived home just in time as the saucepan was bone dry . . . I felt very grateful to my dear mum.'

Later, in a dream, Pam Biron saw herself wandering around the family home holding an electric frying pan and warning some of her grandchildren to be careful of it. The following Saturday two of her married children called with their grandchildren and they sat around the dining table talking.

Suddenly one of the children said he smelt smoke. They dashed around and found that an old frying pan containing a heat pad which her husband used for back pain was plugged into a socket. Both pad and pan were burnt to crisps. They were able to smother the flames before the house went up.

▶ Tales on the Air ▼

I have heard some strange tales of premonition from listeners when taking part in radio programmes. Here are some examples.

Stephanie told the story of an incident when she was twelve and driving with her father. About twenty minutes into the journey, she had a sudden urge to ask him what would happen to the car if the brakes failed. Her father outlined some of the emergency steps that could be taken. Then the brakes on the car did start to fade! By the time they returned home there was hardly any brake power left.

'My father was not pleased with me. He thought I had cut the cable,' Stephanie, now a grown woman, recalled with a laugh. Then she added the strange punch-line: next day a mechanic was called in and he found there was absolutely nothing wrong with the brakes.

'Ian' told the programme about how he was in the merchant navy in 1933 as an apprentice. On his first voyage he sailed from Melbourne to London. One morning, while docked in London, he was sleeping in his bunk when his brother, who was only four and a half years old, appeared to him. 'I saw my brother as clear as a bell, standing in front of me, with a light, of all things, and he said, "Ian, don't worry, I'm not with you any longer, but I'm all right." It was so vivid it woke me up. One of the other apprentices came and asked what was wrong with me, had I been drinking? I told him I had had a weird dream about my brother, who was back in Melbourne. He said, "Oh, go back to sleep."'

The ship returned to Australia via Liverpool and Canada. It had been docked at its first home port of call, Brisbane, only a few minutes when the captain sent for him. He sat him down and told him the sad news that his brother had died of pneumonia in the Melbourne children's hospital while he had been away.

When the family told him the exact time of death, it was the very moment that his brother had appeared to 'Ian' in London. 'I have never forgotten that and I have never had anything like it happen to me since,' he said of the event sixty years before.

A third caller, 'Irene', had yet another story of a premonition of death, which you may have gathered by now is one of the most common forms of premonition.

One Friday night she and her husband found that neither of them was able to sleep. About 11.30 p.m., they decided to make some tea. They sat sipping and talking and suddenly found themselves concentrating on a cousin of hers – what a good person he was, how much he had helped everyone. At midnight the phone rang. It was the cousin's relatives to say he had just died suddenly.

'Margaret' related how, in the middle of the night, she was awoken by a white light in her bedroom. At the same time she heard her grandmother's voice, as though she were passing above the house, calling out, 'Goodbye, Kissy' (Kissy was her mother's name). 'I leapt out of bed and met my mother in the hallway and she said, "That's mum, she's died."' She had died unexpectedly ten minutes beforehand.

▶ Man Who Wasn't There ▼

Professor Hans Holzer, author of a string of books on the psychic, including *The Psychic Side of Dreams*, *ESP and You* and the *Handbook of Parapsychology*, tells of the premonition of a Miss Lauterer of New York. One night, in that stage between sleep and wakefulness, she 'saw' as clearly as a picture the face and body of a man she did not know.

About six weeks later Miss Lauterer went to visit friends in Colombia, South America. She stayed on their banana plantation, near a small village named Turbo. One Sunday, while they were walking through the primitive village with its dirty streets and tin-roofed hovels, a tall, handsome, well-dressed young man caught her attention. He seemed completely out of place in the surroundings and she suddenly realized this was the man she had seen so clearly in New York.

The following day they attended a cocktail party given by a neighbour, the captain of Customs. The captain mentioned that a young flier would shortly join them. He had just arrived on a regular monthly visit, during which he bunked down with the captain's troops rather than staying at the less than salubrious hotel in the village. The flier was the son of the provincial governor. When the man appeared and was introduced to Miss Lauterer, she realized she had seen him the day before – dressed the same way and looking so out of place among the squalor. However, the flier was able to prove to her beyond any shadow of doubt that he could not possibly have been in the village on the Sunday; he had, as the captain had said, arrived only a very short time before.

Conclusion

From presidents down, few of us have not had an insight that defies our conventional ideas of space and time, be it coincidence, premonition, or a combination of the two.

Let us take a final look at the differences. Generally speaking, coincidences are not as emotionally disturbing as premonitions. Premonitions can, in fact, be quite upsetting. Often those affected have no wish to experience more and such a wish can, in most cases, trigger the subconscious into suppressing further experiences of this sort. Others, however, accept premonitions and experience them regularly and often with equanimity.

Whichever way we relate to both phenomena, we should recognize them for what they are – and what they are not! The information on both in this book will, hopefully, enable us to do that.

▶ Ode to Death ▼

In October 1992, the normally effervescent Lisa Gannan did something that was unusual for her. She sat down and wrote a poem, one that was both sombre and yet full of comfort.

Do not stand by my grave and weep,
I am not here, I do not sleep,
I am the star in the dark night sky.
Do not stand by my grave and cry,
I am not here, I did not die.

Less than two weeks later, the pretty eighteen-year-old was dead. A berserk gunman had killed her, her sister Kerry and their father, Tom.

Premonition or coincidence?

CHAPTER FIFTEEN

Diaries

The Austrian biologist Paul Kammerer, as we saw in Chapter Two, came up with the idea of the Clustering Effect. He also kept a diary or log-book of coincidences that came to his attention.

Carl Jung also kept a diary of coincidences, especially those his patients experienced and related to him; they proved very useful in helping him form his theory of synchronicity. Jung felt these 'inner experiences' (as he called them) were significant in the treatment of his patients. He noted that, 'in most cases they were things which people do not talk about for fear of exposing themselves to thoughtless ridicule . . .'

Jung went on to say that he was amazed to find how many people had had experiences involving synchronicity and how carefully their secret was guarded.

Arthur Koestler has claimed that a 'surprising' number of people collect coincidences in personal logs, enriched by newspaper cuttings, either because they believe that coincidences have a meaning or because they too are addicted to what he called 'the secret vice'. He made the claim in 1974, in an article in which he also observes that he finds it odd to hear Jung say that his patients had kept their experiences a close secret. He surmises that this may be because the Swiss, with their numbered bank accounts, are naturally more secretive by nature than the British. He had found that since starting to write on the subject, he'd been inundated by readers' letters describing coincidences. My own experience of writing and talking about the subject leads me to support Koestler. For example, on talk-back radio, no matter where, no matter what time of day or night, mention coincidence is going to be the subject under discussion and the switchboard invariably lights up.

Another insight offered by Koestler's article is his claim that the most revealing among the coincidences he receives are written by people 'solemnly affirming that to attribute significance to coincidence is sheer nonsense, yet [they] cannot resist the urge to tell their own favourite believe-it-or-not story'. Koestler asks: 'Could it be that inside each hardened sceptic there is a little mystic crying to be let out?'

It is true that most sceptics have their favourite coincidence story and are seldom reluctant to trot it out, even though in most cases dismissing it at the end with a disclaiming shrug.

Blair Aldis, a member of a sceptics club, tells the following story. In an audience of 800 people at a cinema one night in 1950, he won the door prize which was a choice between an electric jug and an electric iron. He chose the iron.

The following day he took the iron with him when he returned home and gave it to his mother, who was pleased but said she would rather have had the jug. The following night he went to his local cinema, which had the same door prizes – the manager ran both cinemas. Aldis won again. This time he chose the electric jug for his mother.

Aldis estimates he was dealing with a probability of one in 800 by one in 800 or one and a half in a million. His mother, no doubt, was more interested in the gift than the odds.

However, I am puzzled by Koestler's claim of a surprising number of people keeping log-books and newspaper cuttings. If so, then none of them appears to have had their collection published in the intervening years, during which time interest in the subject has, I would say, increased greatly. It certainly has not decreased. Perhaps these 'surprising number of people', like Jung's fellow Swiss, regard it as a secret vice. If log-books have been offered for research purposes, then the academics I spoke to have not heard of them, nor have I found any listing of coincidence diaries in library catalogues of research papers and books published.

As far as I know, there is not a single layman's coincidence diary in existence in published form or classified. Which brings me to the material which follows, extracts from two personal diaries, those of a woman I met and my own.

The woman approached me when she heard I intended to write a book on coincidences with the material I was collecting. As is the way with such things, she said she too had done some study of coincidences, and she knew of the 'secret vice' tag attached to keeping such a diary and the ridicule that Jung provoked for his interest in the subject. She herself had kept a coincidence diary sporadically in the past, with the vague aim of turning it into a book, but she had never persisted. One thing her efforts had shown her, however, was that coincidence was much more a part of her life than she had realized. That was about the only discovery she had made.

She was hoping now, given my interest, to keep a diary long enough to discern patterns of coincidence, to discover whether the coincidental events were merely random or occurred when needed, as rumoured. In other words, she was keen to try again and the fact that I was going to go ahead with my book encouraged her to make another attempt. I imposed no conditions on the diary and, knowing she did tend to take up interests only to drop them, I half expected to see her last no more than a week or two at the most.

To put the diary into perspective, one literary critic who has an interest in coincidence and guided me in some of my research, Carl Harrison-Ford (he finds having a name similar to that of a film star has involved him in a number of coincidences), observes the diary records only 'quick-hit' coincidences. It does not provide a basis for deeper, longer-lasting coincidences to be discussed, even though they may be 'brewing' away, as they do seem to be doing. Her feelings changed before she abandoned the project, however, and she probably would not now want to encourage others to follow her lead.

The only stipulation imposed by the diarist was anonymity (she has an overriding professional reason for this, but she admitted that, like Jung's patients, she also had some fear of ridicule). I did not object. Her diary, of necessity, dealt with actual people, actual events, time and places. To publish could pose legal, not to say ethical, problems. I feared, first, libel, but apart from that permission to use names would present major logistics problems. Therefore, everyone, including the writer, is presented anonymously; furthermore, I have also had to change some details to avoid breaching confidences, and for reasons of good taste.

Do I know the diary is a true account of events? I know the diarist well enough to be able to confirm she is an honest, sincere person, whose job depends on her credibility, and some of the other details given can be easily verified by anyone with a little effort. Even so, I cannot guarantee that 100 per cent of what follows is true. None of us is perfect and, when it comes to making records of events, accuracy depends to a large extent on the honesty of the witness.

I have not used the diary in full – it starts in December 1988 and ends in March 1989 – editing for space reasons and also because some entries simply did not seem to be describing coincidences to me. Finally, the diary makes it appear she is at work and on leave at the same time. Her explanation is that she was taking a break but calling into the office and doing some work while also planning an official holiday break which never happened.

This diary acts also as a cautionary tale. It shows how easy it would be for coincidence to become a compulsion. On the other hand, you may find, as psychic Alan Vaughan claims, that if you live a stable and secure existence, coincidences simply will not occur with any regularity. He says that synchronicity happens to people only when they need it. Those who live by their wits or in an insecure profession, find coincidences happen all the time.

19 December Visited an art gallery where the portraits selected for a portrait prize had just been hung. One that caught my eye was a self-portrait of the artist in his garden in the suburb of —, according to its title. Although I move around a great deal, I would not go to that suburb from one year to the next, but the previous day had been to see a new client, so the name struck me. A few minutes after seeing this I left the gallery and on the steps saw the only person I know from —. She had been to see the main exhibition, with her young son, and not the portraits.

23 December Had to send a memo to S. in charge of — but realized I did not know the correct spelling of her name and I could not find it on the office directory. As I thought about the problem, I searched among the papers in a tray on my desk for an inter-office envelope. I knew I had a batch of them there, but all I found was one on its own. As I picked it up, I wondered what had happened to the batch, then I glanced at the front of the envelope I was holding and on it was the name of the woman whose spelling I was trying to find. The envelopes have a series of spaces on their front on which the name of the person receiving it is written by the sender. When the envelope is reused, the person who received it simply draws a line through his or her own name and writes below it the name of the person he or she is sending it to. This envelope had come from her. Problem solved. Later I found the batch beneath some other papers. None of them had her name on it.

Later that night was watching a video of *Pride and Prejudice*. As the credits rolled I commented to G. [her live-in boyfriend] on the fact it had been 'adapted by Aldous Huxley', adding that I did not know he had been a movie writer. After making the comment, I looked down at the book in my lap (I managed to read a great deal watching TV) and my eye fell on the name 'Aldous Huxley'. The book was an anthology.

27 December Calling on a client, I could not find his street after leaving the station. So went into a pub and asked a drinker at the bar if he knew where the street was. He didn't but indicated another drinker at the other end of the bar. 'Try him, he lives around here.' The other drinker smiled and said: 'I ought to know where it is, I live in that street', and then proceeded to give me directions. There were more than a dozen people in the bar and for some reason I did not ask anybody near the door, but marched up to the bar. In fact, I surprised myself by going into the bar at all – not my usual style to walk into a bar alone; not my usual style to walk into a bar at all. Then, instead of just putting my head around the door and risking, possibly, some facetious comment, I marched without pause across the room to the bar, as though I knew there was somebody there who would be able to help me.

28 December [Coming across a festival] the whimsical thought popped into my mind: 'I wonder how many well-known people there are in this crowd.' I was just about to dismiss it as such [a whimsical thought] – what well-known person would risk getting mobbed in this crowd? – when I looked over to my left and found myself staring at a whole range of famous people, Marilyn Monroe, Elvis Presley and politicians, pen-portraits by a quick-portraiture artist which he had done to attract customers. Went on my way smiling, the thought had not been so whimsical after all.

30 December G. wants to spend a holiday white water rafting. Having not the slightest wish to take part in such an activity, I have said nothing. But this week he brought it up again, after not mentioning it for weeks. I thought at first it was his macabre sense of humour, but found he did not know (until I showed him the newspaper story) that a woman had died this week in a white water accident. He did not mention the idea again.

1 January G. suggested we visit a holographics exhibition. We did. It seemed like a sounder idea than rafting. Must say I enjoyed it, although it is a surprisingly small centre with not many exhibits. Afterwards I was reading through some of the information they had given me and asked G. why he had decided yesterday we should visit the show. He asked why and I showed him the brochure, which showed it had opened its doors on 1 January 1985. He simply shrugged and had no explanation for wanting to see the show, except that he had always wanted to see it and it seemed like a good idea.

4 January G. said this morning we should take a surfing holiday. Then there was a radio news report about a surfboard rider being attacked by a shark but surviving thanks to the fact a school of dolphins attacked the shark.

The previous week he had been talking of a white water raft trip and there was a fatality, then he decides we should visit the holographic gallery on the day of its anniversary, now the surfing incident. I would have said he knew I was keeping this diary and was playing tricks with me, except I *know* that he mentioned the rafting and the surfing *before* the accidents in both events.

Later, was looking at a reproduction in the children's book section at — when E. from — section [in her office] suddenly interrupted me. He said he could not help noticing the book as he had just picked some photographs he had taken of the countryside mentioned in the book and had come [to the shop] to see whether he could compare the photographs with the drawings. He showed me two of the photographs.

He did not seem at all surprised by the fact that I had been reading the very book he had come to see or that we should both be in the bookshop together or even working on the same day when we are all just coming in occasionally.

Rang C. to thank her for her Xmas gift and we began talking about a neighbour of hers we had met the night we had gone there for dinner. As we were leaving, the car refused to start and he had arrived home at that moment and was able to give us a push. C. said the neighbour, who lived two doors away from her, had been the first neighbour she had met when she had first arrived in town about six years before and had been living in another suburb. She had returned to the United States, come back and had bought her present home, and found the old neighbour had moved into the same street. I am noticing how many people talk of 'coincidences' that happen to them and the way they accept them with only mild interest; also that they are unaware I am keeping this diary.

6 January Listening to radio, I started musing about a political figure whose wife I was due to meet at a social function in a few days. His parents had come from Hungary. For some reason the words 'I wonder if it was Budapest' popped into my mind, to hear 'he was born in Budapest' being echoed back at me on the radio by an announcer giving some background on a ballet he was introducing.

9 January On Saturday G., still hunting for some offbeat sport, had gone on to water-skiing. It was another of those sports in which he fancied himself . . .

I mention this in the context of this diary because upon arriving at the office this morning I saw standing on the coffee table at reception, among the usual business and professional magazines and company brochures, a framed photograph of a water-skier, a professional photograph, showing the male skier banking gracefully, a huge wake dividing neatly behind him. He had on his face a smile of pleasure and achievement. Now our office is the last place one would expect to find such a photograph, especially sitting in our foyer, so my initial reaction was that somebody was trying to make me the butt of a joke. But I rationalized. During the morning I checked several times and the photograph mysteriously remained there. I even asked a few people, but they either did not know or were not interested. Then, as I was leaving for lunch, I noticed it had gone. S. at reception had the answer. It appears that H. had brought the photograph, which was of her brother, taken in America, in to show a friend and had left it there overnight. H. had been late in this morning. So it was not some diabolical trick on the part of my G. Just a coincidence – a further coincidence.

I rang the S — [clients] about a report I had filed with them some months before. Their office has two numbers and I had been using the second on the principle that most people tend to dial the first. As I was hanging up, I glanced at the first number on our record card [the number given was almost exactly the same as the one she had had in the first office – the same digits, only in a slightly different sequence – in which she worked, which coincidentally was almost the same as the telephone number of a London office where she had worked for a period. The coincidence continues: the street in which the office is located has the same name as the street in which she lives, although the suburbs are different. To give the details here would be to breach the promise of confidentiality, but I can verify much of this – her current home number and street address, for example]. I immediately thought, what a great coincidence, it augurs well for a business relationship with all that going for it, and I imagined quietly sealing the deal by bringing up all these 'amazing coincidences'. [A week later she notes in an 'explanation' of the entry dated 9 January: 'None of my calls were returned, which puzzled me, because I am sure the proposal I had put them would have been mutually beneficial. But even more puzzling was that with all these coincidences going for it, there should be no response. But I then began thinking about those former numbers and former addresses. I could associate some successes, some happiness, some career advancements but on the whole I have been in happier, more successful places, had better dealings when my phone number has been nothing like that lot – and as for my present address, G. and I are not exactly what you call living a life-long honeymoon. So why did I assume coincidences would always point towards happiness and success?']

10 January Visiting the newly renovated offices of —. A. came to the foyer to meet me and as we walked along the major corridor that runs through the building I remarked on the new work and colour-coordination. A. stopped beneath the large centre dome and pointed out some of the highlights. 'And who is the architect?' I asked, impressed by all this. As the question came from my mouth, a door opened and a woman appeared. A. laughed and said: 'Meet the architect.' We all laughed and I said something about 'perfect timing', then spent some unscheduled but fascinating minutes discussing the redecorations.

Later today I spoke to a woman who runs a church committee. When I gave her my card, she looked at it, then in accusing tones uttered the name of my sister. Wondering what my sister could possibly have done to offend this church of which I am sure she was never a member, I asked her to explain. As it turned out, it was not my sister at all that concerned her but a person with the same name who had borrowed some items from this church and not returned them. Seeing my card had reminded the woman of that person. I did not inquire whether by 'borrowed' she meant 'stolen'.

13 January After a dinner party our host was running some of us home. Four of us had gone to the party leaving our cars at home, for drinking purposes. He was being directed by each person in turn. As we were proceeding a discussion began about his car, a Peugot. As it was going on, he was directed to make a right-hand turn. 'Hey,' he said, 'here's a coincidence, we're driving past the car yard where I bought this car.' Now, the host had only a rough idea where he was going, the passengers were giving the directions, he had not initiated the discussion about the car, yet as he was talking, we went back to the point where the story of him and his car began.

19 January At a diplomatic reception where a buffet dinner was served, I was talking to woman when suddenly her fork slid off her plate on to floor. I looked down and my fork fell off my plate. We both looked embarrassed. A few minutes later in another section of the room I was talking to a member of the — consulate when his fork fell off his plate. Upon consideration 'fall' is not the word, 'leapt' in each case would be more appropriate. It was an uncanny coincidence. Certainly you don't see diplomats being so clumsy or showing less than perfect social graces, which would have to be the other explanation. I mean, I *felt* my fork jump off the plate.

23 January Watching mini-series starring Burt Lancaster about American businessmen held hostage in Tehran, as usual with newspaper on lap. I glanced down to read President Bush's inaugural address and my eyes fell on his promises to get American hostages out of Iran.

25 January Last Sunday G. had suggested we go for a drive down to —. I could not remember how long it has been since last we took that drive, but agreed readily enough for the sake of a "Sunday outing". Today we were back there for the funeral of a friend. I commented on the irony of the situation, but G. did not seem to appreciate it. Asked him what made him want to drive down there on Sunday when it would have been over a year since we saw the place and he just shrugged. I must explain our mutual friend has been ill for some time and we had not known he had gone there to stay with some relatives, so we obviously did not look him up last Sunday. I feel I must say something to G., about all these coincidences. Can he tell the future?

29 January Put my foot into a bowl of salty water to soak in as part of a treatment to clear up a painful foot ulcer that had developed on the small toe, sat back and picked up a newspaper. Opening it at random, I found myself staring at a full-page article on foot care.

31 January Have not been keeping careful notes of the coincidences, partly, I suppose, because the novelty has worn off and partly because they happen every day and could become repetitive, such as reading and seeing a related subject on the TV. This does tend to happen often.

3 February In bed reading. Heard a faint voice which took me a few moments to track down. No, I was not hallucinating, G. or I had left on the bedside radio, the volume down low. Turned it up and found myself listening to a programme on the history of the Arab-Israeli conflicts. Putting my book aside, I lay back and paid attention. After the programme was over, I picked up the book and resumed reading about much of what I had just heard on air. The book: *Oh Jerusalem*. The BBC programme mentioned some of the characters in the book, some of the battles and the political intrigues of the time. It's pleasant to get a second opinion on a subject, even if it does come about by coincidence.

5 February Going through the bookshelf for something to read, I picked up Antonia Fraser's *King James VI*, thought about reading it, but finally rejected it for another book. Walked into the next room and sat on the sofa with G., who was watching a BBC play about a murder in a British public school on TV. 'This is good, it's written by Antonia Fraser,' he said. I decided the coincidence was telling me I should read her book. I don't know what prompted G. to mention the name of the writer of the play. Like most people, G. will sometimes mention who the actors are as a guide to the quality of the TV show.

7 February The following is the type of thing I am used to and have to push myself to write down, as it is so common a coincidence that by now I feel it is all rather mundane, but for the sake of the record, for the sake of example, here it is. Standing at reception as I arrived in the office this morning was R. As I wanted to discuss the P— project with him and had been unable to get hold of him for some days, I decided to stand back and wait for him to finish a discussion he was having with S., who was slowly edging away from him. I heard him say something to the effect he would make a note of it. He asked — at reception if she had some notepaper 'or an old envelope'. The receptionist passed him an envelope and I could see it bore the logo of P—. Now that kind of thing gives one an uncanny feeling at the moment it happens. It is not as if our office would be over-burdened with envelopes from P—. I would have expected him to have been handed a piece of note or messenger paper. The trouble is, these small coincidences take so much explaining, I tend not to bother writing them down. When I finally spoke with R. I did not, of course, mention the incident. He would have wondered what on earth I was on about. I could have found my contract terminated.

Tonight I enrolled in a keep-fit class, at last. Afterwards walked over to the nearest station to catch the train home. A few minutes later another member of the class arrived on the platform, which would not have been unusual, but we got on the same carriage and struck up a conversation about the class, and alighted together at —. She lives in the street next to mine. This was the first night of the class and we discussed it with some excitement and trepidation. The class is open to people from all parts of town and there were about twenty enrolments. The coincidence of finding we lived in adjoining streets, let alone the same suburb, gave the evening an added zest, as though we had been two old friends. Yet despite the fact we commute from that station and use the same shops, we have never met.

At home G. said he had picked up a telephone directory earlier in the day and it had fallen open on a page containing the listing of a former colleague. He had fallen to wondering what had happened to him; how he was getting on etc., as he had not heard from him for about a year. Later the phone rang. It was the former colleague ringing from London, no particular reason, just felt he wanted to say hullo and find out how things were going . . . G. still does not know I am writing this diary.

8 February On the way home this evening went into a supermarket I don't normally go into but I was looking for a brand of cigarettes I had changed to. I had worked my way along from the station, where the newsagent did not stock them, to a delicatessen, who also did not stock them.

I walked into the supermarket to find my neighbour from the previous night buying cigarettes, the same brand.

28 February Picked up my mail of six or seven envelopes and, after flicking through it, opened the top envelope. The information in it had me reaching for the phone, but, you have guessed it, before I could pick it up it rang and it was the writer of the letter, wondering if I had received it and wanting to discuss the contents. Now, this sort of thing happens so often I believe I could save dialling many times and simply wish them to ring me. But I don't think I have made a particular note of it until now.

2 March For some weeks I have been trying to get information on the — industry. I have checked our usual information providers, but information on this particular industry seems to be lacking. Then, looking for something to read, I chose a copy of a new magazine, flipped through the pages and there was a long article on the industry, the first such details I had seen.

26 March I think this will be the last entry in this diary. Let me explain this remark. On Friday night G. said he wanted to visit the zoo. I made some joke along the lines that he could perhaps learn about water sports from the seals, but I felt uneasy, as I have done recently with G.'s suggestions. In any case, we went, duly saw the seals and, of course, other sections. While at the zoo I overheard a remark about one of its keepers being killed by a tiger not so long ago. That made me feel uneasy. Then this morning I opened the paper to find that it appears a lion killed a man in the — zoo on Saturday, the day we visited the zoo here. You can see now why I do not want to continue with this diary. I don't want to feel responsible in any way for the tragedies, or to cast G. as a person who can foretell them, or to suspect he is playing some kind of macabre psychic game with me. I can rational-ize all of the above, but what I can't do while keeping this diary is to have a human being's normal lack of awareness of the tragedies that are all around us.

Apart from these feelings, I also feel that somehow this is an appropriate time to end the diary, that I set out to prove something and have done so.

This is the end of the material handed to me by the diarist. As far as I know, she did not write more. Some time later, when checking on the facts about the attacks by the lion and tiger, I came across the final coincidence in this episode. The diarist *began* her diary on the day a woman keeper was killed by tigers. She had not consulted me on a starting date. I really did not think a particular date was relevant. I did not discuss it with her. As far as I was concerned, if she managed to keep a diary long enough and with enough detail to make it interesting and appropriate and legally and ethically publishable, then I would consider using it. I must admit that when I sat down to write these notes with the clippings of the animal attacks in front of me and glanced at the date of her first entry, I felt a chill run up my spine.

I keep a coincidence diary for the obvious reason that many of the entries end up in my writings. Naturally, in this chapter or elsewhere in the book, I have not used entries that are of a purely personal interest or would take too much background-ing to be meaningful. The main aim of the sample that follows is to encourage readers to keep their own diaries, or at least make a note of their coincidences (and, possibly, pass the more interesting ones on to me).

A diary or note helps overcome a problem which often arises: people who have experienced a significant coincidence rely too much on their memory when they come to retell it. After being told some amazing story, and I ask for specific details – dates, names, etc. – the narrator is vague about them, or surprised to find she/he has forgotten them.

Even if you do not want to keep a specific coincidence diary, I do urge you to make a note of them, not only for the sake of researchers but also for future generations of your family. A person who told me a fascinating coincidence involving two children, one of them his, born close together who had the same names and other similarities found, when I asked him to check, he had been mistaken about some essential points. And he had been dining out on the story for years.

Personally, over the years of diary-keeping, no startling patterns have emerged, except that, as we have seen earlier, coincidences cluster – there will be a flurry of them, followed by a pause. This, of course, can be influenced by one's own awareness. Working on anything having to do with the subject, my awareness is raised and I tend to experience more coincidences. On the other hand, they can and do impose themselves when least expected.

There is one certainty about coincidences: once people know you are genuinely interested, you become their repository – few people, thankfully (mostly), are inhibited about relating them. Most of us agree that there is nothing like a good coincidence anecdote to stimulate conversation – so long as the facts are correctly remembered.

Now to the extracts (the year is not mentioned because it is not pertinent in any of the following) . . .

14 April A colleague who had called the office yesterday to ask me to place some of his work in another computer directory said he had been in hospital because he had trodden on a needle which had entered his foot. I sympathized and recalled a similar accident had happened to me some years before this. I had to be admitted to hospital for a general anaesthetic so surgeons could probe my foot. Warming to the subject, I went on: 'A nurse came up to me late at night. She looked at the details on my admission form and said in this plaintive voice, "But, it's your birthday tomorrow!"'

As I started to laugh, it suddenly struck me that this was an anniversary of that event. Tomorrow was once again my birthday!

12 August Friend Carol Dodd says she contacted her solicitor for the first time in two years regarding the sale of her house. He laughed and said, 'That's funny, I decided for some reason to get your file out today. It's open on my desk.' She later contacted the builder of her country cottage, where she intends to live once her city home is sold, to ask him to do some additional work on it. He too had her file on his desk. 'I just felt I needed to get it out,' he said, although it had also been about two years since he had completed the work.

12 September Jackie [my wife] decided on an impulse to send a fax to a niece, who has just arrived in New York to work, containing the address of a cousin who lives there.

Received a prompt reply: the niece said she'd been glancing through a magazine that morning and come across a section of photographs of male models, among them was one she recognized, it was of her cousin. She had been feeling frustrated that she could not just pick up the phone and ring him – until, a few hours later, the fax landed on her desk.

16 September Talking to a book editor about coincidences. I felt a need to give him an example he could relate to, so told him about a coincidence that had occurred on 19 July concerning a colleague of his. He did relate to it, only not in the way I had expected. '19 July – that's my birthday,' he said.

29 October Walking briskly with the dogs, the pace whimsically bringing to mind the Sousa march, 'The Stars and Stripes Forever'. It had been one of the tunes on a tape I had played a few days before. Humming the tune, I turned a corner in a street leading to the post office, my destination. As I did so, I glanced at some graffiti scribbled on a wall in childish handwriting: S.O.U.S.A.H.

30 October Reading a magazine out today [although dated 5 November], it says John Sousa was born on 6 November [1854] in Washington, DC (see previous entry).

10 January A friend wanted some information on a man who lives in Norwich and asked me if my agents in London could do some research. He sent me a fax with the details and I wrote a covering note before sending it off. At the time was writing an article in which the name of the MP Aneurin Bevan had come up and I needed to know the date of his death. So, taking advantage of the fax, I asked the agents in the covering note if they could find out that additional information.

Having sent the details, I looked closely at my friend's fax, which I had only glanced at. The name of the person he wanted the research done on was also Bevan.

24 January At a party a psychologist told me she was counselling a woman who was going through the traumas of a breakup with her husband. The woman had said she was not looking forward to the forthcoming 1 February as it was the date of her wedding anniversary. 'Oh, that's my birthday,' the psychologist had found herself remarking. It helped establish some kind of rapport and the woman talked on, more confidingly.

Further into the session, the woman mentioned another traumatic anniversary, 29 July, the date her husband had left her.

'That's the date of my wedding anniversary,' said the counsellor, who is also separated.

A final discovery – the two, who had not met before, each have daughters with the not-so-common name of Kirstin!

11 March Rebecca and Isla, two of my nieces, are staying with us. Had two extra door keys cut. Neither worked. Later today was speaking to a woman about a hall she manages. She said she had just had two new keys cut and neither of them worked.

3 May Have been working during the day on an article about UFOs and become stuck. A question had come up that I knew only Bill Chalker, a UFO expert and a highly reliable researcher, could answer. I selfishly overcame my reluctance to ring him on a Sunday, so I could get some sleep tonight. We had spoken a few minutes, when he said: 'Hold on, we have a UFO sighting!'

As we were having our first conversation in three years about UFOs, a news item had come on his TV of a UFO. We hung up and resumed our conversation after watching the item.

15 October Among our mail yesterday was a letter from Telecom for a 'John Smith' of 170 — Street. The street is one away from ours. We do occasionally get mail for houses in near-by streets with the same number but this number – and street name – are both very different.

Today, due to call on some people in that same long street whom I do not know, to keep an appointment for an interview made for me some days before by an organization which has nothing to do with Telecom. When I glanced at the address to confirm it, it was the same as that of the letter. Coincidence had appointed me honorary postman!

22 October J. tells me he was having coffee some days ago at his university canteen with a fellow student. He asked about a third student he had not seen for more than a year. Just as he did so, he looked up as that student walked through the doors. The student said he had, in fact, not been on the campus for a year. He was passing and on impulse decided to drop in.

23 October Arrived to interview an academic, who asked if I would mind waiting until he listened to an interview with the outspoken American academic Noam Chomsky which was about to start on radio.

Later, having lunch, glanced at today's newspaper to see a long article about Chomsky. It may have been coincidence that I arrived at the academic's house as the radio interview was starting, but there was not much of a coincidence in the fact he was on air and in print on the same day, as a documentary has just been released on him.

However, tonight watching a lengthy documentary about America and who should appear in two brief segments – Chomsky. This doco was made many months ago and had nothing to do with the just-released one on him.

25 October Watching a TV interview with Dustin Hoffman, who started telling an anecdote involving him, Jessica Lange and Baryshnikov. Jackie, my wife, glanced down at the *Vanity Fair* magazine in her lap which she had picked up a few moments before and not yet opened. With a cry of surprise, she held it up. The leggy Lange was the cover picture, with a pointer to the main article: 'Jessica Lange tells it like it was with Baryshnikov . . .'

3 November Medical check-up. The doctor pronounced me in excellent health and I was feeling elated as I left his surgery. 'I'm walking on air,' I joked to him.

Some ten minutes later, still feeling invigorated, I was waiting at traffic lights on my way to a bookshop. When they changed to green, I glanced quickly to my right, then stepped out. I had taken five brisk steps and was almost in front of the vehicle stopped in the second lane out from the kerb when a van sped into the inside lane, brushing past my back and ran on into the intersection, where it came to a screeching halt; oncoming traffic braked.

From the safety of the opposite footpath, heart beating, I watched as the driver reversed the van clear of the traffic. I was angry and shaken. However, I determined not to let the incident totally destroy my feeling of well-being.

As I continued to the bookshop further along the street, I reflected on the coincidences involved – pronounced in excellent health one minute and the next coming within a hair's-breadth of losing my 'health' entirely. A further coincidence – if I had not stepped out so vigorously, I would be lying under the wheels of the van. The hospital would have rung my wife, leading her to say, 'Oh no, he must have had a bad medical report and he's thrown himself under . . .' I even managed a smile.

After buying the book, I left the shop and found to my surprise, outside the shop, the courier van pulled up at the kerb. The driver was sitting with his feet out of the van, looking white-faced. I could not ignore him. In any case, I felt he owed me an explanation.

'My brakes failed,' he said, shaking his head and quite shaken himself. 'I stopped at the previous two sets of lights, no problems. But when I put my foot on the brake at those lights – nothing. Both of us nearly lost our lives.'

I left him waiting for a tow truck and muttering about the mechanics who had serviced the van. Coincidences are full of hidden messages.

4 November Talking to a Canadian woman on the phone when the doorbell rang, asked her to hold while I answered it. At the door was another Canadian woman. She was just passing and had decided to drop off some business papers. It was not until she had departed that I remembered both women, who do not know one another, are from Alberta.

Date lost Returning home this evening, I came across a neighbour and her son. They walked just ahead of me until we reached my house, where we stopped. She turned to me and asked: 'Do you think that's right?'

'What?' I responded.

They had been in deep conversation in the few minutes we had walked together and I had not overheard what it was they had been discussing. She assumed I had.

'That flies beat their wings a hundred times a second?' she said.

I laughed, surprised to realize what they had been talking about. 'I'm afraid I don't know.'

'It's in the *Guinness Book of Records* apparently,' she said, nodding at her son.

'Not a hundred times, a *thousand* times a second,' he insisted, with all the seriousness an eight-year-old can muster when faced with two adults who seem set to disbelieve him, or condescend to his naïvety.

All I could do was try to keep a straight face and repeat, 'I really don't know,' adding, 'Even a hundred seems a lot.'

'It does, doesn't it,' said the mother.

We parted with the exasperated son saying he was going to show her the entry in the *Guinness* book.

Tonight, reading Lyall Watson's *Gifts of Unknown Things*, I came across this reference: 'Flies . . . beating their wings a thousand times a second.'

Our meeting in the street had been unplanned. Although I was intrigued by the proposition, I had quickly forgotten it. I had taken no deliberate steps to confirm the claim and was not reading Watson's book for that purpose. I could have come across his statement at some later date, but I came across it that same night, following the encounter as deliberately as if I had gone home and searched for confirmation, although, quite frankly, I would not have known where to look for it among the books in my house, which do not amount to much in the way of insect life and habits.

15 April Took the dogs to the park. It has been so wet recently, with very few fine weekends, so not surprisingly the park was crowded.

I saw a dog in the distance that looked just like Chloe, one of our two dogs, even to the odd way it walked and its brindle coat. We thought it might have been a relative of Chloe, who is a half-French bulldog (other half unknown), or a breed that may explain that unknown half.

I caught up with the owner. As I did so, the dog wagged its tail and ran up to me like an old friend. Everything in her movement reminded me of Chloe. Even the unusual way she sat, resting on one hip. When we had first seen her she was limping, and the owner explained she had had an operation for a ligament problem, as had Chloe, both on the same leg. The coat, her manner and a comparison of notes about her temperament and intelligence all added up to a similar dog. But she was, her owner insisted, a full Staffordshire terrier and her mum was not, therefore, a flirtatious French bulldog. Jackie joined us. She had taken our dogs to the car. I filled her in on the similarities and she asked: 'So, what's the name of your dog?'

'Chloe,' said the owner.

'That's the name of our dog,' we said in unison.

I felt it was about time we produced Chloe and set off to get her. Half-way back, I ran into Jackie. 'Don't bother,' she said. 'He couldn't wait.' [We have never seen him or his Chloe since.]

3 January At home in front of the TV watching a current affairs show while half listening to Jackie and her friend talk as they looked through some snapshots Jackie had taken of her niece's wedding. The conversation had drifted to snapshots generally and the friend mentioned that a relative of hers had even taken a picture of another relative's cancerous nose. As she spoke, I called out, 'Quickly! Look at the TV screen.' Both women did and staring back at them was a photograph of a cancerous nose. 'Oh, my God,' said the friend, as though she had seen a ghost. 'It was just like that.' She paused to draw breath. 'This is weird.' Then she lapsed into silence.

25 January In the library I noticed an old colleague. He stood as I approached and we shook hands and started chatting. As we did so, I glanced around and saw sprawled in one of the comfortable chairs a man, fast asleep with an open book resting on his chest. He was thin with dark hair and wore a suit and large black-rimmed glasses. It's not unusual to see someone taking advantage of those comfortable chairs to catch up on some sleep. But in this case, as I explained to my former colleague, who wondered why I had started smiling, the same man had been in the same chair in the same position with the book (the same one for all I knew) on his chest exactly one week before, when I had last been at the library.

15 February In search of a copy of Ellic Howe's *Urania's Children*, which had been published in the 1960s, I went to a large second-hand bookshop famous for the thousands of books it keeps but infamous for its lack of organization. I asked for directions to books on astrology and the like, and was pointed towards the appropriate shelves, which were stuffed with books. Others lay in collapsed piles in front of the shelves. Using my foot, I edged aside some dog-earred dusty and broken-backed strays and managed to get within focusing distance of the shelves. The first book I saw was *Urania's Children*, still in a dustjacket, lying on top of a small pile balanced precariously on the edge of a shelf at eye level. It was as though someone had heard me at the counter, run ahead with the book and placed it where my eyes would easily spot it. I must confess I looked around for just such a person, fearing a practical joke, before picking it up to assure myself it was real. Inside the jacket were the words 'out of print'. I had been in the bookshop less than five minutes and had expected to spend at least an hour there and even then come away empty-handed. I tried to look nonchalant as I took it back to the counter, thinking, if I stay any longer my luck will change, the book will vanish!

24 March Walking the dogs when the overused word 'outrage' popped whimsically into my mind. I mused on it, the way it used to come so readily to mind when writing newspaper stories: 'outraged residents threatened' . . . 'this is an outrage,' the minister said, etc. A minute or two later, just as the word which had so haphazardly appeared had fulfilled its job of bemusing me, my eyes fell on a magazine lying face-up on the footpath. Across the top of the cover in large letters was its title: OUTRAGE.

I would like to be able to credit my eyesight with the ability to see about 200 yards down the street and across an inter-section, but am afraid I cannot make such a boast.

Further Reading

Anderson, Ken, *Coincidences: Accident or Design?* (Collins Angus & Robertson, Sydney, 1991)

—— *Extraordinary Coincidences* (HarperCollins, Sydney, 1993)

Ash, Russell, and Lake, Brian, *Frog Raising for Pleasure and Profit and Other Bizarre Books* (Macmillan, London, 1985)

Borel, Emile, *Probabilities and life* (Dover Publications, New York, 1962)

Born, Max, *Natural Philosophy of Cause and Chance* (Oxford University Press, 1949)

Bullock, Alan, and Stallybrass, Oliver (eds.), *The Fontana Dictionary of Modern Thought* (William Collins, London, 1978)

Campbell, Florence, *Your Days are Numbered* (DeVorss and Co., Marinas del Rey, California, 1958)

Chesterton, G. K., *Orthodoxy* (John Lane, London, 1908)

Dent, Margaret, *Conversations with the Dead* (Fast Proof Press, Sydney, 1993)

Dunne, J. W., *An Experiment with Time* (A. & C. Black, London, 1927)

Edwards, Frank, *Stranger than Science* (Bantam, New York, 1959)

Eysenck, Hans, and Sargent, Carl, *Explaining the Unexplained* (Weidenfeld & Nicolson, London, 1982)

Fairley, John, and Welfare, Simon, *Arthur C. Clarke's World of Strange Powers* (Collins, London, 1984)

FitzGerald, Michael, *Storm Troopers of Satan* (Robert Hale, London, 1990)

Flammarion, Camille, *The Unknown* (Harper, London, 1990)

Fontbrune de, Jean-Charles, *Nostradamus: Countdown to Apocalypse* (Pan, London, 1983)

Gardner, Martin, *The Annotated Innocence of Father Brown* (Oxford University Press, Oxford, 1987)

Goldman, Albert, *The Lives of John Lennon* (Bantam, London, 1988)

Goodman, C. Morris, *Modern Numerology*, (Hal Leighton, North Hollywood, 1945)

Goodman, Linda, *Star Signs* (Macmillan, London, 1987)

—— *Sun Signs* (Pan, London, 1968)

Greenhouse, Herbert B., *Premonitions: A Leap into the Future* (Turnstone Press, London, 1971)

Hassell, Max, *Prophets without Honor* (Ace Books, New York, 1971)

Heywood, Rosalind, *The Infinitive Hive* (Chatto & Windus, London, 1964)

Hicks, Christopher, *The Mind of Chesterton* (University of Miami Press, Florida, 1970)

Huff, Darrell, *How to Take a Chance* (Pelican, Harmondsworth, 1959)

Inglis, Brian, *Coincidences: A Matter of Chance – or Synchronicity?* (Hutchinson, London, 1990)

Jung, Karl, *Synchronicity* (Princeton University Press, New Jersey, 1960)

Kammerer, Paul *Das Gesetz der Serie* (The Law of the Series) (Deutsche Verlage-Anstalt, Stuggart-Berlin, 1919)

Kirby, David, *Dictionary of Contemporary Thought* (Macmillan, London, 1984)

Koestler, Arthur, *The Challenge of Chance* (Hutchinson, London, 1973)

—— *The Invisible Writing* (Collins & Hamish Hamilton, London, 1954)

—— *The Roots of Coincidence* (Random House, New York, 1972)

Laplace, P. S., *A Philosophical Essay on Probabilities* (Paris, 1812)

MacLaine, Shirley, *Out on a Limb* (Bantam Books, New York, 1983)

Manning, Matthew, *In the Minds of Millions* (W. H. Allen, London, 1978)

May, John, *Curious Facts 2* (Secker and Warburg, London, 1984)

Muldoon Tom, *Numerology, the Hidden Meaning* (Wednell Publications, Newport, Victoria, undated)

Proctor, Richard, *Chance and Luck* (Longman, Green and Co., London, 1887)

Progoff, Ira, *Jung, Synchronicity and Human Destiny* (Julian Press, New York, 1973)

Reader's Digest, *Into the Unknown* (1982)

—— *Mysteries of the Unexplained* (1982)

Richards, Steve, *Luck, Chance and Coincidence* (Aquarian, Wellingborough, 1985)

Ripley, Robert L., *Believe It or Not* (Pocket Series, New York, 1964)

—— *The Book of Chances* (Penguin, Australia, 1989)

Robb, Stewart, *Prophecies on World Events by Nostradamus* (Liverwright, New York, 1961)

Schul, Bill, *The Psychic Power of Animals* (Coronet, Sevenoaks, 1977)

Shallis, Michael, *On Time* (Penguin, Harmondsworth, 1982)

Siegel, Bernie S., *Peace, Love and Healing* (Harper & Row, New York, 1989)

Silva, José and Miele, Philip, *The Silva Mind Control Method* (Pocket Books, New York, 1977)

The Unexplained, part-work (Orbis Publishing, London, 1981)

Vaughan, Alan, *Incredible Coincidences: The Baffling World of Synchronicity* (Corgi, London, 1981)

Watson, Lyall, *Supernature* (Hodder and Stoughton, London, 1973)

—— *The Gift of Unknown Things* (Hodder and Stoughton, London, 1976)

Weaver, Warren, *Lady Luck and the Theory of Probability* (Doubleday, New York, 1963)

West, John and Toodner, Jan, *The Case for Astrology* (Macdonald, London, 1970)

Wilson, Colin, *The Occult* (Granada, London, 1971)

—— *The Psychic Detectives* (Pan, London, 1984)

—— *Strange Powers* (Latimer New Dimensions, London, 1973)

White, Suzanne, *The New Astrology* (Macmillan, London, 1986)

Wolf, Fred, *Taking the Quantum Leap* (Harper & Row, New York, 1989)

Zohar, Danah, *Through the Time Barrier* (Paladin, London, 1983)

Readers are invited to share their coincidences or comments on the subject with the author. Please write to: Ken Anderson, PO Box 429, Newtown, NSW, Australia 2043.